WOMEN
TALK ABOUT
BREAST
SURGERY

Also by Dee Ito

THE HEALTHY BODY HANDBOOK

WOMEN TALK ABOUT BREAST SURGERY

From Diagnosis to Recovery

AMY GROSS *and* DEE ITO

CLARKSON POTTER/PUBLISHERS
NEW YORK

Copyright © 1990 by Amy Gross and Dee Ito

Published by Clarkson N. Potter, Inc., distributed by Crown Publishers, Inc.,
201 East 50th Street, New York, New York 10022

CLARKSON N. POTTER, POTTER and colophon are trademarks of
Clarkson N. Potter, Inc.

Manufactured in the United States of America

LIBRARY OF CONGRESS CATALOGING-IN-PUBLICATION DATA
Gross, Amy.
Women talk about breast surgery:
from diagnosis to recovery/by Amy Gross and Dee Ito.
p. cm.
1. Breast—Surgery. 2. Women—Surgery—Decision making.
3. Women—Psychology. I. Ito, Dee. II. Title.
RG104.G76 1989
618.1′059—dc20   89-22793
CIP
ISBN 0-517-56353-3

Text design by Beth Tondreau Design / Mary A. Wirth
10 9 8 7 6 5 4 3 2 1

First Edition

For the women, our heroines,
who gave us their stories and taught us
how to get through surgery

ACKNOWLEDGMENTS

We are tremendously grateful to the doctors, nurses, and health professionals who generously and patiently explained what they do and how they think: Constance Brickson; Amy Chou, R.N., M.A.; William Grace, M.D.; David Hidalgo, M.D.; Joel Ito, R.Ph.; Patricia Kelly, Ph.D.; M. Margaret Kemeny, M.D.; Robert Korn, M.D.; Marilyn Kritchman, M.D.; Bernard Kruger, M.D.; Pat McGuire; Marilyn Miklau; Fredrica Preston, R.N., M.A., O.C.N.; Ruth Ravitch; Carol Rogers; Mark Rounsaville, M.D.

Our thanks, also, to our editor, Carol Southern, for her support and enthusiasm.

CONTENTS

THREE · *Consultations with Specialists:*

FOUR · *The Hospital: Routines, Procedures, and Services*

WOMEN TALK ABOUT BREAST SURGERY

O N E

Introduction

THE PATIENT AS EXPERT
THE PATIENT AS PILGRIM
THE PROCEDURES DESCRIBED

THE PATIENT AS EXPERT

This book is a collection of stories—conversations with women who have been through breast surgery. They've had a biopsy and a lumpectomy or mastectomy—or both. Some went on to reconstructive surgery, to rebuild a breast after a mastectomy. Their collective experience adds up to the inside story on surgery.

Most of the women we interviewed are models of the New Patient: well-informed, skeptical, opinionated, insistent on getting involved in treatment decisions. As they moved from diagnosis to recovery, they became experts on their surgery. In their stories they suggest how to proceed, which questions to ask. They recall the details a doctor is too busy to list, doesn't know, or is reluctant to share for various reasons. They point to unexpected sources of help. Implicitly and explicitly, by their mistakes as well as their triumphs, they offer lessons in how to be the smartest possible patient and how to get the best possible care for yourself.

The underlying power of their stories is the proof they offer that one survives these experiences. These voices have all been to the front and returned to tell what happened. In a sense, theirs are adventure stories. They are about heroics, about fighting back, being brave, keeping your wits about you. They are about surviving the shock of surgery, whether it is a needle biopsy or a mastectomy.

Two decades after the medical-consumer movement began, surgery is still a mysterious event, and it shouldn't be. Ignorance is not bliss, and it's not protection. What you don't know can hurt you; it can throw you just because it's unexpected. Thanks to drug management, pain is no longer the major hurdle of surgery; fear is, whether the procedure is considered minor or major. Some fear is an inevitable reaction to a disease or to the risks inherent in surgery and general anesthesia. But the fear of the unknown is unnecessary. Instead of panicking when a doctor says you need surgery, you can know what to do next. Instead of feeling victimized and disembodied by hospital routines, you can understand the purpose of a procedure—and you can even refuse it. Instead of feeling blown in, like Dorothy walking in Oz, you can be grounded in the knowledge that you have mapped your own route. As one woman said of her calm the night before surgery, "I felt that I'd done my homework. I had researched my surgery, checked out doctors, and felt confident in my choices. Now I could relax."

One of the themes running through the interviews is the patient's need for a sense of control. Surgery is more than a physical assault; it's emotionally battering. You're in a weakened condition, surrounded by an unfamiliar, impersonal environment. You're dependent on strangers. You could be at the mercy of a nurse who's slow to bring painkillers or a sitting duck for medical students eager to practice their interview techniques. Our women resisted falling into a state of helplessness. They fought to stay aware and active. We saw that keeping a grip on what's happening is not simply "nice" for the patient. We suspect that unnecessary surgeries take place when a doctor is intimidating, moves to schedule an operation too quickly, and frightens the patient into submissiveness. The most important point in this book may be the reassurance that a patient can always take the time to research and get second or third opinions, so that she can feel comfortable with the decisions she makes.

We were astonished by the thoroughness with which some women attacked the project of surgery. They might have been planning a war. They responded to the diagnosis of breast cancer by giving themselves a crash course in the disease. They read everything they could find on the subject and some now fluently speak the language of pathology reports. They comparison-shopped for doctors and then weighed surgeons against radio-therapists and chemotherapists. They applied the same energy, competence, sense of responsibility, and urge to manage that make many of them tremendous successes in their work.

Their expertise was so awesome, in fact, that we had to adjust our definition of this book. We had planned to interview only patients, relying on them as the experts. The women's stories, though, were so loaded with medical information that we needed to check and clarify facts with surgeons, specialists in anesthesia, radiotherapy, chemotherapy, and oncology nursing, as well as other medical personnel. We met some extraordinary professionals, who gave us what amounted to tutorials in their fields. Their interviews amplify the women's narratives and clarify points that no book so far has explained to our satisfaction. We decided to include these conversations because they are a good, accessible source of information, and because they offer an invaluable view into how these medical professionals think.

The women range in age from their thirties to their sixties. They are all middle-class, with enough money to afford whatever care was required, so we believe that—for better or worse— they've drawn a portrait of the American health-care establishment at its finest.

The women are not scientists (except for one who is a physician), and they are not saints. Their personalities, as you'll see, shape their experiences, as do their fears, their values, and their personal health theories. (Some assume, for instance, that stress and a high-fat diet played a role in causing their illness. To lower the odds of a recurrence, to take control of their health, they changed their lives—at least for a while.)

We limited ourselves to interviewing women who had their surgery within the last five or six years (with one exception—a woman who had had a mastectomy ten years before, whom we interviewed because we wanted to hear the voice of one of the many women who have survived breast cancer). The narrow time frame was necessary because the procedures, and the doctor-patient dynamic (which colors the surgery), have changed so much in the last ten years. Before mammography and breast self-examination became widely performed, most cancers were found late; the most common procedure was the grossly mutilating Halsted radical mastectomy; and doctors essentially directed the course of treatment. A surgeon would schedule a patient for a biopsy, and if the lump was malignant, he would perform a mastectomy while the woman was still under anesthesia. Waking from surgery, she would learn what had been done to her. She would be hit simultaneously with the news that she had cancer and that she had lost a breast.

That one-step procedure is pretty much a thing of the past. Now, good treatment is divided into distinct steps and leaves openings for a woman to insert her opinions and desires. The medical-consumer movement, combined with advances in breast cancer therapies, has genuinely improved the experience a woman faces. She is talked to instead of talked about. She is no longer routinely subjected to the radical mastectomy; there are alternative surgeries and therapies.

Medicine is obviously responding to the revised expectations of patients. As one woman gynecologist told us, "Doctors know where their bread is buttered."

We believe that it was women who started this so-called medical revolution. Women patients in general tend to ask more questions of doctors than men patients, and women like the ones interviewed here are still pushing doctors to open up the medical clubhouse. But if the changes in the system demand more from doctors (to give more time to each patient, to develop the verbal skills and the patience required to explain and persuade rather than just prescribe), the same changes put new burdens on the patient.

The old-style patient assumed, first, that she was incapable of understanding anything medical, and second, that Doctor, like Father, knew best. Now we know doctors are fallible and have biases: surgeons like to perform surgery, and chemotherapists and radiotherapists are advocates of their specialties. That knowledge, that loss of innocence impels the new-style patient to educate herself. She can't just lie back and smile gratefully at her surgeon, the god. She's got to manage her own treatment. She's got to see herself as *hiring* a surgeon rather than crawling to Lourdes. She's got to stay alert.

This is no easy job. It is vital, though, and as the interviews show, fully possible. A mild woman who would never be taken for a warrior warns: "Resist the process of becoming a patient." Resist especially, we might add, becoming a "good"—compliant, obedient—patient. The women here must often have irritated their doctors. They hired and fired doctors to get the procedure they wanted. They pinned down their surgeons with long lists of questions. One insisted on a biopsy, although her doctor was content to wait and see how a lump developed. Another argued with her chemotherapist about which protocol she should receive— and persuaded him to administer the one she wanted.

This doesn't mean that the medical establishment has been brought to its knees. The women's angriest complaints were against surgeons, accusing them of brusqueness, of withholding both information and small gestures of humanity. One doctor "never had the grace to sit down in my room," a patient raged.

Another doctor frustrated a patient by his stinginess with facts: "I wish he had answered my questions. I wish he had told me exactly what he was going to do, what feelings I would be having. He just said, 'Oh, it's nothing.' It was much more than I had anticipated. His technique is to give the least possible information, usually regretting that he's given anything. And his nurses are the same." (The politically correct response may be to find another doctor, but there's a dilemma: One is reluctant to give up a surgeon who is technically excellent.)

The women crave information from all sides. At the end of her interview, another woman said, "I think there should be some sort of support system before you go in, where you could talk, as we're talking now, with somebody who has had the surgery, answering those questions the doctor will never answer, and making the whole thing more acceptable."

We are mystified that such a system isn't in place for patients facing all kinds of surgery. We hope this book will serve as that sort of support and encourage hospitals and doctors to invent such systems. We want this book to be both a source of information and a place of comfort—offering reassurance, courage, and perspective from the women who have been through the surgeries. These experiences, imagined as insurmountable, can be managed. The stories here are evidence of that. They are inspiring because the storytellers are just regular women. They are us, and if they can do it, we can do it, you can do it.

THE PATIENT AS PILGRIM
Mapping the Routes from
Diagnosis to Recovery

All the stories here start with a heart-stopping moment: A
woman discovers a lump in her breast or is told that a
mammogram has detected something suspicious. Ninety percent
of all women, after such a moment, will soon be reassured that
the lump is benign. The other ten percent will begin a search for
the right treatment.

Not everyone, of course, wants a choice. One woman's husband exploded when a surgeon explained his wife's options. "We
don't want options," the husband shouted. "Just tell us what to
do." As the wife recognized, though, "That's not what breast
cancer is about." You may, if you choose, go on automatic pilot:
entrust yourself to a surgeon's care and allow yourself to be
guided. But if you are like most of the women here, you won't do
that.

Instead, you will go on a pilgrimage from one specialist's office
to another, toting your lab reports and mammograms. You will
interview surgeons, radiotherapists, and chemotherapists. You
will decide who is going to treat you and how. You might even
have to negotiate between doctors who disagee with one another.
And all along the way, time will be biting at your heels.

The first step may be the decisive one: moving quickly and
decisively (and bravely) to find out the nature of the lump or
mass. "Make an appointment as soon as possible with a breast
surgeon," suggests medical oncologist Bernard Kruger, M.D. (attending physician at New York City's Lenox Hill Hospital).
"Don't rely on your gynecologist. Don't rely on your internist," he
says. "Breast surgeons are much better at this than anybody
else."

One of the most surprising—and dismaying—findings of our

8

interviews is how often doctors told the women not to worry about the lump, that it was "nothing," though it would turn out to be breast cancer.

One woman discovered a hard, almond-size lump in her breast. A series of doctors told her the lump was nothing—and in fact, it did not show up on the mammogram taken by the leading radiologist in her city. Yet she continued to feel it, and when it was finally biopsied approximately a year later, it was found to be malignant. When we asked Dr. Kruger how this kind of error is possible, he asked the age of the woman. "Thirty-five? It's harder to do a mammogram on women thirty-five and under—their breasts are denser. This is a real problem in diagnosing, and it's a little scary."

Doctors may be trying to protect women or themselves from anxiety—and probably both: Delivering bad news is hard work. One oncologist admitted that there's a reluctance to "scare the wits out of a patient. I think you don't want to send everyone for a biopsy," he said. "Some women have tremendous reactions to just having a biopsy—this violation of their breast." Another factor, he suggested, trying to explain the doctors' seeming nonchalance, might be a selective patient deafness. "I think a lot of women hear what they want to hear. What often happens is, a doctor will say, 'I'm not sure what it is, we probably ought to aspirate it, but I don't think it's anything.' And what the patient hears is, 'I don't think it's anything.' "

It *is* scary. A doctor can "feel" that a lump is benign, and be completely wrong. A mammogram can completely miss a lump: Estimates of the false-negative rate range from 5 to 20 percent. There are ways, though, to minimize the chances of an error.

First, "If the doctor says it's nothing, but you still feel it, go back in a month," Dr. Kruger says. A doctor may ask you to come back in a month, to make sure that the lump is not just a cyst swelling in response to the onset of menstruation. But, Dr. Kruger says, "You don't have to wait a whole month to go back. If you find a lump and it's changing rapidly, don't wait. And don't ever go away for six months. If a breast surgeon tells you to come back in six months, find another breast surgeon."

When you do go back, it still may not be clear whether the lump is a cyst (a fluid-filled sac, almost always benign) or a solid tumor (which could be benign or malignant). To distinguish between the two, a *needle aspiration,* an office procedure, may be performed. A local anesthetic numbs the skin and then a fine-gauge needle is inserted into the lump. If it's a cyst, the needle will draw off fluid, collapsing it. If it's solid, a biopsy will be necessary. A few of the women we interviewed suggested preempting mammography and asking for an on-the-spot aspiration. But mammography should precede aspiration, Dr. Kruger says, because it can help guide the needle placement.

After the biopsy, you have two to four weeks to decide what to do. You are told that once the cancer is cut into, there's a danger of cells "jumping around." This sounds rather unscientific, but according to M. Margaret Kemeny, M.D. (chief of surgical oncology at New York City's St. Vincent's Hospital), "Cancers grow, and there's some truth to the idea that possibly, if you cut into one and don't take it all out, you might spread cells into the bloodstream or into the lymphatic system. So you try not to wait too long between biopsy and excision. Whether a week makes any difference, I really doubt, but a month might make a difference."

What does Dr. Kemeny think of the way patients now run around for two weeks, researching their cases? "I think it's good that women are becoming informed consumers. You can take it too far—and going for more than two second opinions is probably taking it too far, because you're just kind of wasting time. But it's not wrong, because a lot of times you'll be faced with doctors who, for instance, only do mastectomies. I think it's time that women know that they have other options."

When we began this book we hoped to spare women the anxiety of all that running around. We planned to offer a "decision tree": if you have *this* kind of cancer, *this* is how to proceed. We wanted to map the way to certainty. And as we interviewed the women, we listened for the Right Answer: Lumpectomy or mastectomy— which is safer? Chemotherapy—who needs it and who can get away without it? What about reconstructive surgery—should you have it now, later, or never?

We learned many things about breast cancer, but one thing we learned is that there's no one right answer. Take the lumpectomy versus mastectomy debate. Some doctors insist that lumpectomy in combination with radiation is as effective as mastectomy. Dr. Kemeny, for example, reports that the "great majority" of the surgeries she does now are lumpectomies, whereas ten years ago mastectomies predominated. "It was appropriate then," she says, "because you didn't know that lumpectomy was as good an operation. Now, I try and steer away from doing mastectomies if I can. I'm convinced that lumpectomy and radiation therapy is as good as mastectomy. So I don't have to worry about cancer efficiency. Now it is just a question of who wants what operation."

Other doctors worry that the studies supporting lumpectomy are only fifteen years old; what if twenty-five-year studies find that survival rates are higher with mastectomy? What if radiation itself causes cancer later in life?

The debate continues. "We can all cite statistics to support our position, and we do," one doctor admitted to a patient. These positions seem to emerge from the deepest aspects of personality, from the individual's worldview. They are as temperamentally determined as the inclination toward liberalism or conservatism, toward the avant-garde or the traditional. For some women, a sense of safety is achieved only by getting rid of the affected breast. They sometimes have to defend their decision to have a mastectomy much as women ten years ago had to argue for a lumpectomy.

A seventy-four-year-old woman just diagnosed with breast cancer was leaning toward a mastectomy, while her daughter was pushing for a lumpectomy. In this argument, the daughter represents modernity, the cutting edge of science. She is the new patient—the militant, educated consumer of medical services, with a less-is-more attitude toward surgery. The mother symbolizes adherence to the old ways. Who is right? At this moment, we know of no proof that mastectomy is more effective in reducing the rate of recurrence; nor is there proof that lumpectomy is superior.

The guidelines are ambiguous. They are also tentative. When we began our research, in 1985, oncologists saw no reason to give chemotherapy to women with clear lymph nodes. But in May 1988 the National Cancer Institute recommended that *all* women, even those with no node involvement, consider either chemotherapy or hormonal therapy after surgery (the exceptions are women with noninvasive, in situ tumors). Three separate studies had found that chemotherapy reduced the odds of recurrence. Women who had felt lucky to escape the rigors of chemotherapy now worried that they had missed out on a measure of protection.

The frustrating truth is that there is no totally reliable treatment for breast cancer. That's precisely why we as patients have "options." When the breakthroughs come along, the choices will fade away. In the meantime, a woman handed a diagnosis of cancer must choose among the available therapies, making vital decisions on the basis of information learned yesterday.

Professionals in the field are aware of the strains on the patient. In imagining the ideal cancer center, they start where the patient does. "The question of how to find the best surgical oncologist, radiation oncologist, and medical oncologist is a troubling one for both patients and cancer specialists," says Constance Brickson, administrative coordinator of oncology at St. Vincent's Hospital. "More often than not you're working with disciplines that may be in opposition to each other. It's very stressful for a patient to be seen in one hospital for surgery, another for chemotherapy, and even more stressful when the patient is the person coordinating these efforts.

"In the state-of-the-art cancer center," Ms. Brickson continues, "if you called for an appointment, you would be referred to the clinic for an initial mammogram or diagnosis rather than to a specific doctor. The laboratory would be in the same building and you wouldn't have to make five different appointments with five different people. Multidisciplinary conferences would be held on your case; your disease would be discussed with all three disciplines."

The ideal cancer center, Ms. Brickson says, "would take into account that most of its patients are in the early stages of the disease—healthy working people with families and a life. We think there should be evening clinics and Saturday hours. Such centers exist, but as far as I know they do not have the range of services we feel is necessary for the future.

"The key to success for these centers is that the three disciplines work with one another. Now, we have our separate bureaucracies, and our separate funding needs. We don't need three separate laboratories. If we pooled our overhead, we would address the needs of our patients so much more."

Considering the contradictions and ambiguity that characterize breast cancer treatment, we sympathize with the women who choose to put themselves in a doctor's hands. And we remain profoundly impressed with the women who become pilgrims in search of the best possible care.

THE PROCEDURES DESCRIBED

BIOPSY

To find out if a solid lump is malignant or benign, one of a number of biopsies may be performed. If the lump is deep in the breast, inaccessible to palpation, *needle localization* is used to pinpoint the exact spot prior to the biopsy. With a mammogram as a guide, the radiologist marks the breast, applies a local anesthetic, then inserts a thin, hollow needle threaded with a wire the size of a strand of hair. Another mammogram is taken to check that the needle is in the correct position. The needle is then removed, leaving the wire as a guide.

A *needle biopsy* may be an office procedure, although it is often done in the hospital on an outpatient basis. After the area is numbed with an anesthetic, a small incision is made with a scalpel. A hollow needle with a sharp edge extracts a sample of tissue.

The *incisional biopsy* takes a larger sample of tissue. Surgeons prefer this procedure to needle biopsy when the suspicious mass itself is large. The procedure can be performed in a surgeon's office, but it, too, usually takes place in a hospital. Under local anesthetic incision, a section of the lump is removed and the incision is sutured.

An *excisional biopsy* removes the entire tumor along with an adequate margin of normal tissue. As mammography becomes more common, and malignancies are discovered earlier and smaller, it makes sense during biopsy to remove the whole lump rather than just a portion of it. The procedure is performed in a hospital, under local or general anesthesia. For some women, this biopsy will turn out to be their *lumpectomy*, essentially the only surgery they'll need except for lymph node excision (see below).

The *biopsy report* indicates whether the tissue is benign, in-

13

vasive, or in situ (noninvasive).* It also gives clues to the nature of the cancer and suggests a direction for treatment. With the increasing sophistication about breast cancer, oncologists can respond to such factors as whether the cancer is slow- or fast-growing (to find out how aggressive it is), and whether it can be attacked with hormonal therapy rather than chemotherapy (see Chemotherapy or Hormonal Treatment, page 16).

LUMPECTOMY OR MASTECTOMY

It's very likely that a woman will be able to choose between the two operations. One, *lumpectomy*, is considered "breast-sparing." It takes only the mass, surrounded by enough normal tissue to guarantee that the surgeon did indeed get all of the malignancy. Lumpectomy always should be followed by a course of radiation—usually five days a week for five to six weeks. Reactions to radiation were mild. The women described feeling fatigue from the therapy, and, if they were treated in major metropolitan cancer centers, the long (up to four-hour) wait for a treatment that lasts a few minutes was irritating.

In deciding who is a candidate for lumpectomy, one of the less abstruse factors surgeons consider is the size of the lump relative to the breast. "The point of breast-sparing surgery," Dr. Kruger says, "is really to spare an acceptable breast. If you have a small breast and a big tumor, you're not going to have an acceptable result." In the landmark 1985 National Surgical Adjuvant Breast Project study that found lumpectomy-plus-radiation to be as effective as mastectomy, the tumors were all under 4 centimeters. "That was the cut-off used by the study," Dr. Kemeny said, "and it's a reasonable cut-off. Once the tumor is bigger than 4 centi-

---

* *In situ* is the kind of cancer Nancy Reagan had, and as Dr. Kemeny says, "It's a very controversial area, because there are some people who feel that this is a cancer and others who feel it isn't a cancer." At the National Surgical Adjuvant Breast Project, she says, the "two arms of treatment"—the choices—"are a lumpectomy to take out the nodule or lumpectomy and radiation therapy. Other people feel you have to do a mastectomy. The argument in favor of mastectomy reasons that in situ is the one case in which we can be sure the cancer hasn't spread; a mastectomy will completely eliminate any chance of metastasis. Personally, I don't think they have the evidence to justify mastectomy, since 100 percent of their patients are alive after surgery. There's no cancer that will give you 100 percent survivals." Another option with in situ is to do nothing at all. "But then you must get checkups every six months," says Dr. Kemeny, "and a mammogram every six months."

meters, it's getting a little large, especially for a normal-size breast." She suggested, though, that outside of a national study, the parameters are somewhat flexible. If you have a large tumor in a large breast, you can still consider lumpectomy. One of the women we interviewed, in fact, was warned that she would not get a good result from a lumpectomy. They were wrong, as it turned out. She went ahead with the breast-sparing surgery and considers it successful.

The second operation, *mastectomy*, performed under general anesthesia, removes the whole breast—nipple, areola, underlying tissue and skin—through a single incision. The kind of incision depends on where the lump is and can often be adjusted if the woman is planning to have reconstructive surgery. A patient should discuss the positioning of the incision and might ask a plastic surgeon to consult with her surgeon (see Breast Reconstruction, an interview with David Hidalgo, M.D., page 251). The modified radical mastectomy may also remove the minor underarm muscle. (The Halsted radical mastectomy is rarely if ever used today. It takes not only the breast, but the underlying connective tissue, major and minor underarm muscles, and all the lymph nodes.) Doctors may use medical terms imprecisely when discussing a procedure, so a patient should ask exactly how extensive the surgery, whether lumpectomy or mastectomy, will be in her case.

LYMPH NODE EXCISION
Removing the malignant mass through surgery is only part of the treatment. It is also necessary to stage the cancer—to find out whether it has spread beyond the breast, and if so, to what extent. If it has spread, it will most probably have reached the lymph nodes on the affected side. (The nodes are small "stations" along the lymphatic vessels, which collect the waste products of all the cells. The nodes filter out foreign organisms like cancer cells and produce cells that combat such organisms.) During mastectomy, the nodes scattered in the armpit and up the chest to the collarbone are sampled: the incision is long enough to lift the skin. In lumpectomy, the nodes are reached through a separate incision, two to three inches long, under the arm on the affected side. The number of nodes taken can vary from a dozen to approximately thirty. The underarm area is bandaged, and a tube running under the skin is left in place for a few days to drain the area. The

procedure is also called *axillary dissection*. (For more about staging, see Glossary.)

CHEMOTHERAPY OR HORMONAL TREATMENT

Chemotherapy for breast cancer used to be recommended only to women whose malignancy had spread beyond the breast. The latest thinking is that all women with invasive breast cancer, even those whose nodes are clear, should consider either chemotherapy or hormonal treatment. According to studies, adjuvant therapy reduces the risk of a recurrence. In general, premenopausal women are likely to be candidates for chemotherapy; postmenopausal women might best be helped by hormone treatment if their tumor is estrogen-receptor positive (see "Hormonal Therapy"). Postmenopausal women with advanced cancer might receive chemotherapy in addition to hormonal therapy.

Chemotherapy uses drugs to treat cancer systemically—to catch and destroy any malignant cells that may have wandered from the original site. In breast cancer, chemotherapy is always referred to as "adjuvant" because it is used in conjunction with surgery.

The drugs work by interrupting the cell's growth cycle. Some drugs can affect the cell in any stage of development, while others specifically attack the DNA, key to the cell's control system, in one of its phases. Either way, the strategy is to prevent cell reproduction. Increasingly, combinations of two or more drugs are used. Malignant cells vary within a given tumor, and at any given moment various cells are at different points in the growth cycle. Blitzing the cells with a troupe of drugs has been found to be more effective than using one drug alone.

The course of chemotherapy for breast cancer is getting shorter —the average is six months now—and more intense. The premise is that it's most effective the first time. Treatments are at least partially administered intravenously. If a woman has poor veins, or is receiving long-term chemotherapy, she may ask for or be offered a catheter, surgically inserted into a vein, as an alternative to the needle.

Unfortunately, though cancer cells are particularly vulnerable to chemotherapeutic drugs, the toxic effects of the drugs also affect normal cells, particularly in the stomach and intestines, hair follicles, mouth, and bone marrow, thereby causing the well-

known side effects of nausea, hair loss (almost always temporary), skin irritation, and weight gain.

Hormonal therapy is an alternative to chemotherapy and
sometimes an adjunct. One characteristic of a cancer revealed
in the biopsy is whether it is estrogen-receptor positive or negative. If it's positive, its cells have more than the usual number of
sites available to estrogen; the cells thrive on the hormone. When
an antiestrogen like tamoxifen is administered, it binds the sites,
preventing uptake of estrogen and starving the cancer cells. Tamoxifen causes so few side effects that John Glick, M.D., chairman
of the University of Pennsylvania Cancer Center, has called it
"the least toxic drug in oncology." It is the treatment of choice
for postmenopausal women whose cells are estrogen-receptor
positive. For postmenopausal women whose cells are estrogen-
receptor negative, chemotherapy might be advised, perhaps in
combination with tamoxifen.

According to Dr. Kemeny, "We really don't know what people
need—which chemotherapy, whether to have chemotherapy at
all, for how long, which agents. All of these things have to be
studied, so we are trying to get everybody to put their patients
into the national studies so that we can get some answers. That
would be what I would tell women to do."

Doctors in the national clinical trials have the advantage of
cooperative research, the benefit of "the expertise of many physicians," according to Connie Brickson, administrative coordinator of medical oncology at St. Vincent's Hospital. "Cancer
specialists from almost every major institution belong to groups
that meet regularly to discuss data as it comes in on a particular
research project," she said. "Then maybe the ten top specialists
on a specific cancer within the cooperative will meet and decide
—again, dependent on the data we already have—which new
chemotherapy drugs should now be combined because they are
as efficient as the standard treatment." She pointed to the mass
of journals in the library. "It's impossible for any one physician
to read every piece of literature on every solid tumor site or to say
he or she is giving you unquestionably the state-of-the-art treatment for your specific cancer. With these groups, several specialists in my specific disease are in constant consultation and have
daily data on how patients respond to treatment."

The trials work toward developing a treatment program, called
a protocol, for specific diseases at specific stages. "When a pa-

tient comes to this office, she undergoes a number of baseline tests to determine the stage of her cancer," Brickson says. "Is it localized? Are nodes involved, and how many? What is her estrogen-receptor status? What is her menopausal state?" If she meets the eligibility requirements of a protocol, the patient can be treated on the protocol.

"It is a very scientific approach to treatment, and very clearly regulated. If you have any specific toxicity on it, if your white blood count falls to a certain level, the protocol dictates how the dosage should be reduced or if it should be stopped," Brickson says. "Before the treatment is administered, the data manager or research nurse reviews all the blood counts, any toxicities, and observes if the tumor has responded. You are controlled and followed by a team of medical specialists."

If a patient doesn't meet the requirements of any particular protocol, the physician may offer her standard treatment, or "if he feels an investigational drug is appropriate, he might speak to researchers at NCI, and if they feel that a particular drug would benefit her, they would approve the use of the drug," Brickson adds. The decision then goes to the research committee of the university affiliated with the hospital and finally to the institution's review board. The board checks the protocol again and the patient's consent form. By law, if a patient is receiving any investigational agent, she must be completely informed of any toxic effects she may expect, and of her rights—for example, the right to stop treatment at any time and to ask for other treatment or protocols (see Chemotherapy Consent Forms, pages 233–241).

(To find a physician in a cooperative group, Ms. Brickson suggests calling the National Cancer Institute [1-800-4-CANCER].)

RECONSTRUCTIVE PLASTIC SURGERY

A sign that reconstruction has become mainstream is that some breast surgeons take it on themselves to set up appointments for their mastectomy patients with plastic surgeons. The procedures are not without discomfort and complications. All the women we interviewed, however, said they would choose to go through it again. Essentially there are two routes to reconstruction, two ways to construct "a breast mound." Either an implant is inserted, or the patient's own tissue is transplanted from her abdomen or a buttock.

With an implant, it is often necessary first to stretch the chest skin with an expander in order to be able to cover the implant. The expander is described by plastic reconstructive surgeon David Hidalgo, M.D., as "an inflatable plastic reservoir that is placed under the skin of the chest and is inflated with saline during weekly office visits." This process takes about eight weeks; the expander is then replaced with a silicone implant. With an implant there is a risk of "capsule formation," scarring so thick that it distorts the shape of the breast and makes it feel uncomfortably, unnaturally hard. This complication requires one out of three patients to have further surgery. There's also the risk of an implant bursting and needing to be replaced. With implant reconstruction, it may also be necessary to reduce the size of the opposite breast, or lift it, to match the implant. A third procedure, optional with either implant or tissue reconstruction, would add a nipple and areola.

With tissue reconstruction, there's no capsule formation, the breast feels more natural and is shaped to match the other. The disadvantages are that the surgery is longer, more complex, and creates another scar at the donor tissue site.

After deciding on the method, the next question is when to have the surgery. In the past, patients would delay until the mastectomy wound healed or to make sure that the implant would not obscure a recurrence. Now, there seem to be no reasons either to wait or to rush into reconstruction. "I do it immediately if a woman wants it," Dr. Kemeny says.

Recognizing that the techniques are complicated, Dr. Hidalgo describes the various procedures and choices in a two-page letter that he hands out to his patients. In the last paragraph, he cautions patients that "it is unlikely that all of your questions will be answered at the first consultation. More will undoubtedly arise after you have left and have considered the discussion further. Please call the office if you have additional questions. It may be helpful to have a second consultation if there is confusion about a number of points."

Every patient should feel that invitation—implicit or explicit—from her doctors.

(For more on reconstructive surgery, see the interview with Dr. Hidalgo, page 251.)

T W O

Breast Surgery: The Stories

LUMPECTOMY
MASTECTOMY
MASTECTOMY AND RECONSTRUCTION

LUMPECTOMY

"THIS SCARE ABOUT BREAST CANCER HAS REALLY AF-
FECTED ME. I KNOW I HAVE TO BE LESS CASUAL ABOUT
MY HEALTH."

*A fifty-year-old director of admissions for a private second-
ary school in New York City, divorced, with three teenage
children, who had a lumpectomy for a benign tumor when
she was forty-five.*

How did you find the lump?
I had been feeling this particular lump for about three years, but
because I have cysts in my breasts all the time I didn't pay attention to it other than having the gynecologist check it during my
annual exams and say it was fine.
What did it feel like?
It was just a hard little lump less than an inch wide.
Weren't you concerned that it might be serious?
To be perfectly honest? No. I'm one of those women who has
always been terribly offhand about things that happen in my
body. Maybe I think I'm indestructible. But a friend of mine—the
man I see—said, "You've been talking about this lump for a long
time. Maybe you should have it checked out." He was really more
concerned about it than I was.
Did you go to the doctor?
Yes, but the appointment was precipitated by one of my cousins
dying of cervical cancer. I ran to the doctor in a cancer panic,
and again he said it was just a cyst and not to worry. But about
two weeks later a finger on my right hand swelled up, so I went
to a doctor at HIP and said, "I can't understand why this is happening." He said, "Let me check the lymph nodes under your
arm." And he found they were very enlarged. I said, "Isn't that
interesting because I have a lump in my breast on the same

23

side." He asked me how long I'd had the lump, and I told him three years. He said, "This is not a cyst, it is a tumor." He told me to go back to my gynecologist. So I did and said that the HIP doctor had said it was a tumor. He quickly did a needle aspiration in the office. And when he couldn't remove any fluid, he said— very brutally, I thought—"It is a tumor, and you're going to have to have a radical mastectomy. You have to get yourself to a breast specialist." That's when I really got frightened. In all the excitement I never found out why my finger was swollen. The swelling went down as mysteriously as it had appeared.

Did you consult a breast specialist?

Yes. But first I called a friend of mine who is an oncologist and told him what had happened. And he recommended a specialist —a good friend of his, whom I went to see. He examined my breasts very thoroughly. I had never had an examination that complete before. Then he aspirated the lump again, and he couldn't remove any fluid, either. After I was dressed I went back into his office and overheard him talking on the phone, and he was saying, "You're right. It is a tumor, and I think it's malignant." I figured out he was talking to my friend, who he thought was my oncologist, assuming I knew I had cancer and was coming to him for confirmation. That's when it came through loud and clear that this was really much worse than I thought. The doctor then told me that the lump was not a cyst and that he wanted me to go into the hospital immediately.

What kind of surgery was he recommending?

He said he was certain the lump would be malignant and he recommended a mastectomy, but he said he could also do a lumpectomy if I preferred. I have several friends who knew about my problem, and one of them said to me, "Listen, when you have the surgery don't let them take the breast. Just have the lumpectomy, and even if it's malignant you'll have time to think about what you want to do." She also said that one pathology report was not enough to go on. She said once the results were back I should make sure the frozen section was analyzed by at least one other pathologist.

How did you decide what to do?

I was really anxious, and I kept saying to everyone, "I really don't know what to do." And my friend kept saying to me, "Yes, you do. You'll just have the lump removed." She kept pushing me not to have a mastectomy. Then I called another friend who happens to be a radiologist, and he said, "If you don't want to have your breast removed, you don't have to." I also have a friend who is an anesthesiologist who said, "If it's necessary to have a second surgery, you'll do it." There were so many people telling me not to have my breast removed—most of them doctors—so I decided to go with their advice and have only the lump removed.

How is it that you have so many friends who are doctors?
I went to Lincoln University, the first school founded for black men in the country. Most of them studied medicine or law. My grandfather and then my father attended the college, and when I was ready for college I lived with a Quaker family on campus while I went to Lincoln. There were only two or three women in every class until the school was sexually integrated in 1965—I graduated in 1962. Anyway, many of the men I graduated with are doctors, and the camaraderie and friendship we shared in school is as strong as ever. They have been an incredible support system for me.

How was the surgery?
It was scary. But my doctor was very sweet. He's Japanese, and he was fascinated by my legs. I'm about six feet tall with legs so long that they didn't really fit on the operating table. He wrapped my feet in a blanket. After I came out of the anesthesia and saw him, I burst into tears. He told me that the tumor was benign but my condition was considered premalignant. He called it hyperplasia—that's when the breast cells have a greater likelihood of becoming cancerous than normal cells.

Did this surgery change your thinking about your health?
Well, I know I have to be less casual about my health. I've had a number of different surgeries—a hysterectomy, a hernia repaired, varicose veins removed, and each time I was hardly in bed at all and back to work almost immediately. But this scare about breast cancer has really affected me. I want my daughters to have their breasts checked regularly, and I now go for a checkup every six months.

"PROBABLY NO ONE EVEN NOTICED, BUT I KNEW I WAS IN CONTROL—I HAD DECIDED THIS WAS GOING TO BE *MY* SURGERY."

A fifty-three-year-old gallery owner with a history of tumors had a double lumpectomy in 1984. She is divorced and has two grown children.

Is there a history of tumors in your family?
No, just me. I was exposed to radiation as a child—not because of a war or anything. I was a musical prodigy in voice—I sang in Carnegie Recital Hall when I was thirteen years old. So I was constantly vocalizing and as a result had sore throats all the time. My father was a doctor, and my father's brothers were all doctors—ear, nose, and throat men. At twelve I was taken to see my uncle, who said, looking down my throat, "She has very large tonsils. Maybe we could shrink them." My father was with the U.S. Public Health Service during the Second World War, and it so happened that the health service had this new Roentgen Laboratory in a hospital on Staten Island. Being the overprivileged child of a medical family, I had access to the newest treatments available, and it was decided I was an ideal candidate for Roentgen therapy, named after the man who invented the X ray. I was taken to the new lab, where there was what they called the Roentgen box—it was a special room where I was radiated with X-rays in several weekly sessions for a few minutes each time. Needless to say, it didn't shrink my tonsils. When I think about it, it's amazing I'm alive. It's amazing that I had healthy children. Years later my father said, "My God, how could we have done such things?"
Do you think the breast tumors could be traced to the early childhood radiation?
Well, I'm certain it didn't help my body. Also, when I was sixteen or seventeen, I wrenched my back, so my back and spine were subjected to even more X-rays. I think a lot about the possibility that the reason my whole life has been complicated by serious health problems could be the result of the long-term effects of radiation. It worries me a lot. I was married when I was twenty to a doctor, and when I was pregnant with my children I gained a lot of weight, putting stress on my already weak back. The pain was impossible, so I took all kinds of drugs—being married to a doctor, all I had to do was write a prescription and go to the drugstore and get it, which I did. I was on the road to drug addiction. By 1971 my back condition was so bad that I had to have a triple spinal fusion. In 1973 I developed a tumor on my thyroid

and had a thyroidectomy. In 1975 they found a tumor on my right ovary and that was removed, and all the time I was doing drugs. My marriage was in trouble, and I knew I was addicted. I also knew I had to take myself in hand or I'd kill myself, so I left my family—my daughters were teenagers at the time—and went to Florida to stay with my mother to recuperate. I went into psychotherapy. I was there for six weeks when I found out from my daughter that my husband was making plans to commit me because I was a drug addict. I knew I had no choice but to cure myself. Needless to say, I left my husband.

When did you discover the breast tumor?
It was four years ago, just a couple of years into my second marriage. I felt something on the side of my left breast, so I had a mammogram. Then I went to see the breast man—because of my history of tumors I'm constantly supervised by an internist and a breast surgeon—who confirmed there was a suspicious tumor. But during the exam he also felt something on my right side, pretty much in the same general area as the left, which the mammogram didn't show. I was still menstruating then, so he said we should wait a month. The tumors went down a bit, so we waited another month. They came back again. At this point he said, "Let's not play around with this. Let's go in there and do a biopsy. If I have to do more surgery, I'll wake you and let you know first." He was very kind, and I was treated well because he knew me from my previous life as the wife of a colleague. He proceeded carefully and was both concerned and considerate. He was also worried, knowing my history.

Did you get a second opinion?
Oh, yes. I wouldn't have any surgery without it. But the man I went to, who came highly recommended, was the *worst* human being I have ever met. He was so callous and had such rage. He said to me, "Cut it out! What do you need it for, anyway?" So of course I went with my first breast surgeon. I had great faith in him, and I don't have faith in most doctors.

What do you remember about this hospital experience?
It's difficult because I'd had so many major surgeries before this, but it was my first experience going into surgery without the connection of a medical husband paving the way for me. This time I was going in as an ordinary patient. Before, all the details had been taken care of and I just went to my room. This time when I checked in I sat there and waited along with everyone

else, and I was scared out of my mind. It's funny: privileged treatment is always better, but on the other hand I was grateful to be knowing what was happening to me. All of those years I had put myself in someone else's hands and I wasn't permitted to make any decisions about anything.

Was your husband there to give you moral support?

He came with me, but he left. I was pissed, but I recognized that he couldn't deal with it at all. He said, "Listen, I have to be at the office." And even though I was upset, it was better, because I had to deal with this all by my little old self like a real grown-up. I was not Mrs. Doctor anymore. I was just me. I was able to go through this in a very adult way.

Once you were in your room did you find ways to handle your anxiety?

First, I insisted on a private room, and then, knowing what a dehumanizing experience it is to be in a hospital, I never wore a hospital gown and robe. Instead, I wore a kimono or jogging pants and a shirt. It was part of my way to keep my own identify so I didn't feel like a patient. Also, once I changed my clothes I took a walk up and down the hall to keep myself from worrying alone in my room until I was called to come in for the usual tests —blood work, EKG, and X-rays. I refused a wheelchair to get to the labs—it was my own little rebellion—because I felt I would feel like a sick person if I permitted that. I know it sounds crazy, but I had decided this was going to be *my* surgery and no one was going to tell me how I was to go through it. Probably no one even noticed, but I knew I was in control. I anticipated having to deal with unpleasant, overburdened, overworked technicians who wanted to get their work done as quickly as possible, but everybody was very nice and very kind.

Did you see your doctor once you had checked in?

That was important. He came in and we talked. It's what I was waiting for. He told me what I could expect and what might happen. I know he respected me and my competence as an intelligent patient. He said if he found a malignancy, he would wake me first and tell me what he would like to do. He said he didn't think it would have to be a mastectomy. He would try to do a lumpectomy. He told me not to worry, that it would all be fine. By this time, my husband came back with some wine and a corned-beef sandwich. So we sat together and drank and ate. Some friends came by that evening, and we sort of schmoozed until about midnight. I was given a sleeping pill and it was a kind of a toss-and-turn night, and I prayed that it would be all right. I was prepped for surgery the next morning about seven—I'm very hairy, so they shaved under my arms and around my breasts. I had asked them to give me Valium as a relaxant, and they did. My doctor came over to me while I was waiting in the supermarket line outside surgery. He lowered his mask and said, "You're going to be just fine." So I went in and went out.

What is the first thing you remember after surgery?

My doctor was shaking me, and I was on a gurney outside the operating room—not even in recovery yet. He said, "You're okay. It's fine. There's no malignancy. I took out a little bit, but I moved things around so you can't tell." What he did was some reconstructive surgery—I think he moved the fat around a bit so there's not much of an indentation. Then he said, "Have a good sleep." So I did go back to sleep, and the next thing I remember was being wheeled to my room. My daughters and my husband were there. He looked very pale, poor soul. I remember saying to him, "I'm sorry you got such a lemon."

How long did you stay?

I stayed one day. I had a little pain that night, but a nurse was with me until midnight. I was happy to see her go, and then I slept. The next morning I was a bit shaky, but my husband came to pick me up and I went home.

When were the bandages removed?

A week later when I went back to the surgeon. I put vitamin E on the incisions, which were very red and puffy.

How long were the incisions?

They were each over two inches. It's four years and they're just beginning to disappear. I'm a keloid former, but I was very lucky and I healed well.

Were you in much pain from your lumpectomies?

That's difficult for me to answer. I have a very high tolerance for pain. Compared to spinal surgery, where the pain is unimaginable, the pain from this was manageable. I had one pain shot in the hospital because I thought to myself, What am I trying to prove? And when the anesthesia began to wear off it hurt, but as an ex-abuser of drugs I'm very careful about any drug taking. I would say that every day after the surgery the pain lessened. I was, however, knocked out for six weeks because of the anesthesia. Not only was it physical exhaustion, but emotional as well—the apprehension, the fear, and the trauma of it all.

What kind of preventive health care do you practice now?
I see the doctor every six or eight months and get a mammogram once a year as I always have. I started having mammograms every year from the age of forty as a preventive measure—at that time it wasn't considered standard health care—and I keep doing it.

*But despite all the radiation and X-rays in your early years
and all the way up to the present, you've never had a
malignancy, right?*
Wrong. In 1986, they discovered a small growth on my groin. It couldn't have been bigger than a pimple. I said to one of my doctors, "It feels funny. It happened almost overnight." He said, "It's nothing. I'll give you a salve." Thank God I know my body, so I went to a dermatologist immediately, and he took a biopsy. It was a squamous cell carcinoma, and I was told after the surgery that if I hadn't had it removed when I did, I might have had to have a vulvectomy. The exposure to so much radiation at an early age puts me at risk for serious skin cancer.

*Coming from a medical family, do you have any advice for
women on choosing a surgeon?*
Most breast surgeons are so intimidating, but it's important to get beyond that and find out what your doctor's qualifications are. What hospital is he affiliated with? What was his rank in medical school—that's very important. Is he a teaching professor? Is he part of a staff doing research on breast cancer? The point is, is he involved in teaching the methods of breast surgery? Generally, the best doctors are on staff at the best hospitals.

How do you find the answers to those questions?
There is a book in every physician's office where every doctor is listed—where he or she went to medical school, when he graduated, his academic standing, whether he is a full or clinical professor, where he did his residency, whether he is board-certified. I think it's very important for a surgeon to be board-certified with a residency and a specialization in breast surgery. You don't go to a general surgeon for breast surgery.

"THE FIRST THING I DID AFTER SURGERY WAS PUT ON MAKEUP, THE FULLEST FACE OF MAKEUP YOU COULD

IMAGINE. MASCARA. I CURLED MY EYELASHES WITH
ONE HAND—I COULDN'T USE THE LEFT ARM. AND I SAT
THERE IN THAT BED, DETERMINED TO DIE PRETTY."

*An actress who had a lumpectomy a year before this inter-
view. She was divorced at the time of the interview and is
now remarried.*

How did this begin for you?
My menstrual periods had become highly irregular. I was fifty
years old, which is a pretty tough age to have this kind of thing
happen because you feel like you're losing your powers anyway:
"My God, I'm fifty." I really was kind of dotty because I knew
something was going on with my marriage and I didn't know
what it was. Being involved in little emotional crises, not knowing what was going on in my life, I was walking around kind of
touching myself. [She puts her hand to her chest.]
Holding your chest?
Holding my heart, actually. So I found this little bump. Very
small, about the size of a pea, at the top of my breast. I had
always been glandy—I mean that during my menstrual periods,
I had always had a certain amount of swelling and lumps. I don't
have a cystic condition—the mammary glands just get very active, and since I don't have much fat on my body, you really feel
the breast. So I noticed this thing, and my first thought was, Well,
it's just a gland. I had never done any self-examinations, and I
had never had a breast examination.
*You mean that your gynecologist never examined your
breasts?*
He may have, I didn't notice. I think maybe once. And I hadn't
been to a gynecologist in ten years. Understand: I come from a
family rife with cancer. My sister died of cancer ten years ago,
and that's the last time I went to a gynecologist. I think there's a
certain negation that comes in. You don't want to go. And the
last time I had been to a gynecologist, I had a Pap smear that
tested out as Class V, and I went through four more Pap smears
and a month of everybody saying, "Oh, my God, she's got cancer
of the cervix." But it turned out to be a tiny erosion of the cervix
and required only a simple little D&C.
    So that put me off wanting to get examined. I had an internist
I went to every once in a while for a mild checkup, and I think he
may have felt around on the inside, but that was it.

Anyway, I found the bump. I thought, Well, it's the period and it's going to go away. I was getting my periods about every two weeks instead of every four weeks. Actually, it seems the periods were connected to the cancer: the kind of breast cancer I have is heavily connected with the hormone system, which is heavily connected with the emotional system. So there are all kinds of thoughts about stress. They don't think stress helps with breast cancer. My oncologist said to me, "Well, the latest findings are that not a little stress, not anything light, but some deep sadnesses seem to coincide with a higher percentage of breast cancer. There seems to be some correlation."

And meanwhile, your marriage was in the process of breaking up.

Yes, but I didn't know it. I didn't know that my husband was planning to leave me. But I felt it somewhere. I had a puppy I was paper training, and my husband kept saying to me, "Stay in the country. Don't come in—I can't stand those papers around." I was very involved in a class I was teaching, so I kept saying, "Well, I'll finish the course and then I'll pay attention to this."

I went down to Florida for some charity thing in November. I went with a group of people, since my husband wasn't going, and I told one of the women there that I had this little bump. She said, "Well, why don't you go to my internist here, who's a wonderful doctor, and let him check it out, just to relieve your mind." So just to relieve my mind, I went to her doctor. I really was not frightened. I walked in there, absolutely expecting him to say it was a little gland. But he didn't. He started to feel it, and to feel around the breast, and then he said, "Since you're fifty, and you've never had a mammogram, let's go have a baseline mammogram, just to check it out." He said, "I think maybe you're getting a little cystic."

What did the lump feel like to you?

The lump felt hard, and it hurt—a sharp little pain I'd been feeling for only about a month. Everybody said pain was a good sign: "If it hurts, it's not cancer."

I went for the mammogram, and the girl who was doing it said, "Oh, that's going to be nothing. It's a little calcification." Then she took the mammogram. They had me wait in this room. Suddenly, the head of the department came out and said to me, "I'd like to take a sonogram." And he starts feeling around with the sonogram. And I'm watching his face and I am getting an odd feeling. He said to me, "I don't know. I feel there's something wrong with this breast, but I don't think it's that lump." Then he said, "I want to talk to your doctor about it."

My doctor called me later that afternoon and said, "Listen, even though that lump looks benign, we don't feel comfortable with that breast. We want to take that lump out and check it out. You've had so much cancer in your family." Though not much breast cancer—one aunt had breast cancer, years ago.

I said okay. He said, "It will be a little daytime procedure. We'll just give you a local, and you can come right home." I said fine. This is when I realized that my husband was leaving me. That afternoon I called him to say, "I have to have a biopsy," and he said, "Oh, I'll put you on with the secretary who'll give you your insurance number." I said, "I'm going to be at the hospital to-morrow." He said, "Well, give me a ring from there." That's all he said!

The next day, I'm in this goddamn operating room trying to be a hero. It's an uncomfortable procedure. If you're awake, you don't feel the pain, but you feel them cutting and pulling. You know that they're invading your body, and it's not nice and you don't like it. But the surgeon was saying, "It's coming out all of a piece, perfect. It's benign. Don't worry about anything. It's won-derful." He said, "You'll have a little scar." I said, "I don't care if you sign your initials to it, as long as it's benign." And I remem-ber saying to him, "God, something's going wrong with my mar-riage, but I think I care more that I'm going to save my left breast." And I'm talking with the nurses and he's saying, "All right, I'm going to close you up now." Suddenly he says, "Wait a minute. I want to look over here. Do you mind? Are you still anesthetized? Do you want another shot?" I said, "No, I'm all right." He said, "There's something here. There's something else here." "Else" was the word. A gong went off in my head, and I thought, Oh, my God, that's it.

So he took it out and said, "I'm bringing this up to pathology myself." And he said to his assistant, "You close her up." And as the assistant is closing me up, the thought started that maybe this was going to be more than this benign lump. I thought about the mammogram doctor who spent about an hour with that so-nogram! He felt something was wrong with that breast, but he didn't know what it was.

Underneath the lump they removed was the cancer. The lump

was not the cancer. They found this ductal carcinoma that was so young it had been there less than a month, maybe, and was so "voracious" or "pernicious"—one of those ugly words, I forget which—that in another month it could have taken over the whole breast and chest. Its tentacles were quick-growing. It didn't show on the sonogram; it didn't show on the mammogram. They took out the lump and they found this thing. [She knocks on wood.] The luck involved is incredible. By the time it might have showed up I would have lost the entire breast, ninety chances out of a hundred, and maybe more.

Where were you when you found out the diagnosis?
I was dressed, in the hospital office, signing something. They had told me to wait, the doctor wanted to talk to me. About forty-five minutes later he came down and said to me, "We're of course going to send it out to a lab, but there's no question that this is cancer. And I'd like to take it out immediately. *Immediately.* We've cut into it and it's tentacled, and it's moving toward the side." He said, "I'd like you to stay in the hospital right now, and I'm going to set up an operating room for either tonight or later this afternoon. I want to go in there and take it out, and I want you to allow me to do it, and to take as much as I need."

I panicked and said, "What do you mean? This is all too fast!" This was Thursday. I said, "I want to wait until Monday." He said, "I don't want to wait till Monday. We've cut into it, we've disturbed it. It's very young, and I think the chances are we can get it all out right now. Let me do it." I said, "No, no, wait a moment, wait, I have to call my husband." So I called and said, "Listen, it's cancer," and I started to cry. I said, "What should I do? Should I come to New York and go to Sloan-Kettering? Should I stay here? When are you coming?" He said, "Do what you want. I have other plans." I said, "Don't you want to talk to the doctor?" I still couldn't get it through my mind that he didn't give a damn—after thirteen years of marriage. And he said, "Well, let me know how it comes out. Have him call me after it's over." In fact, he said, "Have him call me collect." I put down the phone.

So I was a little numb. There was no question that I was going to let this doctor do it. What else was I going to do? But I'm not totally dumb, so I said, "Listen, I can't do it without second opinions." He said, "I'll bring you two opinions." He said, "I'll get someone from this hospital: he's a very old man who doesn't operate anymore, but he's the best breast cancer expert in all of south Florida. And I'll get another expert. Let me do it. I'll get them both in here early tomorrow morning."

At this point, my medical doctor and a lovely old woman who is the mother of a friend of mine come into the room, and everybody's sitting there trying to decide what to do. And the medical doctor says that his son is a cancer specialist at Sloan-Kettering and maybe I should go up to New York to see him, and the surgeon says, "No, I want to do her now, I think we can do it now."

That's the way I went to sleep that night, not knowing what to do, but they're taking all these tests and they're drawing blood, and I'm terribly confused! I don't know what to do! And you're intimidated, because what they're talking to you about is life and death.

In the morning, early-early, the two oncologists arrive. One at seven, the other at eight. The first one takes a look and says, "Let them do it." He's very abrupt, and he goes. The second, this old doctor, was wonderful! As soon as he put his hands on me, I knew he was wonderful. Southern accent. Old man. He was touching me here and here . . .

Around your neck and face . . .

Yes, and I told him the family history, which involves my mother, two brothers and my kid sister dying of Hodgkin's disease, and my father of cancer of the kidneys . . .

Are you the only one alive in your immediate family?

Yes, that's right. I'm the only one alive. I've been waiting for that shoe to drop all my life.

So now he's feeling around, this wonderful old man, and he says to me, "Listen. Your lymph system feels good to me. It's active, but I think it's active in response to the cancer." He said, "They're worried that they found some swellings under your arms, but I think they're benign." He says, "Now I can't guarantee you this. But I say, let them go in and get rid of the cancer. Let them take out as much breast as they want. Do not limit them." He was saying, "Now, you're a beautiful woman, and you'll still look all right. We can always balance it out later, dear." He was calling me "dear." And he said, "In my opinion, from what they tell me, from what the slides show, you're not going to need any radiation or chemotherapy." Then he said, "The surgeon wants to take out 25 percent of your breast." I said,

"That much?" He said, "Yes, but that's all right. Let him take it. I think the tissue around will test clean. I could be wrong, but it just feels like that to me."

So, twenty minutes later, they're wheeling me to the operating room, somebody's taking off my nail polish on one hand and with the other hand I'm signing permission for them to take out as much as they want. Whatever they want to do.

Now, in the operating room, I was wide awake and feeling a little bit like Ethel Barrymore or someone. I mean, I suddenly felt that I had to perform in the grand manner. I thought, God! I may die on this table—I don't want them to think of me as a coward. You know what I mean? And also, I think I was in shock from my husband and determined to behave well.

So that's how I was. The anesthetist said to me, "We don't usually get such a pretty lady to work on." And they all apologized, because they were the same crew who had reassured me of the benignness of the lump during the first operation. This time, we're in this big, full-scale operating room, not like the little daytime operating room. And I was so concerned about the cosmetic thing that I was making them crazy. "What is it going to look like?" "Is it going to be distorted?" "Don't take off the nipple."

Now let me say something here for other women: If I had had any sense, or my wits about me, or the experience to know, I would have asked for a cosmetic surgeon to come and do the closing-up stitching. That can be arranged. This doctor was a kind of clumsy surgeon in terms of cosmetics. He was very proud of the fact that he kept the shape of the breast normal, but, the scar which is above the nipple, is horizontal, and it keloided, so I can't wear anything that's cut straight across, like a strapless dress. I can wear plunges—and I'm so glad to still have a cleavage—but the scar looked to me like he stitched it badly; it looked like the way I stitch a turkey. I don't know if I'm going to repair this. The man I'm involved with right now says to me, "Why are you looking for trouble? Forget about it—it doesn't bother me." But it bothers me. I know that they can correct that stitching. They could take out the keloiding and restitch. I'll have a line, but it will be a smooth little line. And with a little makeup over it, nobody will be able to see it.

I also have the feeling, with this scar, of a tightening, like a wire. I don't know if that's the keloiding. And I do not have any sensation under the arm and along the back of the arm, where they cut a muscle and a nerve to get at the lymph tissue: that doesn't come back. It feels like there's a glove on you, and I hate it.

What did they find when they analyzed the nodes?
The doctor came in on the fourth day and said; "The nodes have tested out clean." They found no "wild cells"—that's the expression they use. I could have let him just do a lumpectomy and then had radiation and chemotherapy to make sure: I would have had the full breast and a much smaller scar. But I let them cut. You see, I have seen radiation treatments and chemotherapy all my life, and they make a battleground of the body. The image I always have of it is pictures after World War I of trench warfare. I mean, they may have won the war, but look what they did to the land. Nowadays, it's probably better than it ever was, but oh, my God, given a choice of cutting or the other kind of treatment, I'll take the cutting. I want to know it's out. And clean. And I was lucky enough that that's what happened. I was lucky enough that the twelve nodes were all clear, and that the adjoining tissue had no sign of cancer.

What do you remember about your recovery from the surgery?
It seems I didn't want to come out of that nice anesthetic. I don't know how much of that was psychological. I really was prepared to die. A part of me expected to die on that table—that's why I was so brave. I remember them shaking me and hitting and waking me up and flopping me around. Then I came back to the little hospital room and saw this wonderful woman, my friend's mother, sitting there—an old lady, with a pacemaker—and I had my first nonpsychedelic experience of hallucinating. I kept seeing her changing into other people, like my husband.

The next morning, I woke up and there I was with two drainage tubes. I was taped across my chest. I didn't know if there was any breast or not, and I didn't even want to ask. There were lots of flowers, and that was nice. The doctor came and I still didn't want to know what was taken off. All I asked was, "What did you find out about the lymph nodes?" So some part of me, I guess, wanted to live, since I was no longer asking cosmetic questions. I was now resigned to the fact that I may have lost my left breast, but I have a pretty face and I'll put makeup on. I was in the hospital four days. That's all.

How did you get through those days?

Well, you're scared and you're in pain. I took painkillers the first two days, and then as soon as I felt that the pain had reached a tolerable level I went off them and took the pain. I'm afraid of medication. The only thing I did take was the sleeping pills at night.

By the fourth day, the doctor asked me did I want to stay another couple of days or did I want to go home. I said, "What's your advice?" He said, "Well, you're recovering remarkably. The drainage is minimal. My advice is to get the hell out of the hospital." And I thought he was right. I think bad things happen in hospitals.

Did you have private nurses?

I had a private room. My future ex-husband had said to me on the phone, "Order private nurses." I had a nurse the night of the operation and the next day, but I didn't need one after that. I didn't want somebody I didn't know sitting there looking at me.

So you didn't need radiation.

No, and I didn't need the chemotherapy, for which I am constantly thanking God. But now—this is interesting—I'm due for another mammogram this month. And I'm terrified. I have to have one a year for the next five or six years, and then after that, maybe once every two years. I'm going to go to Florida and do it. I don't want to deal with different doctors. I want to get the same doctor who sensed that something was wrong with the breast. He's obviously savvy. I was very lucky. I've been *very* lucky.

When did they remove the drains?

The day they sent me home. I want to say that they did that crudely and hurt me like hell. The surgeon took off one tape, yanked out the drains, and I almost fell to the floor. I screamed. He said, "It's better to do it fast." I said, "Not like that." I think women can ask if there is a way to ameliorate that kind of shock. It's horrible and painful, and you feel uncared for when they do something that way.

When did the bandages come off?

Not for a long time. About two weeks. I stayed in Florida for a month, and they changed the dressing for me.

How did you feel when they took off the bandages?

How did I feel? I felt horrified when I saw the scar. The skin had sunk in under my arm. It's filled in somehow now—it looked much more Picasso than it looks now. I felt that if a man liked Picasso's work, he'd think I was all right.

How did it heal?

I went back to New York still with stitches in me—they were going to fade away on their own—and I spent Christmas and New Year's here. Wore a low-cut gown. I'm telling you, I powdered the damn thing carefully and went out and looked fine. Then I went to Florida and went into a totally psychotic depression. What scared me the most was when they said there was a 40 percent chance of a recurrence. And I had seen the divorce lawyer. I took what my husband offered me. I couldn't fight. I was afraid to, because when I had asked the oncologist, "Could this have come from stress?" he said, "Well, we think maybe yes." I was afraid. . . .

To go through more stress?

Yes. So I just took the settlement and thought of murder for a few months. I still do, occasionally, now.

Do you feel physically healed now?

No. I don't know if you ever feel healed. Those percentages they give you of recurrence hang over your mind. And even now, as I'm talking to you, I feel that scar. And my arm doesn't stretch quite like the right one. Almost, but not quite. I am never unaware of it physically. I heard something that I liked. This wonderful guy, a governor . . . I fell in love with him on a TV program. He lost a leg in the army or something like that, he's an amputee. And the interviewer asked him if he was in pain. He said he's always in pain. Then he said this wonderful thing. He said, "But it's good to be in pain." He said, "It's good to always be a little in pain. It keeps you human. It keeps you cognizant of all the pain that's out there in the world."

And you feel pain serves that purpose for you—takes you
beyond personal pain?

Yes, it takes me beyond it. It makes me incredibly empathetic to anybody else in any kind of distress. It makes me aware all the time to be grateful to God. It makes me aware of people.

I'm only terrified of this coming mammography. I will talk to the doctor, I will ask him if he really feels I have to have it. And then I'll have it, if he really feels I do. But I don't want to. I don't want to walk into that center again. I don't want to look at the mammography machine. I would like to pretend. . . .

This is the interesting thing: there's a part of you that keeps saying to yourself that you didn't have cancer. "They made a mistake." I insisted on getting a copy of all the reports from

Washington, from all the labs. When I saw it on paper—where it said "ductal carcinoma, widespread, pernicious"—I fainted. There was something about seeing it written like that that was more scary than anything. It may not be an uncommon thing for women to think that—you don't want to think it's cancer. You'd rather think the doctor has made some terrible, awful mistake than that he saved your life!

But healed? I don't feel healed. At first, I went out and bought a bunch of brassieres, which I have never worn in my life. And for the first couple of months, I wore them constantly. I wanted it covered, I didn't want the breast to pull or drop. So maybe I was healed when I stopped wearing those brassieres, which probably was sometime in April. I suddenly thought, The hell with brassieres. I have no need for them, I never wore them, and I'm not wearing them now. Then I was able to wear lower-cut things and not care that there was a scar. I don't think it's such a horrible scar. I think I'm very lucky. I know a woman down in Florida who had a total mastectomy of her left breast. She didn't want to have reconstructive surgery, so she was considering having the scar tattooed and making an adornment out of the scar, like a patch. She was going to do something with a flower. I thought that was very brave of her.

———————

"THE MINUTE HE SAID THE WORD *CANCER* I HARDLY HEARD ANYTHING ELSE—MY MIND WAS LIKE COTTON."
A fifty-six-year-old rancher in northern California, recently divorced, who had a lumpectomy in January 1987, followed by radiation therapy in April of the same year. She has three grown children, two sons and a daughter.

How did you discover you had breast cancer?
My regular gynecologist had retired, and I was starting with a new group of doctors. One of their policies is to give you a complete physical, which included getting a baseline mammogram. The mammogram showed a questionable area, but the doctor couldn't find it—it wasn't palpable. Even though I didn't have any symptoms, my doctor felt I should see a surgeon and gave me four names to choose from. But I went to see my regular gynecologist first, even though he had retired, because he's a

friend of the family. He had done a benign biopsy on my left breast a few years before. No big deal, I thought, this is the same thing all over again. But he looked at the mammogram and said, "This looks different. I'm afraid you've got to go and get this taken care of."

How did you choose a surgeon?

I really didn't know what to do. I mean, do you go to the Yellow Pages? Is it a personality contest? But finally I decided to go to a surgeon who was another friend of the family, and he removed the lump. Small lumps can be excised in the office under local anesthesia.

What was the size of the lump?

It was small—five millimeters, the size of a peppercorn—but the surgeon took out a piece of tissue the size of a Spice Island bottle cap, assuming, I guess, that he would eventually remove the whole breast. But he left a little part of the cancer in there, and it turned out later to be a factor in making the decision to have a mastectomy or lumpectomy.

How did you take the news that you had breast cancer?

The minute the surgeon said the word *cancer* I hardly heard anything else—my mind was like cotton—but I know he talked to me about the different kinds of breast cancer and some of the ways to treat them. But when he said he thought I should have a mastectomy, I heard that loud and clear. And this flush went up the side of my head. I felt hot and like the world was crashing in on me. He said, "Go home and assimilate this a little bit. And when you have, come back and we'll discuss it more if you have any questions." But before I left he said he was going to be on vacation so we should schedule it in February—this was about the middle of January. And then he said, "If you don't mind, I would like to recommend that a plastic surgeon attend the surgery. He could put in an implant simultaneously with the mastectomy." It was all going so fast, I went home stunned.

Was there anyone at home you could talk to?

I'm seeing a very caring man who is very supportive. Ironically, his mother had had a total mastectomy twenty years ago, and it had been very traumatic for her. They just chopped away—it was all they knew in those days—and I think she never really recovered from it. She still can't even open the garage door, simple things like that. So when I told him, he said, "Wait a minute, let's get some second opinions before you do this." He read my pathology report to a doctor friend, who said, "This surgeon is using very conservative treatment. I think you should get a couple of second opinions." So I just kind of let go and said, "Okay, I'll do whatever you want me to do."

It's a new romantic relationship with this man. I've known him for a long time, but we hadn't gotten close until a couple of months before this crisis. It turned out to be a good thing for both of us, because he was totally honest with me. He said, "This really scares me. I had a terrible time with my mother." He said, "I don't know if I can face you without a breast." I said, "Well, I'm scared, too." And I thought, God bless him that he can say his truest feelings.

Did you ever see the first surgeon again?
Yes. I saw him a second time when he told me he had arranged everything with the plastic surgeon and they would both be available on February first for my surgery. So I said I was not ready to make a decision until I had more information. He never gave me any literature. I had to ask for it.

How did you go about getting those second opinions?
I went to the university hospital where there is a group of breast specialists. The head of the group was a surgeon. My question was, "I want a second opinion on the surgeon's decision." My question should have been, "What are my options?" We got permission from the doctors to record everything they said. My friend was with me in the examining room so he could hear what they said as well. While I was lying on my back being examined by all these people, I heard this voice saying, "Are you interested in conserving your breast?" I thought, Of course! I don't want to die, but if I have the choice, I'd like to keep my breast.

Anyway, the consensus of the group was, yes, I should have a mastectomy. But before we left the hospital, a radiologist—it turned out he was the one who'd asked if I wanted to conserve my breast—said, "There are options. If you would like to discuss it further, please call me." And he gave us his card. So when we got back home we phoned, and he gave me the names of people at three hospitals in the area. Before we went to see them we listened to the tape—it was a crash program in what it was all about and what my choices were.

Did you get different opinions from the doctors you consulted?
I saw three radiation oncologists and a second surgeon. The sur-

geon said, after looking at the mammogram, that if I were his wife, he would recommend a mastectomy. He pooh-poohed the idea that radiation therapy equaled mastectomy in survival rates. He looked at my slides and, because of the malignant cells left by the surgeon who had performed the lumpectomy, said he thought I should have an axillary node dissection as well as mastectomy to make sure the cancer had not metastasized. But by the time I saw him, I had already consulted a cancer risk specialist—she compiles medical, personal, and family data to determine your risk for a recurrence of cancer—and discovered that my personal margin of risk based on the size of the cancer and a second pathology report was just 1 to 2 percent with radiation therapy. You see, the original pathology report said I had intraductal cancer, but it didn't say noninvasive or invasive. All the surgeons assumed the cancer was invasive until the second pathologist examined the slide and said, "It's not invasive." The three radiation oncologists all felt I was a candidate for radiation therapy, but more important, by this time I was convinced that having radiation therapy would keep me in a safe range where I could keep my breast and still be protected against the return of the cancer.

How much radiation did you have, and what was the therapy like?

I had 1,000 rads, twenty-eight treatments, five times a week. Before the treatments began I had a CAT scan to determine where the organs were in my body; then they designed the focus of the beam based on that information. They put a little pinprick tattoo on my breast, and each time I went for a treatment they lined up the machine with the tattoo. It wouldn't wash off for the longest time, but it's gone now. You're in a room alone, and it's kind of scary at first. I decided I was going to ask every question I thought of, and if something bothered me, I would tell the staff —they were so dear and patient with me.

You lie on this table that rises, and then a kind of *Star Wars* machine—a cobalt machine—swings around, and they adjust it so that the right beams of radiation reach you. Each treatment takes about twenty or twenty-five minutes, but the radiation part takes only a few minutes—the rest is preparation and positioning the equipment. You can't see or feel the beam.

After the series was over I went into the hospital for a couple of days for "booster" radiation therapy. They said that most women who have external radiation treatments have the added therapy. On me they used an implant of radioactive material. In an operating room, under a local anesthetic, they threaded thin plastic tubes through the tissue where my original lump was removed. Then I was taken back to my hospital room, where they inserted iridium, one of several radioactive substances used in radiation therapy, into the tubes. A Geiger counter records the amount of exposure, and when you have what you're supposed to have, they take out the implant and you go home.

Were there any side effects from the radiation?

A lot of fatigue, primarily. I called the nurse about it, and she said, "Don't worry about fatigue. It varies with people, but it can be like getting over major surgery because all your cells have been blasted. Even the good cells are in the process of a kind of reconstruction." After that I kind of enjoyed it. It slowed me down and I had an excuse to nap in the afternoon. The radiation didn't really change the look of my breast. I had all these wonderful Mondrian lines, all red and black, that they drew on me to focus the radiation beam. But the skin on my breast is still soft. I just got a little brown-skinned, like a sunburn.

Do you still worry about the cancer returning?

I don't really feel like I have cancer. I know it sounds strange, but I don't feel sick. And yet I don't want to delude myself. I go in two different directions. Sometimes I have the fear of it metastasizing or returning, but at the same time I feel I'm just going to *live,* dammit! And finally, I say my risk of dying of breast cancer is 1 to 2 percent. That's probably the same risk I run of being killed by a truck. Meantime, I certainly intend to have close follow-up—it's something that women my age ought to do anyway. And if worse comes to worst and the odds aren't in my favor, I can get a mastectomy.

Do you have a regular schedule for reexamination now that the treatments are over?

Every six months I come back for a mammogram. I don't know when I begin coming yearly. But I'm in touch with my doctors.

Do you have any advice for women who have been diagnosed as having breast cancer?

The only thing I would emphasize is, keep your own mammograms and the pathology slides of your biopsies, and after you've sent them out for a second opinion, count them when they come back. Sometimes they get lost or they're not returned. And remember that the world is filled with human beings who have their own opinions and prejudices. Listen to them, but you have to find the treatment that suits you and your body. You can get terribly confused with lots of second opinions, and finally you have to zero in on the doctor or group that is for you. My decision about the doctor and the hospital where I had the radiation therapy was not an intellectual choice but more of a feeling choice—I felt comfortable in the atmosphere. The staff was businesslike and friendly. It came down to simple things like the blue upholstery in the waiting room in the radiation department—it just looked delightful. And then I found out the radiation oncologist had horses, too, and that made my decision—he and I even had common interests.

"MY SURGEON SAID, 'YOU HAVE A MALIGNANCY. YOU HAVE SOME CHOICES TO MAKE.' MY HUSBAND WENT WILD! HE SAID, 'WE DON'T NEED CHOICES. I WANT YOU TO TELL ME WHAT TO DO AND WE'LL DO IT AND IT WILL BE OVER.' I FELT THAT WAY, TOO. BUT THAT'S NOT WHAT CANCER IS ABOUT."

A literary agent who had a lumpectomy, followed by chemotherapy and radiation, in 1986, when she was forty years old.

How did you learn you had breast cancer?
I found a lump. I was reading or something and sort of feeling myself (like I'm playing with my hair now; I guess it's a nervous thing), and it felt as though there was a hard green grape inside my breast—larger than a grape, but that's what it felt like. And I knew that there was something definitely wrong. I called my gynecologist right away, a well-known feminist doctor who is terrific. It took a couple of weeks to get an appointment with her —they wanted me to wait until after my period.

I did go to see her, and she examined it and immediately tried to aspirate it, which was great. And she couldn't aspirate it.
Why is it "great" that she tried to aspirate it?
Because in the last two years, I have learned that what happens

a lot of times is that doctors say, "Oh, it's a lump. How interesting. Let's wait and see what happens with it." They don't aspirate it, they don't send you for a mammogram, they don't do anything! And this happens so often. It happened to a woman I met, who waited for six months, finally couldn't stand it, had the mammogram, and by this time she had cancer and it had spread to fifteen or sixteen nodes. And right now she's dying. She has two young kids. And I could kill the doctor. I just don't understand why he would wait. And last week, I had lunch with a woman in publishing, and she had just learned she had breast cancer. She had found a lump almost a year ago, and the doctor said, "Let's wait, let's not do anything." When I was in the hospital, all the women on my floor had mastectomies, not lumpectomies. And a lot of them had been told to wait for six months, "till the next checkup." Or else the doctors say, "Listen, don't worry about it."

What did your doctor say?

She said, "It feels benign. It does not feel like cancer. Nonetheless, I want you to see someone who is the best surgeon, and he's going to make you get a mammogram beforehand. I'll tell you who to go to, so that you have the mammogram in your hand when you see him, because it's going to take you a long time to see him." She knew the whole thing already. It did take me a long time to get to see him—two or three weeks—and I was panicked.

She also asked me questions. Do I have breast cancer in my family? No. A couple of other questions. I was convinced that I didn't have breast cancer. It just seemed so unlikely.

Do you have any kind of cancer in your family?

My grandmother died of leukemia very young. And two of her sons, my mother's brothers, died of cancer—colon, stomach cancer, something. In my father's family, there was no cancer. Heart disease and diabetes, but not cancer. I have since learned that I am a terrific candidate for breast cancer, because I had many pregnancies late—in my thirties; early pregnancies somehow protect you. And I had just had two unsuccessful pregnancies. My lump, the cancer, was estrogen-receptive, so the pregnancies made it grow very quickly. I'm Jewish, and I grew up on a Jewish high-fat diet—chicken fat and chicken fat and chicken fat. And butter and mayonnaise and all kinds of things like that. Then, when I looked into the profile of a cancer victim . . . I don't want to use that word, *victim*. Cancer *patient*. Emotionally, I was ready for cancer. I had been through enough in the past two years to fit the profile of a cancer patient. I had a difficult marriage. I was under a lot of stress. I was living in one place and working in another and trying to make this marriage work. I was trying to start a business and running here, running there. I was under a lot of pressure to have children. My first pregnancy was devastating to us because it was so far along. I had amniocentesis. They discovered multiple genetic malformations, and I had to have an abortion. It was a baby we really wanted, and I didn't get pregnant for a while after that. Then I finally did, and I had a miscarriage two months into it. It was like one heartbreak after another.

The Chinese call breast cancer "the childless woman's disease," because it's so connected to women who had no children or who had lost children—it's connected to loss. Cancer in general is connected to loss. If a woman is married to a man for a long time and he dies, that woman is much more susceptible to cancer. Your immune system is down. My surgeons and my radiologist would say this is a bunch of baloney, but I think there's something to it. Certainly it was true with me. I was in bad health and in bad emotional health. It was just about the worst period of my life. I had money problems . . . just everything conceivable, all within two years or so.

What happened when you finally saw the surgeon?
He examined me. He did not try to aspirate it. He said that if my doctor had tried and failed, that he was going to accept that. He didn't want to screw around with the lump. Apparently, you can spread the cancer further. And he looked at my mammogram, and it looked like an okay lump. But he wanted me to go into the hospital. He didn't even *think* of not doing anything. He said, "You have to have a biopsy." And he wanted me to have it under general anesthesia.

How did you decide what to do next?
I started to read. And I learned that I had an option of having local anesthesia. So I went to another doctor—I made the appointment to go into the hospital, but of course, that took another week or so. In the meantime, I went to another doctor, a woman doctor, whom I was happy to see. She would do a biopsy under local anesthesia, in her office. But she was about to go on vacation, and I did not want to wait.

How was the biopsy?
I went in in the morning, and as I was coming out of the anes-

thesia—they did the frozen section right away—my surgeon said, "You have a malignancy." They don't say "cancer." He said, "The one thing I'm going to tell you about cancer is that you're going to have a choice. You're going to have to make some decisions." And he told this to my husband, who was with me. And he went wild! He said, "We don't need choices. We don't need decisions. I want you to tell me what to do and we'll do it and it will be over." I felt that way, too. I wanted to be in the hands of someone who is going to know the best and do the best, and it would all be fine. But that's not what cancer is about.

At this most frightening moment of your life, you suddenly have to become a researcher and make cool decisions about a field you know nothing about.

That's right. Like auto mechanics. "Should we do the carburetor or the pistons?" Well, define *piston*. But I have to say, this doctor was great, wonderful.

What makes a surgeon "great"?

He was a real human being. I come from a family of doctors, and although I love my family dearly, I have to say that doctors are fairly arrogant. Surgeons, especially, are arrogant. So I was surprised to see that he was so warm and wonderful. He didn't have a huge amount of time, but I didn't feel hurried out of the office.

What struck me was that here I am in New York, and the doctors I grew up with, the doctors I'm comfortable with, are all in Chicago. And I wanted them all to talk to each other, to confer, to know everything about my past, and to decide the best for me. And that never, ever happened. It wasn't important for this surgeon to know what happened to me when I was eight years old— that always surprised me. I wanted him to know the whole me and to make the decisions. And he just was not going to do that.

Before the biopsy, he told me what was going to happen, and he said, "When you wake up, I'm going to tell you what we found. You may not remember." And I said, "Believe me, I'll remember!" They put me to sleep first, intravenously. It made me high and then made me fall asleep. It was pleasant, whatever it was. And he was there when I woke up. He told me.

Were you in any pain?

I was just groggy, I think. I don't think I felt any pain from the biopsy. It was more inconvenient than anything else. Try taking a shower without getting water on your breast. I couldn't go swimming, I had to wash my hair over a sink. That's what I remember most about it, physically. But I felt fine! I mean, I didn't feel like I had cancer. I didn't have any symptoms that I knew of.

He had done a very good biopsy—in effect, a lumpectomy. He took a lot out—the lump with a good margin around it—so that when I eventually decided not to have a mastectomy, I didn't have to go back and have more surgery. That's not always true.

What was your next move after the biopsy?

It took three or four days for the lab results to come back—to see what kind of cancer it was, to do the hormone testing, to see if it was slow-growing or fast-growing. I made an appointment to see the surgeon in a week. By this time, I was taking in advocates. I had friends who went with me to appointments—I just did not go alone. I was pretty freaked out. I couldn't remember information. I'm fairly smart, but you just don't remember. Especially when there's all this technical information and they are telling you stuff you just don't want to hear.

So my sister-in-law, who's a doctor, went with me to the appointment with the surgeon. He spent a lot of time with me, going over my options and what kind of cancer it is. And he told me that I do have a choice between mastectomy and lumpectomy. He said to me at that time, "I recommend the mastectomy because of the kind of cancer that you have and the way that it's positioned." He also said that I should see other doctors and should definitely get other opinions. And he said, "You should also see a radiation therapist, and then let me know."

I did tons of reading about what I was supposed to do. I went to the Library for Medical Consumers* with a friend who is a very good reader of that kind of material. She plowed through things with me. I started to get inundated with statistics about my percentage of this and my chances of that. I went to see two other surgeons with my mammogram and my slides—I mean, I had this whole dog-and-pony show. The woman surgeon I had seen before recommended a mastectomy. The second surgeon I went to because he'd written a paper about lumpectomies and quadrantectomies and he had his people read the slides. It's a lot

---

* A medical resource library open to the public. Address: 237 Thompson Street, New York, N.Y. 10012.

to coordinate! It's like putting together a big party: the slide people have to see the slides and report to the surgeon before you see the surgeon. Anyway, he recommended a mastectomy.

In the meantime, my brother, who's a doctor, had a friend, his boss at a teaching hospital, who said that I should see an oncologist at another hospital. So I went to see him, with my husband. And he was the first person to say, "I don't know that you have to have a mastectomy. I think that you really might benefit from a lumpectomy. But you should see a radiation therapist."

During all this time, I am desperately trying to get an appointment with the man who is Dr. Radiation. His name kept coming up in all my reading—the research that he had done. I had no clout, but my friends came through for me—one was married to an investment banker whose senior partner's wife had breast cancer. Anyway, they made the calls and got me an appointment to see him. I was thrilled. But by now it's almost the fourth week after my biopsy, and in the meantime I'm running around seeing all these other doctors and doing the research and the reading. I was under a lot of pressure from my family to make the appointment for the mastectomy. And, in the meantime, I'm talking to my surgeon on the phone—he called me from his vacation and spent an hour with me, from wherever he was, going over everything again and why he thought it should be a mastectomy.

I went back to my gynecologist, and she spent an hour and a half with me, which she did not charge me for, going over all my options. She said to me, "I would go with what your surgeon says." And she was a feminist! I thought she would have been into saving the body, but she later told me that if she ever got cancer in one breast, she would have a bilateral mastectomy. She said she has just seen too much recurrence. But she understands that people feel differently.

I made an appointment to see a doctor who was going to do immediate reconstruction. But first I had to do some research to figure out how to interview him. In the Library for Medical Consumers there was a whole list that somebody had left of how to interview for reconstruction. And one of the magazines had just run this fabulous article showing a picture of a reconstructed breast. It looked perfect. It gave me such hope. Everybody was talking about it. It made the idea of a mastectomy possible.

So I'm finished with the doctors. I've scheduled a mastectomy and immediate reconstruction for Tuesday. On Monday is when

my appointment is with Dr. Radiation. I felt bad about setting up
the surgery, but I really was under a lot of pressure, and I
couldn't wait another two weeks to set up surgery if I decided to
go ahead with the mastectomy.

I see Dr. Radiation on Monday afternoon with my brother. I'm
supposed to check into the hospital that night. Dr. Radiation has
the slides, the report, and he doesn't travel anywhere unless it's
in a pack, so he has all his fellows around him, and the nurse,
who is great. He says to me, "Yes, you're a perfect candidate for
a lumpectomy and radiation. And here's why." He had the hormone count and this and that. He was so professional and so
good, and I had been so thrilled to see him, that I felt very confident. So I canceled the appointment for surgery. The surgeon was
pissed. The other doctor was pissed. You can imagine.

Did you speak to him directly?

No, I left word with the receptionist. And I wrote him a long letter
afterward, apologizing, because I really felt terrible. Then I had
to see another surgeon, because I still had to have the node dissection, and the radiation doctor wanted to do a radium implant
at the same time. This surgeon is like Central Casting for surgeons—brilliant but rude. Horrible. But now every time I go to
other doctors, they just clap! It is great, what I look like. His node
dissection was perfection!

So those are all the doctors. At the same time, I started talking
to women who had breast cancer, and they all gave me the names
of other women. I mean, I started a network. I used to be a research chief at a magazine. And there I was, with my pad and
the phone, and it was great—because I felt like I was in control.
Day and night, I talked to as many women as I could find. And I
talked about lumpectomies, radiation, chemotherapy, mastectomy, reconstruction, not reconstruction, immediate, not immediate. And all the women disagreed! But it gave me a better sense
of what I should do for myself. And I read, every book I could
possibly find. I was looking at my type of cancer and trying to find
what they say for this type—it was all mix and match.

What kind of cancer was it?

It was a carcinoma, not a sarcoma. It was a fast-growing cancer.
The lump was 1.5 centimeters. It was estrogen-receptive and
progesterone-receptive, too.

What clinched the decision for you?

I decided that I believed one can really make the medical choice between a lumpectomy with radiation and a mastectomy. Some doctors say no, some say the jury is still out, some say yes. For me, I decided yes.

Then I had to find out whether lumpectomy was an option for me, and all the doctors said it was, for my type of cancer.

And the third decision was a real personal one; how do I feel about my body, how do I feel about the choice for myself? Some women, no matter what anybody says, react, "Cancer? Take it out, I want it out." Other women would hang on to their breasts no matter what—that's how they define their femininity.

I was not in either of these camps. I really could have lived through a mastectomy perfectly fine. This is where my husband was really helpful. He said to me, "You have just had several major losses in your body. You have no body confidence right now —your body has failed you on so many levels. If you have an option of hanging on to your breast, I think you should do it. Go for the thing that's going to be the least intrusive to you." And as soon as he said it, I knew that was the right thinking.

What was the surgical procedure?

They took me fairly quickly, by the end of that week, I think. They wheeled me in, and the surgeon, such a prick, said nothing. He could have found *something* to say. And Dr. Radiation was late, and everybody was mad—it wasn't a great atmosphere for an operation. Anyway, Dr. Radiation arrives, all smiles, a sweet guy . . . and I'm out.

I wake up with about twelve radium rods through my breast, coming out the side. The next day, they put the radium in, like the mercury in a thermometer, and then they all ran away. I'm in a private room and nobody will come near me. There's a big lead barrier at the edge of the room so that people who come to visit me can't come in. The guy who delivers the papers won't walk into my room. The nurses slide my meals in.

And I was just out of surgery, and it was a heavy-duty operation. It's not a little thing like the lumpectomy. I'm all bandaged —the nodes are all down your side, under your arm, and you have to keep your arm up on a pillow. I was having a hard time moving, and I needed help. I could hardly go to the bathroom on my own.

Did you speak to your doctors?

Yes, but I was just so stunned by everything, I wasn't quite sure what to complain about. I'm not good at thinking on my feet. I'm a great person for afterward thinking what I should have said.

How long does the radium stay in?

Two days. I asked the radiation doctor, why was it okay for me if everybody's so scared of it? And he said over and over again, "Don't worry about it. You have this dose, and you're going to leave. We are in contact with it all of the time, and I want to keep our contact as minimal as possible." They all run around with little monitors.

How was the rest of your recovery?

I was in the hospital for a week and a half. After they took out the rods, I was perfectly fine. And everybody was great. They have lots of programs. They have a social worker, we had physical therapy every day—that was sort of interesting. We'd take our hands and try to walk up the wall. My God, we'd get to a point and go, "Aaaah, never!" And they taught you lots of things about how to live the rest of your life with no nodes on the side. Not to get shots on this side, not to have your blood pressure taken, not to get mosquito bites . . .

It's hard to avoid mosquito bites on one arm, isn't it?

I don't even pay attention to it. I get pricks in this hand all the time and it's all right. They heal. I have a personal trainer and I do a lot of physical exercise. My doctor said I should stop working out with arm weights. So I did, but I'll live without it.

What was the result of the node dissection?

It took about a week to find out. They usually take maybe nine nodes, fifteen nodes. They took out fifty-two nodes. Three levels of nodes. I don't know why. And there was a huge debate about the results, whether I had a positive node or not. The report said that on the first level, a follicle of a node was positive but the node itself wasn't positive. They had never seen this before and couldn't believe it. This was not great news. It made it Stage II. And I really didn't want to have chemotherapy. I was still trying to have a baby, and chemotherapy meant that I possibly, probably would become sterile. The doctors kept saying, "First things first. Let's make you well. Getting pregnant is down the line; this is what we have to do now."

I went and saw more doctors, to find out whether I should have chemotherapy or not. But in the meantime, my marriage was crumbling. The only thing really holding us together was the fact that we were going to have children. And the threat of chemo-therapy was going to push it over the edge.

And, in fact, that's what happened. It was here that my hus-band just flipped out. He now was really pressuring me to look into holistic alternatives, like some clinic in Germany where you eat seaweed or something, and diet and visualization, a whole New Age cornucopia of stuff. Which I have done, too! But I use it as a supplement. In Boston, at Mass. General, I hear they give you a diet plan—they take nutrition very seriously. Here, I went to the hospital's nutritionist and it was a joke. The woman didn't know what she was talking about. She'd say, "Oh, you're going to have chemotherapy? Well, eat peanut butter and ice-cream sodas, and eat as much as you can and gain weight because you'll lose weight during chemotherapy." An idiot! The oncologist I went to said, "That's complete nonsense. Don't even listen to her. That's if you're going to have major chemotherapy—like stomach chemotherapy. Breast cancer is a very light kind, and breast can-cer patients shouldn't have high-fat food anyway."

So that's what I mean. None of them believed in visualization or meditation, or any kind of imagining yourself well. And my husband was just flipping out. We set him up with the staff psy-chiatrist, and she was an idiot and she was about to leave. They don't really have it all together.

What did you do when you left the hospital?
I recuperated for a few days at a friend's house so I'd have some-one to take care of me, and it was within the week after I left the hospital that my husband told me he wanted out of the marriage. He couldn't take it anymore. It was the worst thing I've ever had to go through. And it was August by this time, so there was not a single marital counselor in town.

And you were about to start chemotherapy?
Yes. My mother helped me go through it. I hated the doctor and I hated the chemotherapy. He wanted to give me stuff I didn't want, and I refused to have it. I had done some more research, and I knew what I wanted to have. They really overdosed me. See, they have to give you premedications so that you can take the chemotherapy. I got incredibly nauseated and tired. It was just horrible. I had two courses of chemotherapy, one a week. Then I went up to Martha's Vineyard for a couple of days.

What happens during the chemotherapy?
First of all, I had to wait something like four hours to be taken.

Then I'd feel sick while it was dripping in. I could hardly walk out of there, I was so whizzed out. I'd go home and sleep for twelve hours, wake up, throw up, go back to sleep.

You said you refused the mixture your chemotherapist wanted to give you. Do you mean you argued with him and won?

Yes. I wanted him to give me estrogen therapy. He wanted to give me tamoxifen [an estrogen blocker—see Glossary]. And I said, "No, I don't want to go into menopause." I'm still thinking that I'm going to have a baby somewhere down the line. And Dr. Radiation said, "You don't have to have the tamoxifen if you don't want it. We'll work it out between us."

Eventually, what I did, while I was going through radiation, was look for another oncologist. I interviewed one guy, a rising star, who wanted to give me drugs that my doctor didn't want me to have. He wanted to give me Adriamycin. He wanted me to have a lot of drugs two or three times, instead of a few drugs over six months. He said the most benefits are in the first couple of shots anyway, and you only get more side effects as you go on. It's weird. A couple of years ago, chemotherapy lasted two years. Then it was one year. Now it's six months. Actually, now it's three months, and eventually it will just be one or two courses and that's it. He's a smart young whippersnapper—I really like him a lot. But my doctor didn't want me to have Adriamycin because he said my heart had been compromised by the radiation —which was news to me. So there was another big round of ne- gotiations. He talked to the chemotherapist, they each talked to me. By this time I was falling apart. I mean, I couldn't go through another negotiation. I finally said to the chemotherapist, "I'm just going to have to find an oncologist who agrees with my doc- tor because I trust him. What you say makes sense, but I can't fight this out between the two of you." He said, "Look. Whatever you want to do, we'll do. I think it would be better this way, but if you want to do it that way, that's fine."

What did he end up giving you?

CMF—that's Cytoxan, Methotrexate, and 5-fluorouracil.

Most people having a rough time with chemotherapy assume that's just the way it is: chemo is supposed to make you sick. What made you think switching to another hospital would be any different or better?

It couldn't be worse. It might be just as painful, but I couldn't stand the waiting! And I had gotten so sick, and I hated the doctor. I wanted a private office. And I wanted something near my apartment. And with this new doctor my whole chemo was great. I'd wake up in the night and throw up—it wasn't like a day at the beach—but it wasn't that flat-on-my-back stuff I endured. He gave me different premedications. I told him what I didn't want, and he listened to me! He talks to you—"We're going to do this, I'll have you out in no time, and you'll feel like going to a movie afterward."

If you read a book about chemotherapy, you'll see that you don't have to be sick. It's a lot of mind over matter. By this time, I had done a lot of visualization. I had a very good visualization therapist, who used to be at Memorial. She made me some tapes. They really helped. Everything helped. I stopped eating meat, cheese. I stopped eating things that would make me sick and make me fat, and by eating right I felt like I was taking control.

Did you gain weight during the chemotherapy?
A little bit.

How long did the chemotherapy last?
From November to February. Twice a month. Two weeks on, three weeks off.

Did you go into menopause?
My period didn't come in March or April. I didn't get it until September. I was supposed to get it last week, and I didn't. So I don't know if I'm going through menopause or not. I don't have any symptoms.

When did the radiation treatments come in?
After the two sessions of chemotherapy. They wanted me to start in a week, but they let me wait two weeks. They were really in a hurry to start everything. I went in every day in September and October. You have to wait sometimes four hours for the machines. I always thought they could organize it better, but they never could. And sometimes the machines break down. It's really annoying. It takes five minutes really, but you have to sit there for hours. I got angrier about waiting than about anything. I had twenty-seven treatments. Which should have been one month, but it ended up being two months because the machines break down so often.

The radiation people were great. You see the same people all the time. I'd take a book and magazines, and I did a lot of reading.

*How did you feel during radiation? Did you have side
effects?*

I was able to work in the afternoons. And I had no side effects. I
think the breast turned a little pink, that's all. I was told by all
the mastectomy surgeons that my breasts were going to shrivel
up, turn brown and leathery; that cosmetically alone, I would be
better off with the reconstruction after a mastectomy. And it
turned out not to be true for me. My breasts look great!

And how are you feeling now?

Physically? I have a cold, which is the first time I've been sick in
two years. It took me a long time to acknowledge that, "Yes, you
are sick," because I have been on a streak. I signed up for this
personal trainer. I go twice a week. I do exercises. I swim, I walk,
I changed my diet, I went to Weight Watchers and lost fifteen
pounds. I got my hair cut—I lost my hair through chemotherapy,
and it came back again. So I feel great. I feel really, really great.
My life changed. My husband did leave. He stayed with me
through chemotherapy—we found a counselor who helped us
make that decision. Then he left in February of last year. But
cancer changed my life in a lot of other ways, too. I feel better. I
made a lot of decisions about my life and what I wanted.

"I THINK WHAT GOT ME THROUGH WAS BEING ANGRY
AT ALL THESE DOCTORS FOR TELLING ME THIS LUMP
WAS NOTHING. THAT'S WHAT I CONCENTRATED ON:
HOW DID THESE ASSHOLES LET ME SIT AROUND FOR SIX
MONTHS WITH A LUMP THAT WAS MALIGNANT?"

*A thirty-five-year-old woman who was having trouble get-
ting pregnant—consulting with gynecologists, fertility
specialists, and general surgeons—when she discovered a
lump in her breast. At the time of the interview, she had
been married for two years and was working as a librarian
for a state government department.*

When did your gynecological problems begin?

This past year. I was bleeding almost twenty days a month. We
were living in Europe, and I just didn't get good medical care
because my language skills limited me to only English-speaking
doctors.

When we came back to the States in November, the first thing I did was make an appointment with a gynecologist, and I had a D&C in December. The bleeding didn't stop. For some reason the gynecologist decided to do a pregnancy test, and it came back positive. He couldn't decide whether or not I had an ectopic pregnancy. He kept hemming and hawing. I probably should have gone for a second opinion, but I didn't. I thought he knew what he was doing.

He finally decided to go ahead with surgery, and it was an ectopic. There was also a cyst on my ovary, which they aspirated. Everything was okay, and I thought, Now I'll be able to get pregnant. And I tried, I guess for over a year, when I started getting pains on my right side, where my right ovary would be. This was at the beginning of May 1985, and he did a full exam, including a breast exam.

At the end of May, it was getting near my birthday—I was going to turn thirty-five—and I read Jane Brody's health book. I thought I really should start doing breast exams. The first time I did it, I found this lump, an almond-size lump, in my left breast. I never knew what fear was until I found that. I was just absolutely paralyzed. I just started crying.

I was in bed with my husband—we were reading in bed in the morning—and I said, "Feel this." He did, and he was saying, "If it doesn't go away in a couple of days, then you should see a doctor." I was so scared that I didn't want to go. But I talked to two friends who convinced me to have it checked out.

So I went back to my doctor—this is now the beginning of June, a month after I saw him last—and I asked, "Was this lump here in May?" He looked at his records and said, "I don't have any note about it." And I don't believe that he could have missed it— it was just too obvious a lump. So it seems clear that it just appeared. He told me that it was "freely movable," that it didn't feel hard and solid like a stone.

But you describe it as feeling like an almond.
Well, it was the size of an almond. It felt hard to me. I mean, it didn't feel like a cyst. But he said that it wasn't hard like a stone. He said, "I don't think it's anything, but just to make you feel better, I'll send you for a mammogram." Really patronizing. Instead of saying it was good medical practice, he implied it was so I wouldn't worry. He sent me to the man who's the big radiologist for mammography—everybody goes to him. And this man said,

"Oh, what are ya here for? Ya got a lump?" And I said, "Yeah, I do!" So he felt my lump, and he said, "Ach, this is not much of a lump. This is a boring case." And they did the mammography.

At this point, I called a psychiatrist I knew and asked him if I could use his name to get the mammography report. I didn't think my doctor was explaining anything, and you can't get your own medical records in New York. [Under the current public health law, you *can* get your doctor and hospital records in New York. The statute, however, is complicated and there are a number of exceptions.] A hospital will send them to a lawyer, an insurance company, or a doctor—but not to the patient. And I wanted to know what really happened.

According to the report, there were no adverse findings. This report was one sentence. The radiologist kept the films and sent this one-sentence report. I guess I was relieved.

All this time I was bleeding again. So I made an appointment with an infertility guy who was the expert at this hospital and had office hours on Saturday, always a nice thing. I told him about my infertility problems, and I said, "By the way, I have this lump in my breast." He examined the lump and said, "In my heart, I think it's nothing, but I think you should go to a breast surgeon." He gave me two names, no telephone numbers, and didn't offer to make the appointment. I really didn't like him; he was too curt. I couldn't talk to him.

At this point I had appointments with two doctors: one of these breast surgeons and another fertility guy I'd heard about, whom I couldn't see until August. And I still had this incredible bleeding. I thought, I can't handle all this, so I canceled the breast surgeon and went back to my gynecologist, who never mentioned anything about my breast lump and gave me a progesterone injection to stop the bleeding. It didn't work. I was supposed to come back in two weeks, and I did, but with my husband this time. I thought, If my husband comes, there's no way this doctor can avoid talking to us in the office. I mean, they never talk to you in the office! It's always in the examining room. You're wearing your paper dress, you're supposed to bring a little pad and pencil, but you don't have a pocket for your pencil—you're always in this very vulnerable, really inferior position.

Well, the whole time, he talked only to my husband, about "what she'll need" and "this is what we want for her." My father had died in March, and the doctor was saying that the emotional reaction to my father's death could have caused or aggravated the bleeding. "I wanted to do a D&C for a long time, but I didn't think she could handle it," he said. I was enraged.

It's now the beginning of August. I go to another gynecologist, recommended by the psychiatrist, who is part of a big GYN practice. And I say, "By the way, I have this lump in my breast." He said, "If you were my wife sitting there, I'd say you have nothing to worry about. All these doctors have examined the lump and said it doesn't feel like anything, and the mammogram was negative."

Was he basing this judgment on the mammogram report or the film itself?

The report. He didn't actually see the films. He was going on his clinical exam of the lump and the written report. But he recommended a breast surgeon, saying, "Just to make you feel better" —again, like "Don't worry about your little lump." He also said the cause of the bleeding was a cyst on my left ovary. I said, "How is that causing pain on the right side?" "Well, it could be referred pain."* And he recommended surgery.

I go to the breast surgeon, who examines the lump and says, "Well, just to make you feel better, I think we should remove it." So I said, "Okay, that's fine. What kind of procedure is this?" "Well, it can be done as an outpatient, with general anesthesia." He didn't tell me that you could do a breast biopsy with a local. I had no idea that you could. I said, "Well, since I have to have anesthesia for this breast thing, and my gynecologist wants to do abdominal surgery for the cyst, can't we combine the procedures so I only have to have one anesthesia?"

Yes, that was fine. But in the meantime, I went to the fertility specialist I'd been waiting to see. An anesthesiologist told me that he was a really wonderful person and easy to talk to.

I went with my husband, and we talked only about infertility. The doctor didn't examine my breasts. From this first meeting, he finds that I had a chronic infection called mycoplasma that could have caused a miscarriage if I'd ever gotten pregnant. No one ever tested me for it. He always tests for that and for chlamydia because it's just rampant. We decided that he was going

---

* Pain distant from its point of origin, according to Taber's Cyclopedia Medical Dictionary, p. 1463.

to do a laparoscopy and try to correct my tubes as much as possible.

What did you do about the surgery for the cyst?
I canceled it. And because I gave that up, I also gave up the appointment with the breast surgeon. The next time I went back to the new infertility specialist, I said, "I also have this lump in my breast." He would have known that from my records, but he didn't bring it up. He examined me and said that it felt benign, and he said, "Well, if you remove it, you'll have a scar, and the lump itself will probably just come back." I swear that's what this man said. And I like him. I think he's a terrific gynecologist. And he doesn't talk to you in the examining room. You get to sit in the office with your clothes on before or after the exam.

Now, since we were trying to adopt a baby, I needed some medical forms filled out. I decided to go to my husband's internist. And I said, "By the way, I have this lump in my breast." This is doctor number six whom I've told about this lump. He examined me, and he said, "A mammography is only 85 percent accurate. I've seen a lot of lumps and I don't know if they're benign or not until they are removed and until they do a biopsy. And I think you should have it removed, and here is the name of a doctor that I am recommending." It turns out that he is also an oncologist, which I didn't know at the time.

So I've got a laparoscopy set up with a doctor who says forget about the lump, and this internist says have it out, and my husband says bring it up with the infertility guy. So I went back to him. He makes it very easy for you to say what's on your mind. He says, "What's bothering you?" And I said, "Well, I'm scared of the anesthesia and I'm scared about my lump—I think it's growing." He said, "Where are you in your cycle?" I told him, and he said he thought that's why it seemed larger. He examined me again, and he said, "Look, I'll feel better, you'll feel better—let's aspirate it."

Three times he tried to aspirate it. He said, "This is really strange. I can't get any fluid out at all."

Does aspiration hurt?
No. The guy has the most wonderful touch. He's sticking a needle in your breast and you don't feel it. He finally said, "Okay, this is strange. Why don't we have it removed at the time of the surgery? I'll get you a good surgeon." He set up a date in October. Mean-

while, he had cauterized the cervix and pretty much had the bleeding stopped.

The new breast surgeon wanted to see me. I thought, That sounds nice and thorough, instead of just meeting me in the operating room. I told him the story, and he said, "Well, if you'd seen me in June, I would have said, 'Get the lump out.' "

That must have scared you.

It did. By this time I was very scared, even though everybody kept saying, "This is benign." To me, it felt like a stone. I just hated it being there. The breast surgeon also said, "I'm 99 percent sure it's nothing, too, but I think you should have it out."

So I had the laparoscopy and the lump removed at the same time. I think it was fifteen minutes for the lump and forty-five minutes for the laparoscopy. This was outpatient, and when I woke up, they were trying to get me out of bed so they could close up the office. They give you a glass of juice and you stagger into the dressing room and get dressed and leave. But it was all right. I'd rather do any of this stuff as an outpatient than stay in the hospital.

The gynecologist came to me after the surgery and . . . he just has a wonderful personality, the best bedside manner of anyone I've ever met. He told me what he had done, that there was no endometriosis, that he'd moved a lot of polyps. Then he said— this is while I was coming out of the anesthesia—"But I won't rest easy until we get that biopsy on Thursday." I thought, Oh, he's just being thorough.

So I went home. I didn't go to work the next day, but I could have if I'd wanted to. The surgery was nothing. I had one Band-Aid on my navel and one right on the pubic line. And I had a big dressing on my breast that was for support.

Were you in any pain?

I was in absolutely no pain. I just wanted to sleep. So I did.

Then, around two o'clock Thursday, the breast surgeon calls. He says, "Hello, how are you?" and I think, How considerate to call to see how I am. He said. "I want you and your husband to come into the office today. We have to talk about your options." I said, "What are you talking about?" He said, "Just get your husband and come into the office today."

Well, I didn't know how I was going to find him in the middle of the day, but I did, and the doctor just started giving us all this information. He had two pathology reports, and he had run up that morning to look at the mammograms themselves—the guy's a little abrupt, but his heart is in the right place. He's telling me all this stuff. What I knew about breast cancer was an article I read in the *Wall Street Journal* about if you go in one door of Memorial Sloan-Kettering, you talk to a guy who wants to do a mastectomy, and if you go in the other door, you get a guy who says that lumpectomy is great. And I saw a "Cagney & Lacey" television show about breast cancer. That's what I knew about breast cancer until I was told I had it.

He said, "Your choice is: You can have a mastectomy or lumpectomy." He showed me pictures of implants, and they looked like a horror show to me. I couldn't even believe that I had cancer. Then I started to cry. He said, "I'm going to leave you alone, and you can talk to each other. I don't know you very well. Do you want to go out and see eight doctors and get different opinions? Do you want to have the surgery done yesterday?"

At that point, I'd seen all these doctors and they all seemed to be wrong. I felt strongly that I was not going around seeking eight more opinions. And I thought, I probably want the lumpectomy, because I don't want to look like this. But what scared me about the lumpectomy was that you have to have radiation. And my father, who had died of lung cancer, had not done well with radiation. The doctor said, "Don't think about radiation. Your choice is: Can you live the rest of your life being afraid that you'll get cancer in the left breast, or can you live without a breast?" I thought, I'm not scared of getting cancer in the same breast. I'm scared of getting it in the other breast, of getting it everywhere else. If I have a mastectomy, that's not going to take away my fear of cancer.

We left it that I would do more thinking and call the gynecologist, which I did. He's very dramatic and emotional. He said, "Oh, we're devastated!"—and he meant it. "The whole office is devastated!" Then I asked him, "What should I do?" He said, "I think you should have the mastectomy. They're doing very well with implants now." I saw what they were doing with implants. My mother said, "If it were me, I would have the mastectomy. At least we know that works." Then I called my friend the psychiatrist, and my husband and I saw him immediately. The most helpful thing he said was, "Look, the guy is offering you a lumpectomy. That means it is a viable option. Surgeons have been cutting off women's breasts for years. They're not going to turn around and say they've been doing the wrong thing."

I was tending toward the lumpectomy. Then my question was: Should I use this surgeon? And I started asking around and found a doctor who'd done a study on lumpectomy but I couldn't get an appointment fast enough—the guy was away. I called my surgeon back to ask for the name of another doctor. He said, "If you want a plastic surgeon, I'll get you one to talk to." He was not threatened at all by my seeing somebody else.

My husband and I went to see the plastic surgeon and within twenty minutes he made everything clear about the state of the art of breast cancer. What I hadn't understood was that you have to have the nodes removed whether you have a mastectomy or a lumpectomy. The nodes have to go for staging [determining if the cancer has spread, and if so, how far]. By the time we left, my husband and I both thought it was pretty clear that I would have a lumpectomy.

What did the doctor say that made that clear to you?
He explained the research for the lumpectomy, and apparently, the results of five-year studies show that lumpectomy plus radiation is no different from mastectomy. I guess they now have some eight-year data as well. He said, "You have a 10 percent chance of recurrence in the breast if you have a lumpectomy." I thought, What do I have to lose? If it comes back, then I have the mastectomy. And I thought I might as well have the surgeon who did the biopsy do it because he's very interested in cosmetic effect, and I knew he would try to do a good job. So I called him and said, "Set it up."

Before the surgery, I had to see him to remove the bandage from the biopsy. At that time, he explained what he was going to do. As I said, he's rather abrupt. He was saying, "Well, we either do a wedge, or I'll just cut out some from the top, but then the nipple will be a bit low." I got out of there and I was in tears. Somehow, I had thought they were not going to do anything more to my breast—they had already taken the lump.

That was one of the worst times. A neighbor had gone with me, an older, very kind woman. We went home in a cab, and she said, "Can you talk about it?" I guess I just realized I didn't know what they were going to do to my body. Was I going to look mangled? What was I going to be left with?

My mother came up to New York. I checked into the hospital that Monday. It took a horrendous six hours to get admitted. A P.A. [physician's assistant] came over to me, saying, "So, you have breast cancer!" To take your Blue Cross number and make a photocopy of your card took this woman forty minutes, and she couldn't get my doctor's name right. I was in tears before we even got up to the room. And then my neighbor came to say hello and had an epileptic seizure in the room. I was so worried about her that I wanted to postpone the surgery so I'd know how she was before I went in. My doctor's partner said about me, "Thank God she's not my patient!"

Anyway, somehow I got through it. I think what got me through was being angry at all these doctors for telling me this lump was nothing. That's what I concentrated on. Instead of "I have cancer," I was thinking, How did these assholes let me sit around for six months with a lump that's malignant? And they are supposed to be good people. And they probably are. I'm sure they were upset about making the wrong diagnosis.

So I had the surgery, and I had some pain afterward, I guess. I was getting painkillers intravenously, and I had this drain—it's about six inches round, like a small pillow or a little makeup case, collapsible like an accordion, and it would fill with fluid. And I was up, walking around, the next day. A nurse tried to lift me by grabbing my shoulder—that really hurt. I was really cranky, pissed off.

How long were you in the hospital?
I went in Monday afternoon, and I was out Saturday, very early in the morning—7:30 A.M.

How did you feel by the time you left?
Mentally, I was numb while we were waiting for the report about the lymph nodes. We wouldn't know until the end of the week. I think my mother and my husband were in worse shape than I was. I was just relieved that it was over. I told myself, "I'm not going to think about doing anything until I hear the report. If the nodes are positive [indicating that the cancer has spread], then I'm going to kill somebody. I'm going to sue. I'm going to do whatever you have to do."

Thursday night, the surgeon came up. He had just heard. Twenty-three nodes and they were all negative. He came up to tell us in person, instead of calling. He did a great job. Hearing the report made a huge difference to my mother and my husband, but I guess I haven't felt totally relieved since all this happened. I'm still terrified that either my cancer has spread or that I'm going to get some other kind of cancer.

Physically, I felt pretty good. My arm was numb, and it's still numb—six and a half months after surgery.

How is the scar?

I have a beautiful scar. If you raise your arm, you'll see a muscle —the scar is sort of on the inside of the muscle. It's not noticeable at all. And the breast scar, which is about two inches long, is under the breast, and I can't even see it when I look in the mirror. I've been using vitamin E oil on it, and it's practically gone. So he did a wonderful cosmetic job. Even he was pleased with it. Right before he took the bandages off, he said, "Sometimes this doesn't work out so great." So now he tells me, right? But it worked out great, and he was just delighted.

Did you have the radiation?

Yes, the *New England Journal of Medicine* says that whenever you have a lumpectomy, you should have radiation.

What was that like?

I was so tired by the end of it, and then for many weeks after. I started three weeks after surgery. They like you to begin as early as two weeks—as soon as you can get your arm up and out, because you have to be in a position where you can expose your breast and underarm, and I was rather slow about that.

What is the procedure?

You're wearing a hospital gown top and your regular skirt and even shoes. The people are all very nice, very friendly. And the radiation itself had no side effects except for a redness that looks like a sunburn and the incredible tiredness. I didn't need any under my arm, which can cause a lot of swelling and impair your movement. It was strictly to the breast and to the area where the lump was. It lasts less than five minutes, and I went every day for thirty-one days.

We've heard that radiation can permanently damage the skin. Is that true?

I've heard that, too, but I haven't had that result. I had radiation to the breast for twenty-five treatments. Then I had what they call a booster to where the lump was. I still have a rectangular patch of red that looks like a sunburn. But my skin is fine.

Did you use oils or a moisturizer?

Yes. They give you a water-based cream to use while you're getting the radiation because it's supposed to be skin-sparing, and you can't use any oil-based cream. After that, they tell you to put Keri lotion [a brand of moisturizer] on it or vitamin E oil, and it's okay.

How are you now?
While I was getting radiation, I would see the doctor almost every day and I felt safe; somebody was watching me. After that stopped is when I started getting panicked about everything. I still have that, but not as much, because I started going to Cancer Care. I'm not supposed to try to get pregnant because the breast cancer was estrogen-dependent. So we're trying to adopt, and adoption agencies don't want to give babies to women who've had cancer. But we'll see.

"THE DOCTOR SAID I COULD BRING MY FRIENDS INTO THE CONSULTATION ROOM. I WENT OUT TO THE WAITING ROOM, AND MY FRIENDS SAID, 'WHO DO YOU WANT?' I SAID, 'I'D LIKE THE WHOLE WAITING ROOM TO COME IN.' AND EVERYONE STARTED TO LAUGH."
A comedienne who had a lumpectomy in 1985 when she was forty-eight years old.

How was the lump discovered?
I had a pain in my breast that lasted for around two weeks. But I have cystic breasts, so I've had pains before that turned out to be nothing. When I was in my twenties, I had a benign cyst or tumor removed under local anesthesia. And over the years I've had other lumps that disappeared—maybe even the one I had removed would have gone away if I had left it alone. But this time I hadn't felt a lump, just the pain. My gynecologist had been my doctor for years and had done a myomectomy on me in 1974 and later a complete hysterectomy in 1981, but before I had this pain I had made up my mind to switch doctors. I had some very bad hormonal and psychological reactions to the hysterectomy—hot flashes, terrible depression, I used to cry on the street over nothing—and he was very uncaring and impatient. He had prescribed estrogen without progesterone, and when I talked with him about seeing an endocrinologist he said, "There's no point in that. You'll just waste your money." He didn't want to help me explore

my problem at all. So I decided to try a new gynecologist. I wanted a woman because I thought maybe she would understand me better. My internist recommended one, but by the time I could see her the pain had been gone for a week. She found a lump, though, and said, "I think we should aspirate that. If fluid comes out, then it's a cyst, and if fluid doesn't come out, then it could be a sign of malignancy." It was terrifying. Here I was watching nothing come out. But she was all right—not terrific in terms of compassion, but okay as a doctor. She said she thought I should see a breast specialist. I said, "I already have someone I like a lot." She said, "Fine." Then she said I should get a mammogram. I got one that afternoon, and the mammogram was okay. I think there's something like a 17 percent error in mammograms.

What did the breast surgeon say?

He said, "I don't think it's malignant," but he thought I should have a biopsy. He said he was going away, but he would give me the names of some people who could do it. Then he started to talk to me about a mastectomy. And I said, "What about a lumpectomy?" He said, "Oh, well, there's that, too." I said, "What about going off the estrogen until I find out if it's malignant or not?" He said, "You could do that." And then he went on his vacation, and I started to shop for doctors. By the way, about six months ago I came across the bill for that visit. They had charged me for an aspiration, which he had never given me. Every once in a while I think about going back to his office and telling him. It was a very small amount, maybe fifty dollars, but it infuriated me.

Did you have the biopsy?

I saw a doctor who did a needle biopsy in his office. It, too, was negative like the mammogram. But this doctor felt the lump was malignant. And he also talked a lot about mastectomy. I later found out he was not a breast specialist—he was a general surgeon who did a lot of breasts. Maybe that's not very important, but I think women should know if a doctor is a specialist.

Was it intuition that made him feel the tumor was
malignant?

No. The skin was puckered and dimpled—that's one sign of malignancy—but the tumor was underneath my breast, which is small, and the skin was black and blue from being aspirated twice, so the dimpling was hard to see.

What did the doctor suggest as your next step?

He showed me pictures of a woman who had a mastectomy and then he said that if his wife were in my situation, he would recommend a mastectomy. He went on to say that we all know mastectomy is the most conservative method of treatment even though it appears to be the most radical and blah-blah-blah. So it was clear that he wanted to go in, and if the lump turned out to be malignant, he wanted to do a mastectomy.

What did you do?

I went to see a radiologist, who also felt it was malignant, so by then I was pretty sure I had cancer. While all this was happening I'd started talking to all kinds of people on the phone to get more information. I spoke with a very famous woman who had written a book about her mastectomy. She had just had her second and said things like "Now that I'm symmetrical, I don't know what the fuss was all about." It seemed to me such extraordinary denial to say, "What was the fuss?" But I suppose it's human nature for people to want you to have what they had. I remember when I was having the myomectomy a certain relative of mine said, "They should give you a hysterectomy. I had one and I never felt better." Anyway, in all my research one breast specialist's name came up from seven different people, and since I didn't feel very confident about the last surgeon, I went to see this specialist.

And what was your meeting like?

He examined me, and I was pretty sure he thought it was malignant. I could tell just from his manner and the fact that the first thing he said to me when we went into his office was, "Now, you ask what questions you want to ask first." I felt at ease with him. I had some friends with me and when the doctor said I could bring my people in, I went out to the waiting room. You know how tense the waiting rooms are—just horrible. And my friends said, "Who do you want?" I said, "I'd like the whole waiting room to come in." And everyone started to laugh. The doctor said, "I can only have a few because I only have so many chairs that match." There was something so sweet and human about the joke. It sounds stupid that anybody would choose a doctor for humor. I didn't really, but I think it was his humanness that was the deciding factor.

So we decided that I would have a lumpectomy, and if it was malignant, they would excise the nodes to see if the cancer had spread.

And what was the diagnosis?

Not only was the lump malignant, but it had spread. He took out sixteen nodes, and it was in three of the sixteen. I understand that one to three positive nodes falls within the same category. It was a small cancer, but having positive nodes threw my conditon into Stage II cancer.

Do you remember how he broke the news to you?"
I don't really remember, but apparently, when he came into my room, he said to one of my friends, "I need a hug." And someone went over and gave him one. I don't know how these people do this all the time—it has to be really stressful. But this doctor is very interesting. He and a colleague pioneered a process where if he finds a malignancy in one breast, he biopsies the other in approximately the same area in the other breast—I don't know what the percentages are of finding cancerous cells there, but they're high enough so it has become a working method.

Were you in any pain after the surgery?
It wasn't horrible. I was very worried about the use of my arm. I'm left-handed. Some people's arms swell—mine didn't.

How long were you in the hospital?
Not very many days—maybe three or four. There was a drain and I was bandaged, but they removed everything before I left the hospital except for the stitches. The stitches were removed a few days after I left the hospital.

Did you have radiation?
Yes, about three weeks or so after the surgery. I started with a couple of weeks of radiation every day and then began a month of chemotherapy in conjunction with radiation. The chemo went on for between six and nine months. They told me I would have aggressive chemotherapy because I am premenopausal. And the more aggressively my cancer was treated with chemo, the better my chances for a cure.

Was it your breast surgeon who recommended your having radiation and chemo at the same time?
No. The breast surgeon recommended that I see this radiation oncologist, and he is the one who prescribed this routine. I had to go all the way downtown to the hospital. The doses of radiation and chemo are all computerized. I had to stop all the treatments a couple of times because the combination brought my blood count way down. When you have chemo and radiation, your immune system weakens because the treatments kill off the white blood cells, which protect you. The chemo came in the form of

pills that I took at home and injections at the hospital when I went for the radiation treatments.

What kind of reaction did you have to the treatment?
It was a kind of tiredness. If I had to go get a prescription or something, I wanted to lie down on the floor of the drugstore. It's not a regular tiredness. It's like your body is a sponge—just very weak. But prednisone, one of the chemotherapy drugs I was taking, hopped me up a lot. I noticed I was reaching for stuff in my kitchen cupboards like someone who was speeded up in a silent film. I couldn't sleep, either. Then my body finally adjusted.

Did anything happen to your hair?
My hair was quite long at the time. The chemotherapist told me I should cut it short because it would be easier to deal with psychologically when it started falling out. So I got a very short, fifty-buck haircut. It was the most expensive haircut I've ever had in my life, since my hair fell out in a week. Actually, I was shedding for maybe a week or two, and my hair really fell out about three weeks after I began the chemo. They tell you to get fitted for a wig *before* it starts to fall out, also for psychological reasons. And they tell you not to get human-hair wigs because they need to be cleaned professionally to look right.

When did your hair begin to grow back?
Maybe a month and a half after I stopped treatment. That's the worst part—losing your hair. I thought I was being a baby about it, but it seems to be the hardest time for most women. You look like a victim. I got so that I'd put a scarf over the mirror when I went into the bathroom because I didn't want to look at myself. If a delivery man came, I'd have to put a wig on. I still think about that. Today, I went up to get the mail, and I had this wonderful feeling of freedom because I didn't have to put on that wig.

But having the wig did help, didn't it?
Oh, yes. It helped. A lot of people can't find one that's styled like their hair. I was used to having my hair straight with bangs, and I managed to get a wig like that.

Now that you're finished with treatments, are you getting checkups?
Yes. I was talking to a woman in the waiting room the last time I was there, and I said that I'd like to see the doctor every couple of months. She said, "I'd like to see one every day." And I knew what she meant. I was fine throughout the treatments, but afterward I got very depressed. While you're having chemotherapy

you know it's killing something in your body, but it's microscopic and you can't see it. And the fact that you can't see it means you're not sure the job is done. So some people don't want the treatments to end.

And then you read all that stuff in the newspapers—it seems like every day—about breast cancer, the risks, the statistics. And it's a shock over and over again to make the connection between my having breast cancer and the statistics. I recognize myself in the numbers, but at the same time I have to keep myself separate from them. I think when women go for mammograms those times are like rehearsals for the day when they tell you that you have cancer. I've been having a problem with my hand, and about three weeks ago I went to see a doctor. He said, "So are you getting checkups on your breast?" I said, "Yes." He said, "What you're doing is waiting out the five-year survival period so you can sit back and relax." I was so shocked that I couldn't respond. And later I realized he had processed the information about breast cancer, and he had no guard on his mouth and the words just came out. People call me up and tell me about other people they've known who've had cancer and how it comes back. Other people make jokes, too, thinking they're going to make having cancer normal. Since I make jokes about everything, they feel they can do it with me, but joking about cancer returning is different. There was a woman who lived in my building who was driving me crazy. She'd call me at all hours of the day and night after I came home from the hospital. I was tired and upset, and I finally said to a friend, "I guess the only way I'm going to get rid of her is to pretend I have had cancer." That struck me as hilarious. Of course, I was the one making the joke.

"WHEN YOU MEET AN *EX*-CANCER PATIENT, SHE'S ALIVE, AND IT'S PROOF THAT YOU, TOO, ARE GOING TO LIVE. CANCER IS NOT A DEATH SENTENCE AT ALL."

A musician whose cancer was discovered in 1987, when she was forty-six, through a routine mammogram. She had a lumpectomy and, subsequently, both chemotherapy and radiation therapy.

Were you getting regular mammograms before the cancer
was discovered?
Actually, the only other mammogram I had was in 1983. It was
a baseline mammogram, and everything was fine.

Did your most recent mammogram show a suspicious
lump?
No. They found what they called calcification clusters, which I
could see on the X-ray. They were like little white dots kind of
clustered together. It wasn't definitive that there was a tumor
because my breasts are very large and they are made up of very
dense tissue. But the calcifications signaled the possibility of
something serious. I was told there was only a 15 percent chance
that they were tumors.

What are the calcification clusters?
They're a by-product of the way the body metabolizes food, not
calcium. The first thing I thought was I'd better stop taking calcium supplements—I was taking calcium to prevent osteoporosis
—but I was told that had nothing to do with that. And a number
of other women told me that they'd had calcification clusters
which turned out to be nothing. At that point, for me, the risk
was fairly minimal, so I wasn't really worried. I lead such a clean
life, I assumed that I was going to be in the 85 percent whose
clusters were benign. I didn't have a real clear understanding of
the ways in which I actually was at risk for cancer.

How were you at risk?
I have not had any children. I'm a vegetarian, so I don't eat meat,
but my fondness for cheese and butter and things like that put
me at risk for cancer. Somehow I thought that being a vegetarian
was a magic blanket that would protect me.

How soon after you had the mammogram were you given
the results?
Ten days later. There was a delay because they had messed up
my phone number and couldn't find me. I finally called them,
and my gynecologist just said, "I want you to see a surgeon."
That was Friday. He gave me a name, called the surgeon, and
set up an appointment for Tuesday. The surgeon couldn't feel
anything. And I thought, Of course not, there's nothing there,
nothing to worry about. He said, "In a case like this I can't know
anything until we go in and do a biopsy." He said it would be an
outpatient procedure in the hospital under a local anesthetic. He

asked when I would be free to have it done. We settled on Thursday of the same week, which would have been October fifteenth.

What was the procedure like?

I signed into the hospital at 9 A.M. I was sent to the ambulatory surgery unit, where I changed into a hospital gown. I was put in a wheelchair and taken to the same place where I had my mammogram. A doctor and a technician were waiting for me. The technician applied a local anesthetic cream to the general area of the calcification clusters. The doctor's job was to pinpoint the site of the clusters based on the mammogram, to provide a map for the surgeon. The doctor inserted a very fine hollow needle pointing exactly to the clusters. Then the technician took another mammogram with the needle in place. The doctor checked the X-ray and then had to readjust the needle (see NEEDLE LOCALIZATION in Glossary). You see, they were looking for these microscopic little pieces. Once the doctor was satisfied with the positioning of the needle, he inserted this little plastic vial of blue dye into the end and then squished it so that the section where the surgeon was going to cut was dyed blue. They left the needle in and taped it over, then put me back in the wheelchair. I started to feel very faint then—I didn't know if I was going to throw up or just crash out. Everyone at that point was so sweet to me. They put cold compresses on my forehead and talked to me. The technician said, "You were great that you waited to faint until it was over."

Was the faintness a physical or emotional response?

I would say it was emotionally induced. It's not that there was pain, but you *are* being stuck with needles. I told the technician I felt like a voodoo doll. It was very strange to have a lot of people focusing that kind of attention on your breast. Later, when they took my blood pressure, it was so low they almost couldn't find it.

Were you becoming concerned that it might be serious?

Not at this point, because the process wasn't all that different from what I had been led to expect. But going through it was weird, and I'm sure I was much more anxious than I knew. Anyway, they gave me a Valium and rolled me into surgery for the biopsy.

What do you remember about the actual biopsy?

First, they put a little thing on your finger that looks like a plastic clothespin to take a blood smear that's tested for hemoglobin—a low count could indicate anemia. They took my blood pressure and heartbeat and strapped me onto the operating table—they do it with blankets so you don't quite realize you've been restrained until you try to move your arm, and then you know you're being held in.

Were you conscious throughout the surgery?
Yes. The Valium had a slight disorienting effect, but I was aware of everything that was happening. Now I should mention that I had started crying during the needle biopsy and didn't stop until after the surgery. The crying is a very strange thing. I've reacted this way before. It's not the kind of crying where you're sobbing; tears just escape, and they keep coming. Maybe it's just a release. It didn't seem to surprise anybody.

Anyway, they put a kind of blanket over me with a hole cut out over my right breast, pulling up one end in front of my face so I couldn't see anything. But I could hear everything. It was very strange because it was as if I weren't there so far as anyone in the room was concerned.

Can you remember anything they said?
Not much was said during the procedure itself—I didn't realize that he was taking out the whole lump—in effect, doing a lumpectomy. I could smell burning flesh, and I heard this *ppssss* sound. He was using some kind of cutting, cauterizing tool, and there was something unpleasant and disturbing about it, so I just quietly cried the whole time behind the blanket. Toward the end the surgeon gave the tumor to the pathologist, who must have taken it away to do a frozen section. The pathologist said something to the surgeon about not getting the complete margin around the tumor. The nurse then said something about "when we go back in" and I thought, What's going on here? But the surgeon said, "No, we don't need to go back in." And he continued sewing it up, and I have a half-moon incision about an inch and a half long. The whole process took about a half hour.

Did the doctor tell you the results of the surgery?
Yes. Right after he sewed me up, he said, "We found some suspicious tissue, and it looks as if there's about a 50 percent chance that there's a malignancy." But then he said, "If that's the case, I think you're an excellent candidate for radiation, and we'll talk about it more when we get the results." When I was wheeled away, I thought, Oh, God, I've gone from a 15 percent chance to a fifty-fifty chance in the space of a half hour. I'm going to have to deal with this a little bit more seriously. Even then I still honestly didn't think it was going to turn out to be anything. In the

recovery room they brought me some juice and left me there. I fell asleep probably for about an hour, and when I woke up I was feeling very disoriented and strange.

What time did you get home?

I was home by 2:30 in the afternoon, so the whole thing took about five and a half hours. They sent me away with some Darvocet, which is a combination of Darvon and Tylenol.

Were you in any pain?

No, not really—just a little bit of itching. When I first came home I took the Darvocet because I thought the local anesthetic was going to wear off and it was going to get worse. I'm very vulnerable to drugs, so I thought the Darvocet would put me right to sleep, and that's probably a good thing. I wasn't in any pain when I woke up, and I never really needed the drug again.

When did you get the final results of the biopsy?

The next day. And he confirmed that indeed it was malignant, and he wanted me to come in the following Monday or Tuesday. He didn't want to talk about treatment options on the phone. I picked Tuesday—I was trying to buy a little time, trying to get used to the idea that I had cancer. I should tell you that Friday, the day he called with the bad news, was the day Nancy Reagan was diagnosed with breast cancer. She decided to have a mastectomy immediately, and for the entire weekend every news program was all about breast cancer. So I just lay on the sofa in a stupor looking at all this information about breast cancer, trying to sort it all out. He had said I was a candidate for radiation, but I didn't have a clue as to what that meant. My lump was small, like Nancy Reagan's. Did he mean I needed radiation plus a mastectomy or just radiation itself? I think on some level, that weekend, I got the impression that the treatment for any breast cancer was a mastectomy.

But what did the surgeon tell you on Tuesday?

He told me the tumor had been thirteen millimeters, about the size of a lima bean, and it was located at eleven o'clock on the right breast. He also knew the tumor had developed in the past four years because the baseline mammogram had shown no evidence of calcifications. Then he talked about the alternatives. Basically, he said, there were three options in my case, and all three included lymph node excision to see if the cancer had spread beyond the immediate site and if there was systemic involvement. One was a total mastectomy—meaning removal of the breast alone. Two was a segmental mastectomy, where a segment of the breast is removed. The third—his recommended treatment—was no further surgery and radiation. He said he wanted me to have a confirming opinion from a radiation oncologist, then telephoned the one he specifically wanted me to see and said I would be calling to make an appointment.

Were you pleased that he recommended no further surgery?

Well, yes. Right after he said it I was relieved, but let me tell you what happened to change that feeling. Over the weekend, before seeing the surgeon, I called a woman who worked in a breast clinic at a university hospital. She said it was important for me to get another opinion and gave me the name of a surgeon. When I called to make an appointment, the nurse asked me to bring in a copy of the original pathology report, so on Tuesday, during my appointment with the surgeon, I told him I was getting a second opinion. He was perfectly amenable to the idea. He willingly gave me a copy of the pathology report, shook my hand, and said, "Good luck." I walked out, got in the elevator, punched the button, and made the mistake of reading the report on my way down to the garage. Well, what it said was terrifying—words like "invasive" and "aggressive" and the last sentence said "strong possibility of nodal involvement." I felt in perfect health, but it sounded like I was going to die tomorrow.

Did you think the surgeon had been soft-pedaling the truth about your cancer?

Yes, that's probably what I thought. It was very early in my self-education process, but after reading the report I thought he knew I was going to die and was just being nice. I was convinced that after he did the biopsy he had concluded it was useless to do more surgery. That was a misunderstanding. You see, I came out of surgery thinking one of my alternatives was a lumpectomy. It didn't dawn on me that he had done the lumpectomy while he was in there because the tumor was small. When I told him I didn't know he had already taken out the lump, I thought his reaction was very offhand. He said, "Oh, I'm sorry. I didn't know you didn't know." Because of that, coupled with the tone of the pathology report—which bore no relationship to the nonthreatening way he talked about my case—my imagination was working overtime, and I figured he must have known then that my tumor was malignant and he didn't want to level with me. I thought he wanted to break it to me gently that I was going to die.

Subconsciously, I think I believed cancer meant death. By and large, I've noticed, people do not talk about having cancer. Since I've had cancer I've found out that people I really know well had cancer and never mentioned it. My tentmate on a recent trip to India—with whom I lived for six weeks—had cervical cancer, and she never told me. Usually we don't know until people die. I also worked for a number of years in a hospice where everyone was terminal. We didn't take a patient until the prognosis was six months. I know that my attitude toward cancer was colored by the patients I saw then. The net result of all this—the subconscious stuff, the misunderstandings, his personal style, the pathology report—was that I couldn't trust this man to give me the straight dope.

And what happened when you went for the second opinion?

I had been warned ahead of time that this doctor often offended people, that he was very brusque and very direct. That was exactly what I needed at that point. In terms of personality, the first surgeon and I were a poor match—my need for clarity didn't jive with his need not to be direct. This second surgeon did a pretty standard exam—he palpated both breasts—and then sat down with me and in a very clear, straightforward manner gave me so much information that I didn't even have to ask questions. It was like being in a college course—option A, option B, little drawings showing the exact size of the tumor—and his recommendation differed from the original surgeon's recommendation. He wanted to go back in and reexcise the area of the tumor. He said the pathologist's report indicated that there was a small area that did not have enough of a clean margin for him to feel comfortable.

Did he mean that he wanted to take more tissue out of this small area just to make sure?

No. He said he wanted to take out more tissue to test. He said that 90 percent of malignant breast tumors were invasive intraductal, and if the margins are clean, he recommends sewing up the incision followed by radiation. But in 10 percent of cases there's this other kind of tumor, a papillary tumor—he drew it for me—that had a lot of radiating tentacles forming a kind of spiderweb. He said that I had a 90 percent chance of having the first kind.

By then I was very suspicious of statistics, since they seemed to have gone against me, but what he said made sense to me. I knew I had to go under general anesthesia again to have my nodes tested, regardless of what kind of cancer I had, so why not reexcise, look around, and see what was what? But then he said, "I would need you to sign a form that would enable me to do a mastectomy if I find this other type of tumor or if I find an alarming growth pattern." You have to understand that by this time I was convinced I was a terminal case. My concern was not about saving my breast; it was about saving my life. So I said fine. I told myself a breast is not a vital organ. It's not like they're going to take out a heart or lung that might impair my physical ability to deal in the world. And besides, I thought, I could deal with breast reconstruction. At that moment I was trying to psych myself up for the possibility of a mastectomy. Before all this happened to me I had actually seen a woman who had a reconstruction at a fashion event in a really low-cut black dress. She looked like a million dollars and you couldn't see anything, so mastectomy held no terror for me.

Did you decide to go with this surgeon's recommendation?
Yes. It was the first time I felt someone was leveling with me, so I said okay, I want you to be my doctor and I'll go with your recommendation. I was so relieved to have made a decision. As I was leaving, his nurse practitioner came out with a stack of material to give me—pamphlets from the American Cancer Society and a book called *Alternatives* by Rose Kushner. It was a very dense tome. Evidently, a drug company had given the hospital a big box of these books to give out to patients, but I was told that most patients don't want to know that much about breast cancer. I started reading it because it turned out I had the time—they couldn't schedule me for surgery for ten days, so I began getting an education. I learned all this amazing detail about her experience, about the research that's been done. I read over the entire weekend. Then, on Monday, October 26, the phone rang. It was the nurse from the radiation oncologist the first surgeon had wanted me to see. She asked me what I was doing. I told her I was going with another surgeon for a reexcision and possibly further surgery. She said she understood, but wouldn't it be a good idea to get all the information before making a final decision? I was a little resistant, but she was so sweet and persistent. She said, "You don't have to see this radiation oncologist—you

can call the one at the university hospital and get his opinion, but you should see one because you've only talked to surgeons, and surgeons have a tendency to recommend surgery." I thought, That makes sense. I was moved not only by the argument, but by the fact that a woman who had never laid eyes on me was taking the trouble to telephone and try to persuade me to get more information. The quality of her concern was so impressive that I finally said okay, I'd consult the doctor she worked for. She was so pleased—it was like this little victory. I wondered why it meant so much to her, but I did go in, and she was present for most of the time as a kind of patient advocate.

What did the radiation oncologist say?

He took my medical history, and some of the questions were really interesting. Did I live alone? Did I have a support system? Did I have people I could talk to? They were interesting concerns for a doctor—a very humanistic and holistic view of medicine. I thought, I haven't run across this kind of communication before. Then he said, "I'm going to examine you, and then we're going to come back into my office and I want you to ask me every question you have." So I changed, he examined me—palpation of the breast and of the underarm for the lymph nodes. He also checked lymph nodes in the groin. And took my blood pressure. Then I sat down with him, and he spent two hours talking with me. After all my reading, I had a list of questions, and also, by this time I had talked with a lot of other people who had had radiation and chemotherapy and were living perfectly normal, sane, healthy lives. I was past the point where I thought cancer was an automatic death sentence, but I was not completely sure that I didn't need a mastectomy.

Did the radiation oncologist convince you that you could keep your breast?

Yes. It was the same information I had received from the first surgeon, but because our communication hadn't been that good I couldn't trust him. But here was the same information coming from a doctor who explained everything in detail, who was so strong in his belief that further surgery was unnecessary for me that I believed him. He told me I was a very good candidate for radiation therapy because my lump was small. My cancer had been treated by removing the lump. He said, "You may be cured right now—you may not have another cancer cell in your body— but we just don't know, so we irradiate the breast in a very methodical pattern to kill any cancer cells that may be left over." He cited research work in France where they don't even remove the lump—they just radiate—and evidently, there is no significant difference in recurrence or survival between removing the breast and radiation treatment.

Did the doctor talk about the side effects of radiation?
He said there would probably be some fatigue toward the end, but most women continue to work throughout the course of treatment without any real problems. A few women experience nausea, but most don't. Evidently, real progress has been made in refining the treatment. The breast tissue might become firmer, and because I was very fair, he said my breast might take on a sunburn effect, but that would fade away like a sunburn from the sun. I was concerned about whether radiation would make it more difficult to diagnose further cancer in my breast, as I have very cystic breasts. He said it was possible that the cysts might disappear after treatment.

Did you discuss the type of cancer you had?
Yes. The second surgeon had said only that I had an aggressive form of cancer and that it was a deciding factor in determining treatment. This radiation oncologist went into much greater detail. He said it was a garden-variety breast tumor—not anything exotic—but that there were aspects of it that were of some concern, that the cells, under the microscope, did appear to be of a very aggressive type. Mine was in one of the milk ducts but not encapsulated like Nancy Reagan's. Hers was a much less aggressive type of cancer, but she chose a very conservative treatment —probably consistent with her politics.

Did he talk about the controversy surrounding her
treatment?
He admitted there was a lot of controversy in the field—so many points of view—because there were a lot of things they just didn't know for sure. He said, "We can all cite statistics to support our positions, and we do." I had seen that with the second surgeon— he was sure he was right to recommend more surgery; and I could tell this doctor was equally convinced of his position. He talked about the evolution of treatment for breast cancer.

When a few doctors began doing a simple mastectomy instead of the Halsted radical mastectomy, the rest of the medical community accused them of being irresponsible—of not doing the most they possibly could to save the patient. The same thing is happening now with lumpectomy and radiation as a treatment. The doctor went on to say, "When it comes to cancer, a lot of what the medical profession does is overkill. The appeal of surgery is that it is concrete—the bad part is cut away. Radiation seems very abstract." I guess people feel there are these creeping little cancer cooties running around your body and maybe the rays won't get them but the knife will.

So there I was caught right in the middle of the controversy. He said what his nurse had said: "What do you think a surgeon will recommend? Surgery. I've had plenty of occasions to butt heads with your surgeon, but in your case he and I agree—you don't need any further surgery. That should tell you something." I was absolutely swayed by that argument. Well, not totally. But I must say that his caring and his concern and the clarity with which he presented information was very persuasive. Then I thought, God, I'd been persuaded by the second surgeon—am I a wishy-washy person who listens to the last person she talks to?

At that point, I remembered that when I worked in the hospice I'd met a man who was a radiation oncologist. Over the years he had become a friend, and I thought I could go to him as a friend. He cared about me personally, not just as a patient. So I thanked the radiation oncologist and his staff because they were amazing —practicing medicine by the Hippocratic oath in a kind of ideal way, caring about getting the information into the patient's hands. The radiation oncologist gave me my mammogram and my pathology report, on which he wrote a note to my friend the oncologist. My friend was wonderful and concurred with the first radiation oncologist. So I ended up seeing a total of four doctors —two surgeons and two radiation oncologists. Three of the four were absolutely in agreement that no further surgery was necessary, and the other surgeon wanted to go back in to get more of a margin.

How much of a margin is considered correct?
My oncologist friend said that was another area of controversy. How big is a margin? Do you even need a margin? Should one just leave the lump and radiate? The radiation oncologist's perception of surgery is, how can a surgeon find a cancerous cell or two—it's like looking for a needle in a haystack. Only bombardment with radiation can get all those stray cells.

Give us a rundown on the hours just before the node
excision surgery.

I had routine tests the day before and was told not to eat or drink anything after midnight. The next day I arrived at the hospital about 11 A.M.—the surgery was scheduled for 1 P.M. Two good friends came with me to the hospital to help keep my spirits up, and we all went to a waiting area where a nurse took blood and did an EKG. Nurses would keep popping in, asking if I needed anything, like a Valium, which suggests that this period is stressful for many of the patients they see. I didn't feel particularly nervous because I had already had the lumpectomy during the biopsy; I already knew I would keep my breast, so we only had to settle the issue of node involvement. I also underestimated the seriousness of this surgery, labeling it "only" an axillary dissection. I understand now that the recovery is not much different from having a mastectomy.

I was wheeled into the same operating room I had been in for the biopsy. The same pleasant nurse bustled around, strapping me down, while other nurses set up IV bottles and prepared for surgery. They were all very professional but impersonal. I would have loved someone to acknowledge that I was the reason for all this activity.

Did you know what kind of anesthesia you were going to have?

The anesthesiologist told me she would be giving me sodium pentathol through the IV. I have had this before and know how quickly it works. She also told me they would be putting a breathing tube down my throat and that it might produce a sore throat after surgery. It didn't. The sodium pentathol worked so fast and so completely that the next thing I knew I was back in my room, lying on my back, trussed up on the right side.

Were you in pain?

No, not right after the surgery. But later when I tried to move my right arm, which was taped to my side, I did find it painful. And also, once the anesthesia began to wear off, even without moving I felt very sharp zaps of pain that felt like being touched with a burning wire. I would say that during the first twenty-four hours I experienced a great deal of pain, and I was given morphine. After the second shot I started itching and scratching all over, to the point where it was finally intolerable. I was told this is a possible side effect of morphine, so I was switched to codeine. The operation was very difficult for me as well because I couldn't use my right arm in any way so I was restricted to lying on my back or rolling ever so gently onto my left side because of the drain. Also, the hospital bed was angled to keep my head and chest up, probably to help in drainage, so this meant my body weight fell on my buttocks for essentially twenty-four hours a day, and that was extremely uncomfortable. The nurses encouraged me to get up almost immediately. My forays were confined to visits to the bathroom for the first day, but by the second day I was walking up and down the corridor with the nurse. This felt great even though it was painful getting in and out of bed.

Did anyone discuss the drain with you?

When I was more alert the nurses instructed me about the drainage system. There was a large bulb with a stopper attached to twelve inches of tubing that was plugged into my side and kept in place by several black stitches. The bulb filled with fluid that looked like watermelon juice, and the nurses drained it every few hours. I took over the job of emptying the bulb before I left the hospital. The bulb stayed in for another two weeks until it was filling with only about a tablespoon or so in a twenty-four-hour period. When the surgeon finally removed it, I had a big surprise: the external tubing had been connected to about six inches of wider tubing buried under the skin and going from the entry point all the way up to the surgical scar. The surgeon told me not to look when he pulled it out. It was mildly painful, but the procedure was over very quickly.

I was very nervous about my arm becoming infected because the nodes had been removed and that means you have no protection on that side. But I have had no problems whatsoever. I accidentally tore a cuticle and did what I always did—soaked it in soap and water as hot as I can stand for a while—and I was fine. I no longer worry about wearing rubber gloves for doing dishes. Some women do have serious complications, but sometimes, I think, the literature and doctors and nurses alarm patients unduly.

Were you given exercises for your right arm?

That was traumatic. The nurses gave me standard instructions about crawling my fingers up the wall four times each day and making a mark, then crawling up the wall the next day an inch beyond the mark. I took the assignment very seriously and was so results-oriented that it got to the point where I would just look at the mark on the wall and burst out crying. I just wasn't prepared for how painful it would be to regain the range of movement in my arm, and I caused myself a lot of misery by looking for achievement and being impatient with myself. I have always been so physically flexible that it was a great shock to be unable to lift my arm even six inches or so from my body. This wasn't only because of pain from the incision and the drain, but because the muscle was so incredibly tight. About a month after surgery I could raise my arm shoulder high, but I couldn't get it to go any higher no matter how many times a day I crawled up the wall, and the sense of defeat was overwhelming. Finally, I decided to take two weeks off from making this an assignment I was failing. I took a couple of gentle movement-and-stretching classes and simply did what I could without measuring the results. At the end of the two weeks I could lift my arm over my head. Within three months after surgery I had total range of movement in my arm. My advice here is to be patient. I certainly couldn't take that advice, so I give it knowing how difficult it is.

When did the doctor tell you the results of surgery?
On the afternoon of the second day he came in and delivered the news fast. He said I had one positive node [indicating that the cancer has spread] and then ran out. He is a terrific surgeon, but his bedside manner needs help. I was really stunned by the news, particularly because I had no real idea what it meant. But fortunately, almost immediately after he left, my brother and my dear friends came by to express my concerns out loud and feel the anxiety with me. At some point I decided not to listen to any statistics or to any prognoses. I made up my mind that even if I were told I had only a 10 percent chance of survival that I would be one of those people who made up the 10 percent. I felt that since I was putting the full force of my will and determination behind being an exception, it didn't matter what the statistics were and might only discourage me. So I continue to refuse to hear any discussion about statistics or possible future courses of the cancer. It's interesting because people are constantly asking me, "What does the doctor say about it?" as if doctors hold the key to my healing. I answer that *I* tell the doctor what's going on. Doctors can tell you what the side effects of chemotherapy might be, for example. I am the only one who can tell the doctors what the side effects *are* for me.

What did one positive node mean for you?
It meant I was an automatic candidate for chemotherapy. I just read that the National Cancer Institute now recommends pro-

phylactic chemo for most breast cancer patients regardless of nodal involvement because it so dramatically improves chances for survival. At the time, one of the doctors suggested that having one positive node was lucky because it meant I would have chemotherapy automatically.

How did you feel about having chemotherapy?
I was probably more terrified of chemotherapy than of cancer, and I have heard this from other people. Shortly after my drain was removed and the surgery was officially over, I went to see the oncologist with my brother. We were kept waiting for a long time, so I saw quite a few people come in and out, and they were all walking just fine—I had an idea that you became a semi-invalid in a wheelchair. These people looked perfectly normal—they had hair and didn't look sick—so I was quite cheered by watching them.

My mother didn't want me to have any treatment. Her idea was that some sort of faith healing would do the trick. While I believe in the power of positive thinking, I knew I was going to go ahead with the chemotherapy before I took over complete responsibility for my health. The oncologist was serious and professional, and we asked all our questions. At the end I asked, "When do we start?" and he made an appointment for me the next day. I didn't want to wait around and brood about it. I didn't need a second opinion. I knew I was going to do it. I liked the doctor and trusted him right away because he was forthright. Later, I discovered that he was also funny and a delightful person who gave me every injection himself. No medical techies in sight. I understand this isn't standard procedure. Many doctors only check in with their patients once in a while, and their nurses give the actual injections.

Tell us about your chemotherapy treatments.
Well, I showed up the next day and they took blood to get my baseline blood counts and put a big blue icecap on my head to freeze my scalp. By doing this they hoped to reduce hair loss. The doctor explained that when the blood supply to the hair follicles is slowed down by the cold, the chemo has less chance to get in there during the first hour or so after an injection. In my case this worked fairly well—I still had some hair left after six months of treatment. Not much hair, but enough so that someone meeting me wouldn't think anything was wrong. My chemotherapy was CMF, the classic prescription for adjuvant chemotherapy as I

understand it. CMF is an acronym for Cytoxan, Methotrexate, and Fluorouracil. My schedule was two weeks on and two weeks off. Two weeks on consisted of an injection of Methotrexate and Fluorouracil on the first and eighth of each month and tablets of Cytoxan three times a day for the first fourteen days of each month. I'm not sure what I expected to happen after my first injection, but I went to the health food store where I met a friend and was overjoyed to be able to say I was unaffected by the injection.

Did you have any side effects after that first day?
Well, in fact, for the first five months I experienced very little reaction to the injections. In the beginning I had more of a reaction to the Cytoxan tablets. They made me feel slightly nauseated. I found the way to help this was to keep some heavy food in my stomach. As a consequence, I gained over ten pounds. Another side effect in the beginning was the rampant diarrhea. The doctor gave me Lomotil, which I never took as I preferred to try Kaopectate, which is gentler and easier on the system. The Kaopectate worked amazingly well, and the diarrhea disappeared after the first few treatments. But about two months into the schedule I got the terrible flu that was raging at the time, and that laid me up for over a week. I feel that the flu used up some of my energy and emotional reserve. Two other setbacks occurred during the time I was getting chemotherapy—my dog was killed and a very old and dear friend was killed in an automobile accident. These really took their toll. So the last month of chemotherapy left me with no reserves of energy or of psychic resources. That was the only period I vomited. I would go to bed right after dinner—which was almost always mashed potatoes and an artichoke, my two favorite foods—and I accepted no invitations. But except for the time when I had the flu, I didn't miss a day of work because of chemotherapy. I was productive all during the course of treatment, though not at my normal level of energy. I would characterize it as operating on four or six cylinders when you're an eight-cylinder engine.

Were you frightened about the cancer during the course of the chemotherapy?
I thought I was dealing with it very well, but during this time I became aware of how I was sitting and standing and moving. My shirts were always pulling to the right, and when I looked in the mirror I could see that I was carrying my right shoulder lower

than my left. I was moving as little as possible on my right side, almost as if I were trying to protect it. I was also aware of some unusual tension in my upper back and neck, and I seemed to be holding myself with my head and shoulders hunched forward. I was fortunate around this time to become involved with a form of body work called the Rosen method, which made me even more aware physically and helped me understand what a profound impact cancer had on my whole body, not just the cancer site.

I came to realize that any severe illness causes profound changes in one's relationship to one's own body. There is the sense of betrayal: how could my body do this to me? And there's a retreat from the treatments and invasions by doctors and nurses. The tendency for me was to retreat into an intellectual relationship with my body and the disease. I intellectualized what was happening to me to such a degree that I left my feelings behind. My hunched-over, protective posture was an expression of really primitive, unreasoning fear. I came to the conclusion that cancer patients need some form of body work to "get back into their bodies." Simple massage or Alexander method or Feldenkrais would do as well as Rosen. Some women who have had mastectomies have told me that they don't look at their own bodies or that they use a washcloth to wash the area where they had surgery so they don't have to touch it. One woman was appalled when I suggested she do some body work. She was worried that it would be traumatic for a masseuse to work on her body. Body workers are professionals and have seen some amazing bodies in their time and don't need to be protected. I think that for a woman to truly heal from breast surgery, she needs to reacquaint herself with her physical self, and the body work helps.

Could you talk about the final phase of your cancer treatment, the radiation?

That was very unintimidating after all the other challenges. I went every day for five days to spend approximately fifteen minutes under the linear accelerator. The only side effect in my case is a skin rash on my right breast and on my shoulder and upper back where the radiation exits. This phase of the treatment hasn't required the slightest change in my life. I can still wear a bra, and I feel that my energy is actually returning, although I've been told fatigue may be one of the cumulative effects of radiation. So far this hasn't been the case for me.

*Does being very large-breasted require any different
procedure in the treatment?*

Yes. The technician used a piece of loose-knit fabric to tie my
breast into place—it sort of looks like a one-sided bra. The technician then drew lines on my chest and under my breast to indicate where the machine will be directed, and the treatment took
place in three passes. The first aims at my breast obliquely from
the left. The technician leaves the room, and the machine hums
for approximately thirty seconds. Then he aims the accelerator
in exactly the opposite oblique angle from the right, leaves the
room, and the machine hums for another thirty seconds. The last
pass is at an area above my breast to include my shoulder, and
this time the machine hums for sixty seconds. Then I'm done.

*Now that almost a year has passed since your last
treatment, how are you feeling?*

Better than ever—great! I'm eating a strict macrobiotic diet.
When I was first diagnosed with cancer I wasn't sure I wanted to
cast my lot with brown rice and seaweed. But there are too many
studies about the effect of diet on all kinds of degenerative diseases for us to ignore its importance. That's why I became a
vegetarian in the first place, but as I said my fondness for dairy
products as my source of protein probably contributed to a higher-
than-necessary fat content in my diet. There is some evidence of
a link between fat intake and breast cancer. A survey of Japanese
women, who traditionally live on low-fat diets and have low
breast cancer incidence, was conducted; when they moved to the
United States and changed to a high-fat diet, their incidence of
breast cancer increased to the same level as American women's.
I also think work stress and emotional stress contribute to
weaken the body and make it susceptible to disease. And environmental factors can't be discounted. Maybe it's a combination of
all these things. I've given up a stressful full-time job and am
now consulting in arts administration. I'm doing everything I can
to reduce my chances of recurrence of the cancer and increase
my chances of surviving it. I know that an official "cure" means
no recurrence for five years, but I really believe I'm cured.

*What advice would you give a woman who has been told
she has breast cancer?*

I'd tell her to talk to at least one radiation oncologist and one
surgeon, just to get their points of view. If she feels for any reason
that she's not getting all the information she needs to make a

decision, she should see another set of doctors. I would tell her not to stop until she feels all her questions are answered. Approach it like a research project in school. The Reach to Recovery program has volunteers who have had different courses of treatment—they will talk to you. Talking to people who have had cancer is great because they really know what you're going through. They get you past that panicky state of feeling you're going to die immediately. You get into these weird frames of mind where you start considering even a double mastectomy if it's going to save your life, but when you meet an ex-cancer patient, she's alive and it's proof that you, too, are going to live. Cancer is not at all a death sentence.

"I HAD BITTER DREAMS OF MY BREAST FLYING OFF WITH WINGS ON IT."

A West Coast college administrator, divorced, with two grown children, who had a lumpectomy in 1987, when she was fifty-seven, followed by three months of radiation therapy.

Did you discover your breast cancer through a routine examination?
Yes. I had gone to my gynecologist for a checkup and everything seemed fine, but the doctor said he thought I should have a mammogram because I hadn't had one for a couple of years. But I had changed health plans and things were very busy at work, so I put it off. And really, there didn't seem to be any urgency. Finally, a few months later, I went in for the mammogram, never thinking there might be a problem. I was at work when the gynecologist called me and said a suspicious area had shown up on the X-ray and I'd better see a surgeon right away. I just went blank. I said, "I don't know any surgeons. Can you recommend one?" So he gave me the names of two, and I selected one.
What happened when you went to see the surgeon?
The first thing I heard was "suspicious mass," and that meant cancer to me. That connection was drawn right away. The next thing I thought was, I'm going to die. I had asked a friend if she would come with me to the surgeon. When we went in he had the mammogram and said, "This is very serious. It's larger than we

expected. I think we'd better schedule you for a biopsy right away." I just broke down in tears when we left the office. I was absolutely devastated. I didn't know what to do. I was like a zombie. I had no thoughts of my own and was ready to do whatever the doctor told me to do. A few days later the surgeon did an incisional biopsy. It's an outpatient kind of thing under local anesthetic. He wanted a larger tissue sample than he could get with a needle biopsy. The tumor was 2 centimeters. It was in the upper quadrant of the breast, in the center, underneath the nipple, and it was quite deep. He said, "You're going to have to have a mastectomy, you know." And I didn't question it. I scheduled the surgery before I left the hospital.

Did the surgeon offer you any option besides mastectomy?
He didn't, but when I made my appointment for the surgery his nurse handed me a paper. I thought it was just another hospital form and I didn't pay any attention to it until later. A friend of mine who is the head of the biology department at the college called and said, "I have some books for you to read, and I think you ought to do some further research before you have a mastectomy." That prompted me to read the paper I got from the hospital. It is a California state law that surgeons must tell women considering mastectomy about the options available. It was the first time I realized there were options. I had mentally prepared myself to lose my breast.

What did you do?
My hospital plan includes a visit to a geneticist [see interview with Patricia Kelly, page 276]. My sister and my daughter had come from out of town to be with me when they heard about the cancer, and my other sister was here, so I thought, This is the perfect opportunity for all of us to see a geneticist. The four of us walked into her office, and she had a copy of my biopsy report in front of her. She said, "Well, things really don't look quite as bad as they thought, do they?" I said, "What do you mean?" She said, "Well, I'm looking at this report, and it looks pretty good." My sister at that point said, "She's scheduled for a mastectomy."

What was "good" about the report?
The geneticist said, "You still have some time. The kind of cancer you have is noninvasive—it's ductal carcinoma in situ—which means you can postpone it." And I said, "I think I'd like to postpone it." By the way, it sounds easy now, but making that decision would have been very difficult without support. Once you

have a mind-set to go ahead with something drastic, you convince yourself it's necessary. I had had bitter dreams of my breast
flying off with wings on it. I had already gone through the process
of thinking my breast was gone. Now here I was saying, "No,
I've changed my mind, I want to cancel the mastectomy for
now." I don't think I could have done that alone.

*How did you find out your insurance covered the services
of a geneticist?*

I have some wonderful friends at the college who told me our
hospital plan included genetic counseling. My insurance plan led
me to a hospital that had a geneticist on staff.

What did you do then—get a second opinion?

Well, the first thing I did was do more reading. Then I consulted
a radiation oncologist at the hospital where the geneticist practiced. He exploded when he saw the report. He said, "What are
you doing! The kind of cancer you have doesn't necessarily require a mastectomy!" This contradicted what the surgeon had
said, so my sisters and I decided to go a hospital where a friend
of mine had connections with another radiation oncologist. A resident examined me, and after keeping me waiting an hour, he
comes in with my original mammogram—I traveled everywhere
with my X-ray—and he said, "Well, at your age, I don't see what
the difference is if you lose a breast. You can always build another one, or wear a prosthesis or something." We were appalled.
One of my sisters said, "That's the most unprofessional thing I've
ever heard." And furthermore, she said, "How would like to lose
one of your testicles?" He stepped back about three feet, and she
said, "Look—I'm only *suggesting* it and your reaction is horror."
But he gave me absolutely no hope. He said, "You have to have a
mastectomy." He said, "For breast cancer, the gold standard at
this hospital is the modified radical mastectomy."

*So now you had two opinions recommending mastectomy
and one against. How did you make a decision?*

I went back to the first radiation oncologist, and he was still
upset. He said, "I'm going to send you to somebody else." The
surgeon he recommended was a woman who had to be in her
seventies. She calmly explained the pathology report and the X-
ray. She said, "By my background, I've been trained to cut, and I
believed for most of my career that that was the way to cure
things. But, in the last few years, I'm beginning to realize that
women should have more options, and I have changed my think-

ing." Then she examined me, and she said she thought there was a possibility that I could have a sectional wedge taken out. "Now when I tell you this," she said, "I'm not guaranteeing that your breast is going to look the same as it did before, but at least you will have most of your own breast. It has to be your decision."

Again one of my sisters was with me, and we felt really good about what happened. We went home, and I thought about it, discussed it with the rest of my family, and decided to go with her. So I called her up and said, "I'd like you to do the operation," and then I was so upset with her reaction. After I'd finally made the decision she said, "Well, I'm not sure I can—I have a very busy schedule. . . ." She didn't say "no" to me, but she didn't say "yes." We just couldn't understand why she was so evasive. My sister called her back and pleaded with her to do the surgery. It was then we found out we were in the middle of a political situation—the original surgeon was one of her colleagues at the same hospital. I learned later that my case was subsequently taken to the tumor board, which happened to meet at her hospital, and all the surgeons had voted against lumpectomy for me. She would have had to go against all the male doctors in the hospital in order to take my case. My sister continued pleading with her, and finally she agreed on condition that I would tell the original surgeon that I was changing doctors.

You cannot know how terrifying this was for me. But I went back to the first surgeon, and although I kind of fished around for things to say, I was much more knowledgeable this time and I was asking more intelligent questions. I said, "I've been to other doctors," which he thought was fine. I said to him, "I would like you to do a sectional." He was dead set against giving me my choice. He said, "No, I can't in good conscience do it." I wanted to say, "Well, then I'm dismissing you and taking on someone else," but I just couldn't say it to him in person. The next day I telephoned his office and told him that I was going to another doctor.

So then I called my woman doctor back and said, "I dismissed my doctor." Well, it turned out that's what I had to do, what she wanted me to do. She couldn't treat me until I was no longer in the care of her colleague. But you see, you don't *know* any of those things. It was like walking through a maze, moving one way and then the next. All you have to do is find the right way. But how do you know what the right way is?

Could you explain what a tumor board is?

It's made up of doctors from different hospitals who are called together to decide on the treatment of a tumor when the case is difficult or there is controversy about a particular procedure. Once a group of doctors have decided on a procedure, it's difficult, I think, to go against them. I found out later that my doctor never showed up at the meeting, I think to protect me and herself. That way she would not be part of the group decision.

It's shocking to know that hospital politics could interfere with a patient's exercising her options, isn't it?

The story isn't over yet. The doctor said, "We're going to do the surgery in two weeks, but I'd like you to see a plastic surgeon so you'll know clearly what is going to happen to you." This was my fifth doctor in a three-week period. I was emotionally exhausted. My family was tired. I was feeling pressured by knowing that everyone was giving up time from their own busy worlds to be with me. But I went to see the plastic surgeon. Well, he proceeded to devastate me. He said, "This cannot be done!" He drew a sphere. He said, "Think of your breast as an orange." Then he marked off a fourth of it and said, "This is what you're going to look like with a fourth of it gone. You're going to have a big dent in your breast, and it's going to look very bad." Then he brought out all these slides of silicone implants. The ironic thing was, I went in thinking he was going to reaffirm what my surgeon said, so I'd gone by myself. And he totally reversed what she told me. I was ready to walk out and slit my wrists! I was hysterical when I called her. She said, "Calm down. You've made your decision to do the sectional. Before you went to see him you were going to go ahead with it, nothing has changed." She reminded me that she had told me that after the sectional my breast would not look exactly like my normal breast. I understood that, and I also understood she didn't want to raise my expectations about how it would look. Honestly, I didn't expect it to be like cutting my finger or something minor like that, but the plastic surgeon was so certain it would look terrible without implants that he unnerved me.

Was your doctor surprised that the plastic surgeon she referred you to didn't concur with her diagnosis?

I think so, although she never said that. But later I found out that the plastic surgeon was on the tumor board, and he was not going to go against the other seven men. So I went back to the radiation oncologist at my doctor's hospital, and he reassured me that my decision to have the sectional without implants was the right thing to do. He was like my center of gravity. Every time something went wrong, I'd go back to see him and he'd get me back on track again.

What happened with the surgery?
I had the sectional. I was out in two days, and I'm very happy. I'm happy for more than one reason. I made the decision, and it turned out much better than I ever dreamed it could. It was exactly as the doctor said it would be. It doesn't look exactly like my other breast, but it's not in any way deformed. It's fine.

So what the plastic surgeon warned you would happen
simply didn't happen?
Right. But I'm not saying he was unethical. He and the others are coming from a perspective that says, "Let's take off the breast and redo it, because there will be less chance of a recurrence of cancer." It's kind of a self-perpetuating thing. If you have the mastectomy, then you're sent to a plastic surgeon who does the reconstruction work. By the way, I did some research on reconstruction and it's not anywhere near as easy as they tell you it is, at least not from what I read in the medical books.

Did you have radiation therapy?
Yes. The healing process after the surgery took about two weeks, and then the radiation treatments began. For six weeks, five days a week, I had radiation that covered my entire breast, and then for the seventh week, it was a much more focused beam of radiation on the area where the surgeon had removed the tumor.

What was the experience like?
I was one of the very fortunate ones. There were two other women getting treatment at the same time I was there. One was an attorney who had colon cancer and the other a student who had cancer in her jaw. We became fast friends through this whole thing. I'm telling you this because I don't know if any of us would have made it through without the support we received from each other. One of us was always depressed. My mother died in the middle of the treatments. The attorney's mother died in the middle of it. But the staff in the radiation department was so understanding. Many times I think they let us sit there and talk rather than pull us in for the radiation because the talking was as good for us as the radiation was. It was the first time any of us had experienced some humanity through this whole thing, and we all had different doctors. Occasionally other women would come in

and they'd kind of pick up this feeling of camaraderie from us. We were able to help them, and that gave us a feeling of well-being.

Sometimes people with cancer find it difficult discussing their illness with healthy people without feeling a little ashamed. It's hard to explain. You tend to want to keep it quiet. Maybe you don't want people to know there's a chance you might die soon, or maybe you feel that they feel you brought it on yourself and maybe you even deserved it. There actually is some theory that cancer is self-inflicted and that it's brought on by stress. We talked about those things openly among ourselves. It is so difficult having the disease, and we could support each other and empathize in a way that other people can't.

For example, I'm a single woman, and the man I was dating didn't want to see me as soon as he found out I had cancer. I had been seeing this man for three years, and after I told him, he just stopped calling. I never found out exactly why—maybe he couldn't face the idea of being with a woman without a breast. As much as the doctors don't want to admit it, your breast is part of your sexuality. It was comforting to be able to talk about it with people who could understand. I also found out from talking with other women who had breast cancer that the way he behaved wasn't an uncommon reaction from men. Even my grown *son* couldn't handle it. He just totally rejected me during that time. In his case we figured out—I don't know if it's true, but it's what we decided—that to him it meant Mom might die, so "if I'm not around, I won't see it."

How long has it been since you had your last treatment?
It's been five months now, but I'm not back to what I consider normal. I'm a high-energy person and I love to exercise, but I've had to cut back a lot. Just today I stopped by to see the radiation oncologist and told him I still feel tired but that I've found ways to work through it. He kept saying, "Most women want to take a day off after treatment. Take a week off when you're feeling tired, I'll sign a note." But I don't want to. It's better to keep busy, as tired as I am.

What advice do you have for women considering surgery?
Most important—in making the decision, slow down. Read as much as you can. Get other consultations. And don't let anyone talk you into doing something until you feel real positive about it. One thing I've found out is that when women get mastectomies

in a hurry, a postoperative depression hits them because once you've cut off your breast, you can't change your mind. You have the option of waiting and adjusting to the idea because a couple of weeks won't make a difference. If it turned out that in the future I had to have a mastectomy, I wouldn't like it, but after this experience, I could handle it. I know that I am the one who makes the decision about what is done to my body, and I wouldn't give that responsibility to anyone else.

MASTECTOMY

"THE WORST THING A WOMAN CAN DO IS DENY SHE HAS CANCER. DENY IT FOR A MONTH IF YOU NEED TO—NOT MUCH WILL CHANGE—BUT DON'T WAIT FOR SIX MONTHS TO SEE A DOCTOR."

A publishing executive who had a lumpectomy in 1984, in her late forties, then developed another lump two years later and had a simple mastectomy.

Did you know anything about breast cancer before you discovered you had it?

A good friend of mine had breast cancer in 1978. She's one of those women who is always on top of it—finding out the latest developments in everything. She did not want a mastectomy. She wanted a lumpectomy, and she had heard it was a procedure that was done a lot in Europe but not much in the United States. At the time she couldn't find a surgeon who would do it. They all said, "You'll be dead within a certain amount of time unless you have a mastectomy." But she didn't listen to any of them and finally found a surgeon in Washington D.C. who agreed to do a lumpectomy. She had the surgery done there, followed by radiation. So when I was diagnosed with breast cancer six years later I was already predisposed to having a lumpectomy, because I'd been through it with her and particularly because I saw she was fine after her surgery.

Did you discover your tumor?

Yes, by self-examination. At first I thought, Oh, no, this isn't a lump, it will go away. But I kept feeling it, and in three weeks I went to my gynecologist, who was affiliated with a very good teaching hospital. He said, "Yes, that is a lump." He gave me the names of three breast surgeons who specialize in breast cancer at the same hospital. I went to one, and he aspirated it with a needle but no fluid came out, so he said the next thing for me to do was to get a mammogram. I did that, but nothing showed up.

Is it common that a cancerous tumor doesn't show up on a mammogram?

I don't know how common it is, but I know that just having a mammogram is not enough. I personally know a few women who had breast cancer that didn't show up on their mammograms. You have to do a breast self-examination as well. On the other hand, one woman I know had a lump no one could feel, and it took a mammogram to show up the cancer.

Did you go the next step to a biopsy?

Well, actually I had the lumpectomy done in the breast surgeon's office under local anesthesia. I told him to take out the whole lump instead of taking a section of it, and then biopsy it. The lump was a little under 2 centimeters—the size of a nickel. The surgical part wasn't anything—a small incision with no pain or side effects. The waiting for the diagnosis was the worst part, and that took five days. He called and said, "Yes, it is malignant, and I have you scheduled to have a mastectomy in a week. I've spoken with a plastic surgeon here. She's excellent, and you can have reconstruction at the same time." I was stunned that he could tell me all that in such a matter-of-fact way. So I said, "Wait a minute, don't you believe in lumpectomies?" And he said, "No, I do not." He said there was not enough scientific proof that lumpectomy was helpful at all, and he painted a very gloomy picture. So I said, "Can I get a second opinion? Will you give me my records?" He said yes, he would. I went over to get my records from his secretary, and as I was leaving, she said, "You'll come back. They all do." I didn't know then how prophetic she would turn out to be.

What did you do about getting a second opinion?

I went to a very charming surgeon who had treated one of the editors here at work and her sister for breast cancer. The editor works on a lot of medical books and had done a lot of research, so she was sure he was the right person for me to see. He exuded a great deal of confidence. He was listed in a national magazine as one of the top surgeons in the country. He had once been at the same hospital as my original surgeon but left because they wouldn't let him do these lumpectomies. My only concern was that he was now with a small hospital that was not considered one of the best.

But I liked him, and he said what I wanted to believe, that "based on this pathology report, you do not need a mastectomy." But there was invasive carcinoma in the sample of breast tissue, so he wanted to go in and reexcise the area to make sure the other surgeon had removed all the cancer cells and to do a lymph node excision at the same time. That made sense to me, so that's what we agreed on.

Did it take you some time to adjust to the fact that you had cancer?

Oh, yes. And you feel very pressured. So I did a lot of spiritual things like visualization because a woman I know who had breast cancer found it very helpful. She was convinced that her cancer was caused by stress. And at various times I think my cancer was the result of stress as well. The first paragraph of the Simontons' book, *Getting Well Again,* describes accurately what I had gone through. They say that a year or two prior to the onset of cancer, most cancer patients have a period of depression or stress—problems start mounting in their lives. I'm an only child, and I was taking care of an invalid mother. I have a stressful job. And the thing I really believe ticked off the cancer was an incident that happened in the lobby of this building. A very large messenger guy accidentally hit me very hard with the tip of his elbow in my right breast. It was a sharp, pointed blow—it was pinpointed like a force going right through me. I've been hit in the breast before, but it was nothing to compare with this. And the strange part of it was that the minute it happened I said to myself, "I bet I get breast cancer from this." I told every doctor about it, but all of them said, "No, that's nonsense. That's not how cancer is caused." But the surgeon who did my lymph nodes didn't discount it. He said, "It's possible that a sharp jab like that could have jarred the cells into reacting."

By nature I'm practical, not very spiritual, but when I knew I had cancer I joined an organization called Unity which is based on the power of positive thinking, and it made me more open to considering some ideas and concepts that were not totally rational. I call myself a bispiritual—50 percent spiritual, 50 percent material. But a few days before surgery a friend of mine gave me a tape by Bernie Siegel, a surgeon at the Yale Medical Center at

New Haven. He worked with Elisabeth Kübler-Ross and the Simontons. It's an incredible tape. It's called *Love, Medicine &
Miracles*. He believes the physical and spiritual are intercon-
nected. He talks about people who have been told they have terminal cancer and then the disease goes into remission. My
feeling is that everything works and everything doesn't. Spiritual
works for some people and it doesn't work for others, but it's very
comforting. Siegel is a surgeon, and what he had to say really
helped me through the surgery. I had a very positive attitude
about the whole thing.

What do you remember about this surgery?
One of the first things I remember had to do with the hospital.
Now it's possible that I was supersensitive because of everything
I had heard about the hospital, but a doctor came into my room
to get my medical history. Among a lot of other questions he said,
"Describe why you're here." So I said, "I found a lump in my
right breast." He said, "Wait a minute, your right breast? Are you
sure it's your right breast?" I said, "Of course I'm sure." My chart
stated it was my left breast. So there was this flurry of activity
and a lot of people came into my room and they got all my records
together and did an examination. I said, "How could this happen?" They said, "Well, we think when you checked in, the
woman who was taking down your personal history probably
said, 'Left breast,' and you must have corrected her by saying,
'Right.' She must have assumed you were confirming that the
cancer was in the left breast. So she wrote down 'left.' " It was
like a joke. I can tell you it made me even more nervous about
the hospital, but I felt confident about my doctor and made an
effort to be positive. That night a few friends stopped by, and I
played my Siegel tape again before going to sleep. I slept well
that night, but I was very nervous in the morning.

Did you talk with the anesthesiologist?
Yes. I told him I had a bad experience as a child with ether. I got
sick to my stomach. But he said all the right things about how it
was going to be fine. And I figured that things had changed in
anesthesiology in the forty-two years since I was six. They
wheeled me in, and the room was very cold. The intravenous
went drip-drip-drip. But just before I went under the anesthesia,
someone said, "Now, which breast is it?" I thought, Not again!
That was another really scary moment. But the spiritual advice I
was trying to follow said to let go and let God take over because

there's nothing more you can do. So I kept saying that over and over again to myself. Then the anesthesiologist said, "Now you're going to sleep," and that was it.

How did you feel coming out of anesthesia?

I didn't like it very much because my mouth was extremely dry. I kept hearing them say, "Wake up, wake up." I opened my eyes and I was in the recovery room. But when I really woke up I was in my room and all my friends were there. There were about twelve people, and I was one big smile. I kept saying, "I made it, I made it." But I was very tired.

How long were you in the hospital for this procedure?

Just two or three days. I was bandaged up at first. And when I saw my breast it didn't look like it did when I had the office lumpectomy. My breast was sort of flattened out, but the doctor said it would fill out, and it did. The only problem I had was the drainage from the node excision. The area was all swollen, and the drain kept filling up with liquid. Even after I got out of the hospital I had to go back to get the drain emptied.

When did the surgeon tell you the results of the node
excision?

A couple of days after surgery, he said, "Your lymph nodes are negative, so that's fine. You do have a microscopic sample of cancer in a bit of the breast tissue we removed, but it's really microscopic." So I said, "What does that mean? Do I need radiation or chemotherapy?" He said no.

That was a mistake. From everything I know now, I really feel if you're going to have a lumpectomy, you must have radiation. But at that time, he said, "You're experimental." And he told me about this radiation oncologist in Toronto who has been doing a study on women who have a very small breast cancer that has not spread to the lymph nodes. In such cases—I was a perfect candidate—she believes in lumpectomy alone. She maintains that if you have radiation, it makes it harder to detect any future lumps, and if you have your lymph nodes removed, as I had, you can no longer tell if the cancer is back in your system. It was very rational and made perfect sense to me then. Besides, the surgeon seemed convinced it was the right way to go, and he was considered very reputable.

What postoperative treatment, if any, did the oncologist
recommend?

I called her and told her the name of my doctor, whom she knew.

She asked me a few questions about my medical history, then suggested taking a drug called tamoxifen which helps prevent tumor formation. My surgeon had said no chemotherapy, no radiation, so I decided not to take it. After I had a bone scan and found that was okay, I did nothing except self-examinations and see an oncologist for regular breast examinations. The scary part about cancer is knowing that you're dealing with microscopic cells, and even tests like mammograms and CAT scans sometimes don't show anything until the cancer has moved to a more advanced stage.

How was your recovery from the surgery?
Physically, the scar healed normally, and I don't mind looking at my body. But I think a woman's attitude is important. Even if you don't believe in anything, you have to think positively. I have no husband, no lover, but I am fortunate to have friends, and I'm not shy about asking for help. They clean my apartment when I'm sick. They get very nervous about cancer, but I think they didn't mind being around me because I tried not to be down and depressed.

When did you discover the cancer had recurred?
It was nearly two years, and I discovered a lump again in the same breast, almost in the same area. I thought, No, this isn't true. So again I did that denial thing for about a month. I'd feel it and say, "No, maybe I'm getting my period." I'd feel it again and say, "No . . . it isn't anything." I'd ask my friends to feel it. My therapist finally said, "Look, why don't you go to your gynecologist?" I said, "I don't like going to the gynecologist." But the truth was I was embarrassed to go to him because I hadn't been back since he recommended the breast surgeon who did the original lumpectomy and wanted to do a mastectomy. I was convinced he and everyone affiliated with that particular teaching hospital believed only in mastectomies, and I had gone against their convictions and had a lumpectomy. And now maybe they would be proved right. But I finally did go back, and he said, "Oh no, I gave you the name of a few doctors." I explained how frightening it had been to go to the breast surgeon he recommended—he was so intimidating and formal and told me I would die if I didn't have a mastectomy. So the gynecologist said, "Go back to the surgeon who operated on you. He'll know what it is." So I did.

And what did the surgeon say about the second lump?

He came in and said, "Hi, how are you doing?" Then he did an examination, and he was really rough with my body. And he said, "Oh, that? That's nothing." Then he turned to his nurse and said half-jokingly, "Of course, I could be sued five years from now." Then he said to me, "Why don't you see a radiologist about having some radiation?" I said, "But wait a minute, I had my surgery almost two years ago—even I know if you're going to have radiation, you have to have it right after surgery. Why are you telling me this now? I don't want radiation now! Is this lump really nothing, or is there something you're not telling me?" He said, "No, no it's nothing. You're fine. But do go see a radiologist." I was very frustrated, but I decided to call up the Canadian doctor who recommended against radiation, and this time she said I should have radiation now as prevention. Why was everyone changing their opinions now? I think they were scared when I got another lump even if it wasn't anything.

Did you go to a radiologist?

No.

Why didn't you go?

The lump was small, and I was scared and confused. I kept feeling it, but I would tell myself the surgeon should know if it really is something—he's this famous doctor.

Did the lump get bigger?

About a month and a half later I thought it really was getting bigger—and now it was about three months since I first discovered the lump. So I went to a new gynecologist—this time a woman recommended by a friend. But I didn't trust her. She said, "It could just be the lumps you get before your period." She said, "I understand your being worried, and if you're worried you should see your surgeon again."

Did you go back to your surgeon?

That was my dilemma. Do I go back to the surgeon who told me there was nothing there, or do I swallow my pride and go to the first surgeon who did the excisional biopsy? I finally decided to go back to him, but it turned out he was ill so his office gave me the name of another surgeon at the same hospital. This time I wanted to be affiliated with a hospital that had a good reputation. A woman I knew had a lumpectomy done by this same surgeon, and I remember being very surprised because I had somehow been under the impression that it was hospital policy not to do lumpectomies. I called her to check up on him and the hospital, and she said, "He's terrific. You'll really like him." So I went.

And what did this third surgeon have to say?

He was a really nice guy. I told him I was hesitant about coming to the hospital because the surgeon who had done my biopsy was affiliated with this hospital and believed the only way to treat breast cancer was mastectomy. This surgeon just shook his head and said, "He's a friend of mine, and it's unfortunate, but he is very rigid about that." His suggestion was to do a needle biopsy. He said he could have the results analyzed immediately and would call me on Monday—this was Friday. On Monday he called and said, "Yes, it is malignant, and I think since it has returned a second time you should have a mastectomy." But he didn't say it in a heavy way. He told me I didn't need radiation or chemotherapy because I had negative nodes the first time. I was very upset and said, "Maybe I should go back to my surgeon." He said, "Anything you want to do is fine. I've just given you a lot of heavy news, so think about it for a few days and make your decision at leisure."

I had been seeing an oncologist during this last year for my breast examinations, so before deciding on a surgeon I thought I would get his opinion about a mastectomy. I knew he never agreed with the way I was treated originally—not having radiation or chemotherapy—but he was sympathetic about how difficult it was for me to make a decision.

I went for a second mammogram, and again the cancer did not show up. So that's twice the mammogram was wrong and two doctors couldn't feel anything. I asked my oncologist what I should do—have another lumpectomy or have a mastectomy. I already knew the answer. He said, "A mastectomy." The lump that had been removed was at three o'clock, and this new area was at about five o'clock. He said that if I only had the lump removed, the cancer would just keep spreading. I said I would have the mastectomy, and he said, "You've got guts, kid."

Did you ever tell your surgeon that the lump wasn't "nothing" after all?

Well, here's what happened with that. The woman who had recommended him to me was furious when she heard my cancer recurred because her sister, who had also had a lumpectomy from him with no radiation or chemo, also had a recurrence, and it was very bad by this time. She was now on chemo and still under his care. So my friend wrote him a letter telling him about my cancer. He must have been scared when he got it because this man, who is not accessible at all, called me at work and at home. He couldn't reach me so he finally wrote me a letter saying how sorry he was that I had a recurrence and that he would be very interested to know what the pathology report was. So I called him up, and I was nice. I know he was really terrified that I was going to sue him, so I said, "Don't worry. I'm not going to sue you. I'm feeling very positive, and I'm not blaming you for my getting cancer again, but I did come to you for that lump." He said, "Well, I didn't feel anything." I don't blame him for the recurrence—I believe he acted responsibly in giving me a lumpectomy—but what I do blame him for is that when I went to him he never said, "Let's do a needle biopsy. Go and have a mammogram." He just said, "That's nothing." I should have pursued it. The oncologist I went to told me I was taking my life in my hands by not having radiation. As for the second lump, I guess I wanted to believe it was nothing, like the surgeon said, so I chose not to act.

You were already experienced in hospital procedure. Was there anything you needed to know before the mastectomy?

Yes. I wanted some direction in choosing a hospital. I called a plastic surgeon for breast cancer in Washington, and he said not to go back to the small hospital where I had the reexcision and lymph node excision. He told me that the large metropolitan teaching hospital where my gynecologist and the third surgeon practiced was very good, so I decided I would have it done there. I went to see the Washington doctor because I wanted more information about reconstructive surgery. I discovered that if you plan to have reconstruction, the mastectomy must be done in a way to accommodate the reconstruction. That's routine at this hospital, but maybe in Ohio or somewhere else the way the surgery is done would make reconstruction impossible unless the patient speaks up.

Did you decide to have reconstruction?

My surgeon did not recommend having it at the same time as the mastectomy. Other surgeons do. Some women want to have it done so they can come out of the surgery feeling whole, but I'm very boyish anyway and not much into femininity, so it didn't bother me. I also feel the least amount of surgery necessary is the better course.

How was this operation?

I was in the hospital for four days. The surgery itself was uneventful. I wasn't even afraid when the nurse removed the bandages. I could have looked away, but I said to myself, "You have to face this. Look down now." And I did. I looked and looked, and in place of my breast was a neat incision. That's all, and it didn't bother me. I psyched myself up to be positive and to accept it before I went in. You have to accept it as a reality and fight the desire to resist it. I didn't say, "Oh, poor me. Why is this happening to me?"

This doctor didn't put in a drain because my lymph nodes had been removed in the last surgery, but my side kept swelling up, so they would remove the fluid with a needle. When I went home it just kept on swelling until finally the surgeon had to put in a drain. But I never needed a painkiller. I didn't even have an aspirin after the mastectomy.

Wasn't it painful to have a drain put in?

There was some pain, but it was mostly just sensitive and throbbing. A friend of mine came with me, and she almost fainted when she saw the tube being put in my side without even Novocain, but I guess it was something I felt had to be done so I got through it. And he never offered it. There is a little scar where the drain was. The drainage part was really a drag. The liquid that comes out is not red like blood; it's the color of pus. And smelly. I had to keep changing the bandages—the stuff would come through the bandages onto your clothes and sheets. The drain stayed in for about a week or so. And the area was very sensitive by the time it was ready to be removed. So I said, "Aren't you going to give me something?" He said, "Unfortunately, you're going to have to grin and bear it." He put his hand on my chest, pulled out the drain, and all this liquid just poured out of the hole, and that was it. It didn't hurt at all.

Do you think much about the cancer returning?

I think anyone who has had cancer will be scared the rest of her life that it will recur. I always thought when you got cancer that you died immediately. Not true. Ingrid Bergman had breast cancer and didn't do anything. She lived for ten years after the diagnosis. Some doctors will tell you that if cancer doesn't recur in five years, you can feel reasonably secure—my doctor says it's ten years from the first occurrence. But when I have a headache, I sometimes think I have a brain tumor. One day I had a stomach thing and I thought, Oh, God, is it stomach cancer?

I read in the book we're publishing that breast cancer never originates somewhere else and goes to the breast. Breast cancer originates in the breast, and it is serious. The researchers say the survival rate is very good with breast cancer when you catch it early. But there are women who have had lumpectomies with radiation, and the cancer has spread. There are women who have had mastectomies and radiation, and it has still spread. My last surgeon says early detection is not always the key to survival with breast cancer; he says the kind of cancer a woman has can make the difference. I don't really know. I just know that a lot more women are getting breast cancer, and the only thing we can do is find out everything we can.

When my cancer was first discovered I was more conscientious about the kind of food I ate. I made sure I was on a low-fat diet. I wasn't perfect, but even before the cancer I never ate junk foods. I never drank coffee or tea. I never smoked cigarettes—I did smoke grass, but I gave that up. Now I allow myself a glass of wine with dinner, but not every night. I keep going over the reasons why I might have developed cancer. Was it stress? Was it the sharp blow? I've always been in good health, and there has never been any history of cancer in my family. I guess I'll never know for sure.

How soon did you return to work after the mastectomy?
I went to work three weeks after my operation. I not only came back to work, it was sales conference time. I haven't had any vacation since I had my operation, and that was over a year ago.

What do you think women should do when diagnosed with cancer?
Read the most current books on the subject. Even if you're not particularly spiritual, read the Simontons' book. Things are a lot different today from even ten years ago. The worst thing a woman can do is deny she has cancer. Deny it for a month if you need to—not much will change in that short a period. But don't wait for six months or a year. Also remember that doctors can be very intimidating. Try not to be talked into any surgery until you have had time to absorb the information or find out more about your case.

"I CALLED A FRIEND WHO HAD A MASTECTOMY FIFTEEN
YEARS AGO. SHE SAID, 'LISTEN, THE FIRST THING YOU
HAVE TO REMEMBER IS THAT THERE ARE THOUSANDS OF
US WALKING AROUND.' THAT WAS PROBABLY THE MOST
IMPORTANT THING I HEARD."

An executive of an environmental research organization,
who discovered she had breast cancer in her early forties,
four years before this interview. She had a mastectomy and
no chemotherapy or radiation. She is married, with no chil-
dren.

How did this begin for you?
I didn't notice anything myself. I went to have blood tests because I was getting married. The doctor gave me a checkup and
said, "You're in terrific shape, just terrific, except for this lump."
And I didn't pay very much attention to it. I was getting married
in ten days, I was very excited, I was busy planning things.

So we got married, and we had a wonderful time on our hon-
eymoon. When we came home, my mother kept nattering on the
phone, saying I should go back to the doctor. So I did. This was a
good month later. The doctor hadn't led me to believe that I
should be anxious. He poked this thing again, and instantly his
expression changed. He said, "You have to go immediately to
have a mammogram." I think it was at that point that I suddenly
felt acid-cold shivers of terror. A very great disorientation. Just
rumblings in your soul that something isn't right.

A friend of mine said, "I'll go with you." I said, "You don't need
to." But she did. When I got to the lab, I had this awfully nice
technician who began by saying, "You know, most of these lumps
are benign." As he was talking, he was doing the X-rays, and
then he suddenly said, "You know, there's a very high rate of
successful surgery when something isn't fine."

What happened once you'd had the mammogram?
My internist called me and sent me immediately to a surgeon at
his hospital who is supposed to be very good. I was scared to
death. I thought I'd swallow my tongue. I felt completely sus-
pended from the world of reality—like I was watching someone
in a movie. The surgeon said he thought this was a benign situ-

ation. Nonetheless, he felt they should do some surgery and find out—in the hospital, under general anesthesia. He was a very big, reassuring man. He came in before the surgery and sat on my bed and said, "I think it's going to be fine."

When I woke up from surgery, I remember asking, "Where's my doctor?" They said I'd have to wait until I was back in my room to see him. One is very foggy after general anesthesia, but when I was back in my room, I asked again, "Where is the doctor?" My husband said, "He's going to come and see you in the morning when you are awake."

Well, even if you're half-drugged, you know that nobody waits to tell you good news. I started thrashing around and crying and saying, "Get him, get him. I want him here now." I put up kind of a fuss. And my husband went and found him. The doctor appeared next to the door like a caged person. I said, "What's happening?" He said, "It's a disaster, I'll talk to you in the morning." And he left.

I want to say right now that I've never had the courage to write this man a letter or call him and say, "Do you know what you did? Do you know what a word can mean—the single word *disaster*?"

I was awake all night. I was sharing a room with a lady in her mid-fifties of some Slavic, breast-beating origin, weeping and wailing, who had just had a mastectomy and screamed all night long, "Oh, God, they took my breast off." I was totally traumatized. I thought I was going to die. I was sure I was going to die. I remember walking through the halls, dragging the IV thing. I wanted to see light, to see somebody walking around, interns and residents, somebody alive. I recall a young doctor coming up to me and asking me if I was all right, because I was standing in the middle of the hall, crying. He was so lovely. I said, "I've had some bad news today." He said, "I know. We've heard." He said, "Let me just walk you back into your room." I felt that at least I wasn't all by myself in the world. He came and just sat by my bed and held my hand for a while, which meant a great deal.

It was about three in the morning, and I was so scared that I picked up the phone and called a very dear friend of mine, a writer, who had had breast cancer fifteen years before. She's wonderful. She's the first person who ever interviewed Castro. I called her, and she sort of woke up with a start. I said, "I've had this news, I'm sorry to wake you up, but I had to talk to somebody." At first she sort of yelled in her gravelly voice, "That's dreadful!" Then she said, "Listen, the first thing you have to remember is that there are thousands of us walking around." That was probably the most important thing I heard: "There are thousands of us walking around." It helped me a lot. She said, "I'm not quite up on the latest, because I was operated on so long ago, but my husband and I will get books for you to read and we'll talk about it."

So I sort of felt that something would happen. I run a research organization. What I do is examine environmental problems and think about how they can be solved. I'm basically a person who believes greatly in the power of good information as a way of directing what one does. So my friend put me on a slightly different track.

The next morning, the surgeon came in and brought with him an oncologist, who began talking about chemotherapy. They wanted me to go quite soon into surgery. I said, "I appreciate your views. This is not the second opinion that I want. I want to think about this. I will be leaving the hospital, and I will decide what to do next." And I went home that day.

You didn't go for a second opinion before the biopsy, did you?

No, because I said, "I am only authorizing you to do a biopsy, no matter what you find." Different decisions require different amounts of homework. A decision to find out whether you have a malignant tumor is one thing. To go through all the intensive research of all the options—when you don't know you have it— seems premature to me. When I realized that this *was* malignant, then I started doing research.

One of the first things I did was call an activist health organization. Here I was, a person still in some pain, in enormous emotional shock and deeply disoriented, trying to do some homework. I had only about four or five days to decide what to do because once they cut open a tumor, they tell you, "Listen, you can't wait." I called this health group. And they started off by saying, "Never trust a doctor. Never trust American medical care. Everybody wants to cut your breast off. You have to go to Mexico. You have to go to Canada. Come down here and read everything there is. Don't trust anybody."

This was a group that had a political agenda, which was to deal with the biases of medical practice against women. And I listened to the woman on the phone and at the end of I don't know how many minutes, I said, "I have to go," and I hung up. I think I came as close to self-destructing as I have ever come. That's another person I've wanted to call and say, "If you're a person with a political agenda, you stay the hell off the phone with patients. You have no business dealing with people in trauma." To say something constructive—"Have you thought about this?" or "Have you been here?"—is one thing. But to shake someone's faith in their medical advice, at a time when their whole sense of mortality is on the line, is to me very cruel.

How did you shop for a doctor?
I went to another hospital and saw two different people. One was an expert in breast surgery; another was head of surgery, one of the most respected and revered surgeons—a surgeon, not an oncologist. And I saw the head of breast surgery at yet another hospital. I had strong reactions to each of these doctors.

The first, who is a specialist, was clearly interested in doing his research and getting the kind of aggregate figures that would make an impact on the future. He kept talking about statistics: how many people live with surgery, how many live with chemotherapy. At one point I said that I'd had a terrible time getting an appointment with him. He said, with what looked like a certain amount of pride, "My secretary protects me." I thought, Ego—I don't need that.

Then I went to see the head of surgery, who has a sense of calm and gives you the sense, when he is with you, that there's no one else in the world but you. And for me, the sun rises and sets not only on him, but also on this marvelous, tough woman who has worked with him for twenty years. I had called for an appointment with him, but the hospital wouldn't release my slides on less than twenty-four or forty-eight hours notice, which was just impossible. And this woman told me, as if she were my advocate, "You call them and tell them it's your life and you will pick up your slides!" And I did. I took the slides to this doctor, and he confirmed the diagnosis. But this man never sends up alarms—he has a gentleness and a supportiveness.

Expertise is only half of it in this business, I think. A deep shattering in the personality has to be dealt with, and a doctor who is totally there for you is a form of support and adds a dimension that's immeasurable. I have my appointments with him at six at night, and I've sat in his office, reeling out all my information, my books, and my questions until seven. That's very late for a man who is in his late sixties and who starts work at five in the morning. He gives the kind of support that doesn't try to avoid your questions or your anxiety. He has his limits—he won't deal with things I now consider crucially important, like diet and stress—but he is a remarkable man.

And last, I went to the head of breast surgery at a major cancer treatment center, and he looked at my slides, confirmed the situation, and then said, "Where else have you been? What are your plans?" I told him about the surgeon I liked so much, and he said, "If you have him, you don't need me. He trained me. If you need chemotherapy or after-treatment, come back and see me. But he's the best."

What kinds of questions did you ask these doctors?
I asked each what he would do in my case and whether there were other legitimate options that existed. Then I asked why someone would come to him instead of someone else: in other words, what's so special about you?

When you're going out to get a doctor, you're disoriented and scared. You tend not to want to ask a question that may imply the doctor isn't perfect. My feeling is that you are hiring a doctor. And it was helpful to me to ask those questions: "What exactly would you do? Is this what you recommend for every case of breast cancer? Why did you choose this in my case? Why would you not do a lumpectomy and radiation? Would you do it for somebody else? What's the difference?"

Did you consider a lumpectomy?
I thought about going to Mass. General [the Boston hospital known for research in lumpectomy], but everyone has a different sense of who they are and what their breast means to them, and I wanted to run away from an organ that threatened to kill me. I wanted to throw it away. Also, I was only forty-two. A secondary cancer caused by radiation fifteen years later does not appeal to me. So my choice was surgery.

This was the interesting thing: The doctors I went to all asked the same question—"What do you want from your treatment?" I said to one of them, "Isn't that obvious? I want to be alive. I want to be healthy." He said, "No, that's not so obvious. There are many women whose first response is, 'I will die before I'll lose my breast.'" He said, "When you hear that response, that colors what you say next."

I didn't have that reaction at all, maybe because I'm older, I've done things in my life, I have a sense of identity. I always thought I had a terrific body, I didn't feel that my breast was the most important thing I had, and I wanted to be alive—that was my overwhelming desire, to do what would most protect my life.

So you scheduled yourself for surgery.

Yes, immediately. One of the interesting things is that I think doctors, interns, and residents are very uncomfortable with this operation. It's hard on them. It's not like an appendectomy. It's something that disfigures, that has implications for them. They're also conditioned, I think, if they have any sensitivity, to feel that women will be particularly affected by this operation. The night before my surgery, I asked the resident if he would describe how this operation was done. And he looked so uncomfortable. I said, "Let me tell you something. I don't have any power here. All I have is information. I may not be able to control it, but at least I'll know what it is. You have to tell me." And he did.

The next morning, when I came out of surgery, my doctor came into the recovery room and said to me, "Can you hear me?" I must have mumbled. He said, "I think we got it all." And he knew it would go into my subconscious mind. I remembered it days later. That's something he didn't have to repeat.

There was another great comment I just have to give you. My husband came in. He leaned over my bed, and when I opened my eyes he said, "Isn't it wonderful? This is the first time since we've been married that you're well." Isn't that a knockout?

Were you in much pain?

The physical pain is bearable. I remember my doctor saying, "You will have pain, but it's the surface pain of a wound. It's not the internal pain of abdominal surgery, which is a lot more difficult."

Can you describe the surgery?

They take the breast and all the lymph nodes. The nodes go out from your breast like a hand; there are nodes under your clavicle and others that are under your arm. They take all the nodes that drain the breast. Over the next four or five weeks they determined precisely where any cancer had traveled into the nodes. It had traveled into one lower lymph node.

There are all kinds of things a person might want to ask about this surgery that I now know but didn't then. For example, if a person is interested in having reconstructive surgery, they will save a big lump of skin under your arm and leave it there, like a golf ball almost.

Another question—and I think this is very important—is who's going to sew you up. Surgeons do surgery and then, in teaching hospitals, leave an intern to sew you. In an operation that has disfiguring implications, it's very important to have the best suturing you can have. My doctor did the entire operation. He's one of the few people who still makes nifty little knots with black silk thread. Everybody else uses staples. You barely would know I had a scar—I have a tiny white line that runs right from here [the middle of her chest] to under my arm.

Did you consider reconstructive surgery?
No, a breast is a breast. Once it wasn't a breast, what was I going to do with this other thing? I just didn't feel like it would ever be a breast. Again, I think every person has a different set of reactions. To some people, immediate reconstruction is just vital— they can't bear to look at themselves.

How did your recovery go?
It was about five days of real discomfort, helped considerably by Demerol. It was the most fabulous stuff. I had a private room this time, and it made a lot of difference. I didn't need a private nurse. Someone was always there with me. In fact, one of the things that I feel quite strongly about for anyone in this situation is that from the minute they go under a knife, someone should be sitting there quietly. Someone who is smart enough to keep their mouth shut, to speak when spoken to. Because no one recovering from surgery has the energy to be entertaining, nor wants to be entertained; and, particularly in the case of this kind of surgery, the amount of mental activity going on is intense. Simply trying to get hold of your physical discomfort and your life—it's a lot of work.

I was worried about their removing the drains—I had two drains in. I made a deal with the nurse. I wanted to look brave— which makes me laugh now—when they came to take the drains out, when all the interns watch. I wanted to put on a really good show. I said, "Listen, save up all these painkillers and drowsy pills and give them to me so I'll be really out of it." But the doctor came the day before he was supposed to. And I'll never forget the nurse standing in the doorway and shrugging because it was too late to give me all that stuff.

But in fact, when they removed the drains, it wasn't painful. It's a very odd feeling, because they are literally sliding out these long tubes from inside you.

How did you feel when they took off the bandages?
This is the thing that's the most difficult, which every person has to go through. On about the fifth day, they came in, some interns and residents. You feel like this is the reckoning. I understand that some people don't ever want to look: they will go for months without ever looking down. But my reaction was that I might as well get it over with. I was on this kind of stage—because here were all these interns and residents, and here was the doctor giving me a little pep speech. I looked down the minute they took off the bandage, and then I said, "Just like you said—there's no breast." It really stunned the doctors. But it was my way of getting control of the situation. I had to do something—it's a shock.

Had you imagined the way it would look?
Not really. I had read *First, You Cry*, but I think what you do, at least what I did, is you just deal with life minute to minute. You have to deal with the thing, and so you do. I think people have an enormous amount of strength that they can summon to go on. People have enormous reserves of courage, I think, that they have no choice but to put to work. You reach inside yourself and look around for how to cope. You just do what is natural for you to do. When people come and talk to me about this, what I have said to them is, "You will know when you have a doctor you trust. If you haven't found him yet, go see other people. You will know what to do when the time comes. It may be difficult, but you will know how to cope."

How long were you in the hospital?
Four more days. You're gradually healing, getting your strength back until you're walking around a lot. I think one of the scariest things is when you go home. In a hospital, you're in the world of the wounded. I think that a great depression can hit when you suddenly don't have all those support systems a hospital offers. Good or bad, you're the focus of some attention, and you don't have other responsibilities. Suddenly you're walking out of the hospital with one breast, into the world of the normal.

There are lots of different stages of adjusting to who you are, and one is just adjusting to yourself physically. I went to a gym about a year and a half ago where everyone runs around naked, and when I was getting into a shower, I had a kind of moment of truth. I thought, I am not going to hide the fact that I am a perfectly good human being with a body that's a little different from somebody else's. I will not walk around hiding behind a towel when everyone else isn't. I will not do it. And I didn't. I realized that there were people looking and trying not to look. Then I realized the thing that bothered me most was I had gained ten pounds—I was more embarrassed about being fat than I was about having one breast.

But the most important thing you have to get used to is a new sense of your own mortality. Because no matter whether you can say, intellectually, "I am mortal," the fact is you don't worry about it. But once you've had cancer and you say, "I'm mortal," it's a little different.

With only one node involved, was there talk of your having chemotherapy?

Hah! Was there talk? I'll tell you. There are some doctors who categorically recommend a year of what they call adjuvant chemotherapy if there is any lymph node involvement. Some recommend it even if there's no node involvement. Others are much more conservative and decide based on all kinds of things: the size of the tumor, where the node is (if it's way up under the arm, your prognosis is much less good), the type of tumor cell you had —some are terribly aggressive, and some are terribly slow and don't move very far. My doctor did not recommend chemotherapy for me. Both my internist and the oncologist who had seen me first said, "You have to have chemotherapy." I finally said, "If you want to make that case to my doctor, you go and make it. But on what basis are you saying this? Have you seen my slides? Or do you always say it?"

Ultimately, there was a lot of pressure on me to have chemotherapy as a way of wiping out any potentially roving cancer cells. I asked my doctor, "Why don't you recommend chemotherapy?" He said, "I cut your breast off and your lymph nodes out. I did the diagnosis. I know where that one lymph node was, and I cut way around it." He said, "Cancer cells don't just jump around. They move in a logical pattern. I don't think that it moved anywhere else."

I didn't want chemotherapy, but if he had said I had to have it, I would have. I felt there were other things I could do to resist having cancer again that made more sense to me. I'm not Pollyanna—I know I could get it any minute. But my own view was that cancer comes from a weakness in the immune system. Most women who are in my profession, or even if they're not, have a lot of stress in their life. Most human beings have stress. Most human beings don't eat great diets. So it never can hurt to tell somebody to try to get more sleep, to lower their stress, and to eat better. Eat more vegetables, less meat, less fat. It can't hurt anyone to be told that, and what it can do is give them a feeling that they are taking some positive steps to develop greater strength in their life and in their body. Greater resistance. I've always said to my doctor, "What does it hurt?"

Does he argue that with you?

His basic approach with me was, "Just go and live your life." Me, who runs a public interest group, who runs around like a maniac, who used to get three hours' sleep, and I was zinging all over the place, drinking coffee, eating no fiber. I started reading books on nutrition. I revised my diet and went off meat entirely. I revised my amount of sleep—I now get eight hours. I do an hour and a half of exercise in the morning, and then I eat this incredibly healthy breakfast—wheat germ, yogurt, banana, potassium, and I just sit and read the paper. I started a high-vitamin diet. Two grams of vitamin C every day, I take betacarotene, which is a precursor of vitamin A. I take E with selenium: selenium levels have been found to be low in women with breast cancer. And in fact, I was found, in testing, to have low selenium levels. Selenium comes from fish and a variety of things, but you can take it as a supplement with vitamin E, and the two work synergistically.

Who recommended this diet?

I did. I read everything. Again, this might not be what some people would do—they might want to see a doctor about it—but it seemed to me the things I was doing by way of vitamins could not hurt. My view was, as the lady said who recommended chicken soup to the guy in the street who'd been hit by a car, "Take chicken soup." And everyone said, "Lady, he's been squashed by the car." And she said, "It can't hurt."

"IN FRANCE, YOU GO TO A DOCTOR AND YOU START AR-GUING *IMMEDIATELY.* HERE YOU SIT DOWN AND SAY, 'YES, SIR.'"

A sixty-year-old artist, mother of three, who had a lumpectomy in 1978 when radical mastectomy was still the preferred method of treatment. She had a mastectomy in 1987, after a recurrence.

How did this begin for you?
I found the lump myself, which I understand is pretty classic. It felt hard, really hard, and about a centimeter or two. I wasn't particularly alarmed. But I went to a doctor, to have a complete physical examination, which I had never had. I didn't tell him about the lump, and he didn't examine my breasts. It was a very poor examination. Afterward, I said to him, "I have something that I feel a little concerned about. Would you please check it?" And he checked it, and immediately he said, "My heavens, this is absolutely serious, and you have to go into the hospital tomorrow afternoon." I went to have a mammogram that afternoon—he organized that—and immediately it was diagnosed as malignant. So he said, "Come into the hospital, and I will shepherd you through."

I had never seen this man before! So the idea of his shepherding me through I took with a grain of salt. I said, "No."

Then I started a search to see what I could find about breast cancer. I went to many, many doctors. Every day I would have an appointment. They all said, Yes, mastectomy. Finally I was in one office when I could hear a rowdy conversation going on between the doctor, whom I had not seen yet, and a patient. The doctor was just killing her because she had suggested that there might be some alternate methods. She said that she had read a book. So I heard the name of the book, and of course, as soon as the doctor finished the examination with me, I promptly went down to Barnes & Noble and got the book. It was called *The Breast* and was written by a Dr. Cope [*The Breast: Its Problems —Benign and Malignant—And How to Deal with Them,* by Oliver Cope, M.D., Houghton Mifflin, 1977]. He was head of breast surgery at Massachusetts General Hospital, a very loved and venerable doctor, who had a big following and was the first one who wrote about lumpectomies. He apparently decided some long years ago that he just could not see that radical mastectomies were doing anything but demolishing women's lives. And he attempted to do this alternate method, working with radiation, and had some very good results.

I began to get a little more savvy on the subject of lumpectomy, but I still couldn't find anybody in New York to do it. I had a friend who knew a doctor in France, head of radiology, and the doctor said, "Absolutely no, don't have a mastectomy." This French doctor kindly called me up and told me there was one person who would do it in New York, a colleague who had studied with him, and I should please go and see him.

So I rushed out and met up with this extraordinary doctor. He was doing some very adventuresome radiology with lumpectomies and having good results. He had written many papers on it and was very esteemed. He said, "Well, of course, you don't need to have a mastectomy. You can have a lumpectomy, but you'll have to have radiation." So I went through that. In those years, it was very unusual. Nobody was doing it.

Did you think about going to Mass. General for the lumpectomy?

I would have, had I not found this doctor. I would have gone to France, actually.

How was the surgery itself?

He didn't do the surgery—he was a radiologist and worked with a surgeon. And he suggested to me—it was rather curious—that he would prefer me to find my own surgeon because it would be better for the progress of the method if we branched out.

By that time I had an internist who put me in touch with a surgeon at New York Hospital, an elderly Norwegian man, head of surgery at that time. And when I told him what I wanted to do, he said, "Absolutely, I'm all for it. I haven't done one, but I am very willing to do it because mastectomy is ridiculous." He said, "You know, in America, women don't really appreciate their breasts as they do in Europe. In Europe, women will never give up their breasts right away without making a fight for it. Women are much more submissive in this country to doctors than they are in Europe." Which is so true! I mean, in France, you go to a doctor and start arguing *immediately*. Here, you sit down and say, "Yes, sir." It's a very different attitude. That's changing, but it never was that way in Europe.

So he got instructions from the radiologist, and that was that.

The surgery went without waves. It was a difficult time for me —it was tiring and spooky, and I didn't know what was happening. You know. It was frightening. But it mended, and the team was so good.

What do you remember about the surgery—it would be interesting to see if there have been changes in the procedure since then. How many days were you in the hospital?

One night. I went in the night before, the operation was done that morning, and I went home the next day.

So two nights altogether.

Yes. When I left, I still had the stitches in. I had been in contact with a writer who had had a double mastectomy. When she heard I was doing this, she implored me to go to her doctor. She was adamant that mastectomy was the only way to go—but her own case had been very, very advanced. Anyway, I did go to her doctor, with the stitches still in my breast, and he gave a look at that and said, "This is outrageous. You have to have a mastectomy immediately. And if I were you, I'd have both breasts removed."

Why did you go to a surgeon after your own surgery?

When you get involved in this kind of thing, you grasp at *anything*. It's amazing. Your mind is totally occupied with this project, and you'll do anything—you'll go to a hypnotist! I've done that. I've gone to a healer. . . .

But in the end, you didn't have more surgery—you had radiation, didn't you?

Yes, for six weeks, five days a week.

Did you have side effects from the radiation?

I was just very weary.

Did your skin brown?

Yes, and my doctor didn't warn me. In fact, it didn't show itself for two years. I believe it was because they gave me an enormous dose.

What kind of follow-up care did you have?

I had checkups every three months, then every year. Until . . . I think it might have been the seventh year that I stopped. I didn't go. Because at that point it was awfully hard to tell what was going on in my breast because the tissue was so different because of the radiation—it was hardened, so there was a mass anyway. To feel something else was tricky. I didn't feel anything. My doctor felt it.

What made you return for a checkup?

I started feeling a swelling in my lymph node on that same side.

I went to my internist, and he said he wanted to have a biopsy done immediately. I went to the radiologist to double-check, and he thought I should have a biopsy on the breast, not the lymph node. And I did. And it was malignant.

I was going through a separation from my husband at the time, so my mind wasn't quite on this. And I felt a little bit like a veteran, and I was not as full of anxiety as I had been the first time. So I kind of put it aside. I decided I wasn't going to do anything about it. Much to the horror of my doctor.

Did you just ignore it?

I went into all sorts of other possibilities, alternate cancer treatments. I went to a doctor, very much on the fringe and extremely respected by a huge group of people. He's now very active with AIDS. And I went to the surgeon who wrote *Love, Medicine & Miracles,* Bernie Siegel, who also felt that I should have a mastectomy. And I became very involved in a group called Commonweal. It's run by a man called Michael Lerner, who was originally a psychologist out of Yale. He's the son of Max Lerner, and he has a brother who is a cancer doctor at Massachusetts General Hospital. So Max Lerner is the father of two sons specializing in cancer, and all because he had cancer, lymphatic cancer, six or seven years ago, and they gave him up as gone, and he is alive and kicking—it's fabulous.

What is Commonweal?

It's a retreat, I guess, in Bolinas, California. Michael got a MacArthur Grant [the so-called "genius" award] for his work. He is extraordinary. I mean, he's a saint. You go there for a week, and you have access to every piece of literature that has ever come out on cancer anywhere in the world. Then you have all of the alternate medicines and the doctors and so forth. The Simontons are very involved in Commonweal—it's that type of place. They take eight or ten people at a time. The program is based on meditation with some psychological discussions, a macrobiotic diet, and yoga.

What's the thrust of the psychological discussions?

Facing the situation, peacefully accepting what you have. Doing something about it. Being comfortable with your decisions. That kind of thing.

What did this doctor do for you?

His principle is that cancer has an anabolic and a catabolic—a negative and a positive—energy. He analyzes the composition of your tumor. He reads the pathology reports, and he gives you his own medicine. And his telephone is busy with people calling from all over the world.

This is definitely not disreputable in any way. His medicines are made up of all natural elements. And he believed that he was controlling my tumor. I have a feeling it was controlled. It's just that I was with him for nine or ten months, and then I realized that I was going to take this medicine for the rest of my life. I still was plagued with this hanging over me. I decided I would go ahead and have the mastectomy, and then see where I stood.

Where did you go for the mastectomy?
I had a very successful mastectomy, but a very unpleasant situation with the surgeon, whom I detested, really. He was recommended to me by my internist as the best in town. He is a very negative man, a very pompous, egocentric fellow. Very bombastic and outraged if you even suggest that you know there are alternate approaches. When I mentioned the other doctor, he became hysterical, jumping up and down, which was just amazing. And he was soaping me through the whole thing, saying, "But you know, mastectomy is nothing." He really is a good surgeon—I can't fault him—but there must be others who are much more kind.

How was he unkind?
I wanted to be sure that he wouldn't take out more than necessary. He said it was none of my business. The night before my surgery, I wrote him that I would leave it up to him, but I would rather not have any nodes taken out unless it was necessary. He called me up and said, "You made a fool of me on my floor—how dare you?"

I wish he had answered my questions. I wish he had told me exactly what he was going to do, what feelings I would be having. He just said, "Oh, it's nothing." It was much more than I had anticipated. I was perfectly willing to accept this thing if he would give me some information about it. His technique is to give the least possible information, usually regretting that he's given anything. And his nurses are the same.

How was the surgery itself? Did you have much pain?
Quite a lot of pain, for about two days.

How long did you stay in the hospital?
I think six days.

And when did you feel back to normal?

A long time—it was unbelievable. I would say maybe February or March. About eight months. The wound hurts while it's healing.

And the result of the surgery was that my nodes were involved. He took out what he could and advised that I should absolutely have chemotherapy. I went back to the internist and tried to reason with him, to see if there were other ways of doing it, if I could take tamoxifen, and he would have none of it. He told me I was being irresponsible and that I really had to just bite the bullet and have the chemotherapy. But it so happened that I had a friend whom he had filled full of chemotherapy for two years, and it was just an agony to see what this poor woman went through before she died. I thought, My God, I couldn't possibly do that.

When I went to see him, I took a very close friend of mine who is a doctor, an oncologist, whom he started insulting—he was very threatened. I've never gone back to him. My friend said he had never seen such behavior in his life.

That left you without a doctor.

Well, I went back to the radiologist, and he didn't think I should have chemotherapy, since I was postmenopausal, and that instead I should have tamoxifen. I had an unusually high estrogen count, which makes tamoxifen very effective—I was a perfect candidate for it. My oncologist said the same thing, and so did my present internist, whom I'm crazy about. He's probably the only doctor I have found in New York who has an open mind. He's incredible. Hugs you when you go.

So you're on tamoxifen. How is that? Do you have any side effects from it?

Yes, I've been having joint problems, though that's abated enormously. And I have gained weight, about ten pounds—I feel kind of bloated. That's about it. There's a long list of possible side effects—hot flashes—but I haven't gotten any of them.

You said that your doctor didn't tell you any of the feelings you'd be having. What would you tell someone who was going through this, instead of "It's nothing?"

I would tell you that it was something. I would tell you that it was a very bad experience. And that you would be very much involved in it physically. That it would take you much longer to recuperate than they say. They said, "You can go back to work in two weeks." Well, I'm sure you *could,* but I think it would be the worst thing that could possibly happen to you, because you're very weakened. That's not taking care of yourself properly.

Also, I am not convinced that a man can give you this information. He doesn't know how it feels. For instance, I had a long discussion with my surgeon about the possibility of rebuilding the breast at the time of the surgery. And he said, again, "You know it's nothing! They just put a little flap in and it just grows, and then finally they put in a little bit more"—once a month or something like that. I said, "Well, what do they put in?" And he said, "Oh, just a little liquid." Ridiculous. . . .

I think there should be some sort of support system before you go in, where you could talk, as we're talking now, with somebody who has had it, answering those questions the doctor will never answer and making it more acceptable.

What about reconstruction?
I went to a plastic surgeon. He, I must say, did give me the whole business. He was very straightforward. He gave me every detail. And it was horrendous! He is a very good doctor, expensive but very good. But he told me it will never be the same, and it will always feel different, and it would be a six-hour operation. To me, it seemed absolutely out of the question. Actually, the only thing against not having a breast is that you have to put something in your brassiere. Really, that's it. Otherwise I wouldn't pay attention to it whatsoever. It isn't as dramatic as I thought it was going to be. I must admit, I thought it was going to be horrible. But as far as the psychological aspects of it, I find it's not so revolting-looking. I can hardly see the scar. You look very young on one side, and kind of adult on the other.

So I think the counseling should be done by a woman, frankly. I feel pretty strongly about that. The Reach to Recovery group— they're extraordinary people. A woman who came to see me was just smashing. She looked terrific.

And how are you feeling now?
I'm a little tired. That's about it. I went to the doctor today, and he said everything was fine except that I have low thyroid, and he said that I must take kelp.

Are you doing anything for yourself?
I'm doing yoga, and I'm going back to the Commonweal for a week. It's an incredible place.

Did you change your diet at all?

No great changes, no. I tend to eat sensibly anyway—very little meat, a lot of salad and grains. That appeals to me.

Do you have breast cancer in your family?

Yes. My mother. She died of cancer when she was fifty-two. By the time she was diagnosed, there was a tumor on her spine, but every doctor I've spoken to said no doubt it came from the breast.

"THE ONCOLOGIST COMES TO MY BEDSIDE AND SHE SAYS, 'YOU CAN CHOOSE TO HAVE CHEMOTHERAPY OR NOT,' AND I STARTED TO CRY. I SAID, 'HOW CAN YOU PUT THIS DECISION IN MY HANDS WHEN I DON'T KNOW ANYTHING ABOUT IT?' "

A housewife who had a mastectomy in 1987, when she was sixty-two, followed by chemotherapy that was complicated by her multiple sclerosis.

When did you first discover you had a lump?

On December 17, 1987, I went to my internist for a routine physical, and this time he found a lump and sent me for mammography the same day. It was not that he was especially concerned. I have multiple sclerosis, and he knew it was hard for me to get places, so he said, "Since you're downtown, let's take care of the mammogram right away."

And what were the results of the mammogram?

Well, the first set of pictures was okay, and the doctor gave me a clean bill of health. But later the radiologist called me at home and said, "I've been looking through the pictures with a magnifying glass, and I see something that might be suspicious. Will you come back in so I can take a picture with your breast in a different position?" It was in the second mammogram that the lump was found. It's funny because once I knew the lump was right under the nipple, I could feel it with my hand.

Were you frightened?

I was good at that point because I was saying, "Let's not get alarmed. This could be anything." I asked my internist to recommend a surgeon, and I went to him. He did a needle biopsy in the examining room. The needle was so thin, I didn't feel anything at all. I waited for about a half hour until the pathologist's report came down, and the surgeon said, "Yes, you have a malignant tumor." That was really a bad moment. I cried a little bit, and the surgeon just looked at me—he didn't say "I'm sorry" or anything. The report said it was a three-centimeter, ill-defined mass. The diagnosis was adenoid carcinoma—an invasive ductal cancer.

What did the surgeon recommend?
He said there were two possibilities. I could have a lumpectomy or a mastectomy. He was in favor of the mastectomy because of the position of the lump. With a lumpectomy the breast would have looked like a doughnut or something. Also, with a lumpectomy, I would have to go for radiation. It would mean I would have to go for treatments four times a week for six weeks or so. And I knew that in my condition that would be extraordinarily arduous, particularly because it was the middle of winter. The surgeon also made it sound as though my breast would not be in very good shape after radiation—the skin would be wrinkled in addition to the deformation of the breast due to the surgery. "But," he said, "it's your choice. Make an appointment for the surgery with my receptionist on the way out." I looked at him, and I said, "Wait a minute. I have to go home and think about this a little bit." And he said, "I'm a very busy man. Make the appointment." I walked out of there, and I said, "I do not want this person doing my surgery."

Now that is a real change in me. A couple of years before I might have done exactly what he said because he was well-recommended. But his attitude was horrible. Right after that appointment my mother died—she had been bedridden and was really non compos mentis for a couple of years, but her death was still very hard for me. I was joking with my friends that maybe it's better to have two disasters than one because one takes your mind off the other. Otherwise, you're obsessive. And you do obsess about cancer. Once you're into this you can hardly think about anything else. I think losing a breast was more in the front of my mind than having cancer. Some women I've spoken to have said they were glad they had breast cancer because something could be done about that, whereas if it were in some other part of the body, nothing could help.

How did you find another surgeon?
I asked everyone I knew. Finally, I called an organization called SHARE, a self-help group for women who have had mastectomies. I said, "I'd like to speak to a few women and get recommen-

dations from them for a surgeon." A woman who worked in a hospital and her husband, a doctor who was affiliated with a teaching hospital, recommended a woman—I liked the idea of a woman doctor. I also spoke with a doctor I'd seen two years before who had since developed a specialty of oncology. He knew the woman surgeon and said she had a very good reputation. She practiced at a hospital that specializes in cancer treatment, and two friends had their mastectomies there. They told me there was a strong support system in the hospital, so I was not displeased about having my surgery there.

What was this surgeon like?

At first sight she seems very young. But she must be about forty. We decided that, yes, a mastectomy was the best treatment for me for the same reasons the first surgeon stated, but she was more forthcoming with her information. I had one question: "Why is everyone rushing me into surgery when this lump must have been growing for goodness knows how long?" She talked about the rate at which malignant cells can metastasize. I had the sense that the number of cancer cells might double in size in a month so if I didn't do it right away, the cancer would . . . something terrible would happen. I'm still not clear about this. I wished even then that I had the courage to explore alternatives to mastectomy. I remember I went down to the Library for Medical Consumers* looking for alternatives. The only thing I found was a treatment that one of the Scandinavian countries was exploring where they ran an electrical current through your body to destroy malignant cells; but the study wasn't very substantiated. Anyway, I wasn't prepared to go to Scandinavia in the middle of winter with my MS. But I still think that mastectomy is a medieval, horrible operation that will be obsolete in a couple of years.

How was the surgery?

I was fortunate. I had had gall bladder surgery in 1975, which is more drastic than this, and I had come through that with flying colors. This time I wasn't in pain and I wasn't afraid. I had surgery in the morning, and it was evening by the time I was fully awake in my room. My husband and my son were both at my bedside. My son was simply amazed at how I didn't seem groggy

* A medical resource library open to the public. Address: 237 Thompson Street, New York, N.Y. 10012.

and that I was just fine. My recovery from the surgery has been what you call uneventful. No problems.

Did you find the drains uncomfortable?
I can think of things that would be more uncomfortable.

And how was your stay in the hospital?
Actually, it was wonderful to have the surgery done in a specialized hospital. I was on a floor full of women having the same surgery, and by the day after surgery I was able to go to the bathroom and walk around, and everyone was visiting and congregating. The support system was terrific. The hospital provides exercise groups and other support groups where you can talk about how you feel. There's a group for husbands and other family members. This operation has a quality all its own, which is twofold. It's mutilating on one hand, and you're dealing with a life-threatening disease on the other hand. It's almost too much to comprehend. Women usually have had a very short preparation for this surgery, and everyone is sort of in a state of shock that they have actually *done* it. But there is this knowledge that, "I did it. I did what was necessary."

It sounds as if your experience in the hospital was like a women's consciousness-raising group.
Yes, in the sense that when you see all these women with breast cancer, you suddenly realize that it's an ecological disease. It's a political problem. It's not just you. All of them have cancer—a whole floor of women with breast cancer, and we had a meeting every morning with a nurse, a physiotherapist, and a social worker.

The first day after surgery you didn't feel much like going, but they got you up there the second day. You started exercising, you started asking questions. It was a group, and I felt that it was so crucial to be there instead of isolated in a hospital room. You would do the exercises to get the range of motion back in your arm. You'd learn about prostheses. Two volunteers came in to discuss the different reactions the men in their lives had to the surgery. It was wonderful.

What was it like to see your incision?
They prepare you for that. They actually showed me pictures. They said, "You'll have a chest like a prepubescent girl." That's not quite true because there is a scar. But when they took the bandages off it wasn't a shock. It's not unsightly. My surgeon has

a reputation for doing wonderful stitching, and when the nurses see it they know she did it. The incision was the least of it. It's just that you don't have a breast anymore.

When did you get the results of your node excision?
A few days after the surgery, and that was hard. I had two positive lymph nodes out of the sixteen or eighteen they removed. And that's when the second chapter of my case begins. The oncologist came to my bedside, recommended by my surgeon. The oncologist turned out to be another young lady. And she says to me, "You can choose to have chemotherapy or not. It's up to you." And I looked at her, and I started to cry immediately. I said, "How can you put this decision in my hands, when I don't know anything about it?" She said, "I'll go up and look at the pathology report." When she came down she said, "Yes, you should have chemotherapy." I asked her if there were different kinds of cancer. I used an analogy to another discipline. I said if there were such a thing as neurotic cells, then are there psychotic cells as well? She said, "Yes, that's a good analogy. Your cells are psychotic." And she meant my cells were out of bounds. They had lost touch with reality and were going crazy. And then I understood my cancer. I was very scared of chemotherapy because being nauseated is one of my big fears. Just the word *chemotherapy* to me is horrible. The surgeon, who was in the room, said she didn't have the feeling that chemotherapy was crucial for me. It used to be that chemotherapy was not usually recommended for anyone with less than four nodes involved, and I had two. I think the surgeon was basing her thinking on that.

How many days did you stay in the hospital?
I was there nine days. It had to do with the drainage. They don't like to send you home if you're still draining more than a certain amount of fluid.

Did you go for a second opinion on the chemotherapy once you were out of the hospital?
Yes. I went to my old friend, the oncologist. He looked at the pathology report. He looked at the surgical report. And he said, "I have to see the slides." He had the slides taken to *his* pathologist, who did a more elaborate report. The oncologist finally said I had to have chemotherapy. So now two doctors said I should have chemotherapy. I was still very scared and upset. The surgeon had said, "Try one treatment and see how it is. If it's terrible, you can stop." It was very strange, because here's the

surgeon telling me I can stop, but the surgeon is not an oncologist. The oncologist—I must give her credit for this—said, "If you shop around, you will be able to find an oncologist who will give you a different recommendation." And later I found out there is a tremendous amount of disagreement in the field about the efficacy of chemotherapy.

Were you able to overcome your fear of chemotherapy?
Well, I got myself to the point where I said, "All right, I'll try it." And I went for two treatments, February 23 and March 1. It's a two-week-on and two-week-off protocol. At the end of the second week of pills, during the two weeks off I started getting a really horrible diarrhea which was uncontrollable. I called the doctor and she said, to take Kaopectate and Lomotil and eat rice, but nothing worked. The diarrhea wiped me out completely. So somewhere along there I had to start balancing my underlying illness —the MS—with the cancer. I knew that chemotherapy could compromise my immune system. And I said, "What am I doing here? I'm ingesting poison. This can't be good for the MS." I made the decision to stop chemotherapy. It was a very, very hard decision to make. I discussed it with my husband. He's the kind of guy who thinks that if the doctor tells you to do something, you do it. He didn't *not* support me in my decision, but he didn't support me. He thinks that if there is something to be done about cancer, one should do it. This is a man who lost his first wife and doesn't want to be a widower again.

After you stopped the chemo, did you replace it with any other postsurgery treatment?
My estrogen assay was in a gray area. The cancer I have is not estrogen-receptive but rather progesterone-receptive. So I'm taking tamoxifen, which is an antiestrogen. It apparently has the effect of quieting the cancer. It doesn't cure it, but it is supposed to keep the cancer under control. And it has no side effects. I am also looking into various other things at this point. I am casting about for a nutritionist. I am changing my diet. I am eating virtually no meat. Only grains, vegetables, fish, few dairy products, and very little sugar.

Is there a way to monitor your condition?
They can monitor you to a certain degree with a blood test and, every so often, a bone scan and a liver scan. I don't really know how to answer that yet. Since I stopped the chemotherapy, I haven't wanted to talk to an oncologist. I have to settle myself in

my own thinking and research and reading and talking. I have to decide whether to go back to my first chemotherapist—I have nothing against her except that she's young. It's hard to have faith in someone who is younger than your own daughter. If someone recommends that I take poison, I have to have a lot of faith in this person.

So you don't feel the tamoxifen is enough?

My feeling is that, presumably, I do have cancer, and I will have to deal with it sometime. Even though only two of the nodes they removed were involved, I'm not certain the remaining nodes are cancer free—and neither are they. In the long run you have to be your own doctor. You have to take your care into your own hands.

Your surgery was only a few months ago. Do you feel you've adjusted to losing your breast?

I can't talk about it with other people because nobody wants to hear about it. At Easter we went to my in-laws, and my sister-in-law's sister had had surgery on her knee and she was talking about it. And I'm thinking, I've had surgery, too, and it was much worse than your surgery. But they don't want to hear about breast cancer. If it hadn't happened to me, I wouldn't want to hear about it either. It's too horrible, because your breast has so much significance. Aside from the cosmetic importance, it's gender-defining, sexual.

Are you considering reconstruction?

No. Because it's another surgery.

Do you use a prosthesis?

I haven't gotten one yet. For the moment I stuff Kleenex in my bra. I wear a lot of big sweaters.

"EVEN NOW I CAN'T HONESTLY TELL YOU WHY I DE-LAYED SEEING THE SURGEON. I GUESS IT WAS FEAR AND TRYING TO DENY THAT I MIGHT HAVE TO HAVE SURGERY."

A single, forty-eight-year-old curator of a midwestern museum who discovered her tumor by accident as she was watching television in 1985. She had a modified radical mastectomy seven months later.

*What was your reason for waiting so long between finding
the tumor and having the surgery?*

I'm one of those women who didn't have a regular gynecologist,
nor did I get annual checkups, so when I found the tumor I didn't
know who to see. It was a hard lump about the diameter of a
quarter. It came out of nowhere. I got the name of a good surgeon
and decided to bypass a visit to a gynecologist and go directly to
the city where the surgeon had his practice. He checked out the
lump and I had a great many X-rays, after which he said, "This
looks very benign, but if there are any changes, come back." I
was quite relieved. Then, around the first of the year, I thought
the tumor was beginning to grow, but I blocked it out. Even now
I can't honestly tell you why I delayed seeing the surgeon. I guess
it was fear and trying to deny that I might have to have surgery.

How were you feeling?

Aside from the anxiety and not doing anything about the growing
tumor, I felt fine. As a matter of fact, I never felt better the whole
time. I was never sick. Breast cancer doesn't hurt. But in the
third week of April I made a business trip to Washington, and
while I was there, I did a lot of thinking and made up my mind to
go back to see the surgeon. That's what I did, and the first thing
he said to me was, "Have you had a bee sting?" The tumor was
hot to the touch, very swollen, and the pores were all enlarged. I
knew I had a big problem. The surgeon said, "It looks like this is
malignant. We'll do the biopsy tomorrow." Well, I screamed and
yelled, kind of letting it all out right there in the office. But then
I went home and made ready to go to the hospital the next morning. I remember it was a Tuesday.

Did you get a second opinion?

No. I didn't need a second opinion. I knew that I had a problem.
By then I didn't want to wait; it was growing, growing, growing.
And even in October when I first went to him, I thought to myself,
if I ever have surgery, I want this guy to do it. He impressed me.

*Did he say that if you had done something about it sooner,
it would have been less of a problem?*

No one said anything. There were no recriminations. I mean,
what can you do? I'm lucky I got to the surgeon when I did,
frankly.

*Did you have both the biopsy and the mastectomy the next
day?*

No. All my friends said, "Don't let him chop it off!" So I wrote on the bottom of all the consent forms that I agreed only to a biopsy, that I was not giving consent for a mastectomy. I wanted the time to think about a mastectomy once we had the results back.

I went in for outpatient surgery, but I was kept waiting for about three hours lying around on a gurney. The anesthesia wore off, I was in a foul mood, and I was totally undone emotionally. When I finally went in for the biopsy, I think I was really out of my mind.

When did you find out the results of your biopsy?
Too soon. As I was coming out of anesthesia, a male nurse said, "Well, I guess we'll see you in here tomorrow." At least three people in the recovery room told me I had a malignancy, and I hadn't even seen the doctor yet. I was furious at them and the doctor. It was so inconsiderate. And on top of it all, the anesthesia had me so nauseated that I was feeling really sick. The doctor finally came out and said, "Well, I guess you know the tumor is malignant." I cut him off and said, "I won't talk to you about this now, and you're not doing surgery on me tomorrow." He said, "Oh, come on, you're a better sport than that." I couldn't answer him, but I thought, I don't want to be this sick ever again. They took me to my room, and I started throwing up all over everything. My friends and my brother and nephew were there, and I couldn't stop throwing up. That anesthesia was the worst.

When did the surgeon talk to you about the cancer?
The next afternoon. He told me everything. He said, "The tumor's big as an egg, and it's malignant. I feel we should do a total mastectomy. I wouldn't recommend a lumpectomy because of the size of the tumor. We would have to give you such a strong dose of radiation, it could damage your lungs." So those were the options—mastectomy or lumpectomy and damaged lungs. During surgery he would also do an axillary node dissection to see if the cancer had metastasized. He also said he was releasing the anesthesiologist. I said, "Well, thank goodness, he was awful." Not only that, but he was ugly and grim. You face this wretched person first, and then you have to have surgery. I was still feeling physically horrible, so I told the surgeon I couldn't face surgery again in the morning. So he said, "All right, I'll schedule it for Friday."

Was the night before surgery an anxious time for you?
Not really. The thing of it is, I knew the cancer was there and

that I had to get rid of it. Once I made the decision that I was going to lose my breast—I never liked my breasts, they're enormous—I was all right. Now I'm thinking I'd like to get rid of the other one—I'm feeling a little lopsided. Maybe I'll think about having reconstructive surgery later.

Was the new anesthesiologist better?
Much better. He was very attractive and patiently explained everything to me. I said, "I don't mind losing my breast, but I don't want to feel that terrible ever again." He said, "That's no problem. I can control the gases." And on Friday, the experience was totally different. It was so much more pleasant from beginning to end, maybe because I knew what to expect. I remember coming out of anesthesia and, ironically, I had the feeling I was having a wonderful experience.

What kind of surgery did you have?
A modified radical mastectomy. They also removed thirty-two lymph nodes, four of which were positive for cancer. But again, some jerk comes into my room on Saturday after the surgery while I'm having a nice lunch with my friends. This time it was the oncologist, who starts discussing chemotherapy with me. Maybe my own doctor had told me the oncologist was going to stop by, but I know we hadn't discussed any details. What bothered me was the oncologist's manner. He was just so blabbery— telling me how I probably had these malignant cells floating in my bloodstream and how they were going to sign me right up for treatments and blah, blah, blah. I went into a total rage! Maybe it was irrational or emotional. I said, "I have to go to the john," and stormed into the bathroom. When I came back I was a little calmer, and I said, "What if I don't have chemotherapy?" He said, "Oh, come on, you're more rational than that." I thought, the hell I am.

How did you feel physically after the mastectomy?
Wonderful. The first night they had me hooked up to an IV machine that administered morphine by computer. When you wanted some morphine, you just pushed a button. I was up until three or four in the morning watching movies. That's how good I felt. Unfortunately they took it away the next morning. Then they gave me Percodan, but that made me very sick, so they switched me to something called Tylox, which is pretty strong, too. I also had two drains to allow the body to eliminate excess fluids after the surgery. The drain consists of a flat white piece of plastic

with holes in it—it sort of looks like a tiny version of a hose you might use to water the lawn—and it's placed in your side, attached to plastic tubing about a quarter of inch in diameter. That tubing is connected to something called the Heyer-Shulte Jackson Pratt—they call it the J. P. drain. The J. P. drain is a plastic bulblike thing that keeps the suction going, and the nurses measure what's coming out. You have drain one and drain two, sort of like plumbing.

As far as the incision goes, I thought there would be all this gauze and huge amounts of adhesive tape. Well, it wasn't that way. There was just one piece of tape over the incision, and the second day after surgery he took the tape off and there was the incision with this black thread. It was pretty ugly. I said as much, and it really hurt his feelings because he thought he had done this beautiful job. Since then I've decided he really did do a pretty good job—the way he smoothed the skin together. Now I can sort of appreciate the aesthetics of it. By Sunday I was up, running around the hospital. My friends came up to see me, and they said, "Most people who have this surgery can't lift their arms over their heads." And I was doing everything. At one point the nurse said, "Well, you can shower." And I said, "I've been doing that since day two." And she said, "Oh, fine."

Didn't it hurt to lift your arm?

Oh, yes. I mean, it hurt like heck. But I thought, I'm right-handed —I don't want to lose the use of my hand and my arm and everything. I'd been lifting weights for three years, and I think that probably helped.

Did you have a lot of emotional support to get you through the surgery and recovery?

I know this sounds crazy, but I actually enjoyed being in the hospital. People came in droves to visit. My room was like a florist's shop. There were incredible lilies and really inventive floral arrangements. Cards and letters and phone calls—constant phone calls, twenty-four hours a day, from everywhere. I got all this attention, and except for the incident with the oncologist barging in, I loved the whole experience. My brother and my nephew—they're all the real family I've got—were wonderful. They were with me the whole time. You can feel very unloved and unwanted in the hospital. My women friends really rallied around, too. I am very fortunate.

Even on an institutional level, I had support. The nurse called

Reach to Recovery to let them know I had a mastectomy, and this very lovely woman came to visit me right after the surgery. Twenty-eight years ago she had had a Halsted mastectomy, the extremely radical procedure where they remove the breast, the muscles, the nodes, and virtually cut down to the bone. It must have been horrible. Women like her volunteer their time to talk with women who have just had the surgery, and they help you cope with the recovery. They bring you a satchel containing a rubber ball you exercise with by gripping—that helps encourage fluid drainage—and a pillow to put between your arm and your side if you have pain. There are lots of booklets, too. Also, when the nurse calls Reach to Recovery, she gives them your bra size because one of the other things that comes in your personal satchel is a hand-made temporary prosthesis in your size made out of cotton batting wrapped with nylon net. It's pretty heavy. Mine weighs about six pounds because I wear a size 42E bra. The volunteer showed me a real prosthesis and the bra that holds it. It costs three hundred bucks for one bra and one breast. After I went home I tried to make an extra one for myself, but you have to weight it with BB's or something—otherwise it ends up around your chin. She was such a nice woman. She even came back a couple of days before I was discharged just to see how I was doing.

Before the surgery I was having a drinking problem, so I had gone into counseling. And my counselor called me, too, and said, "I'm available if you need me." As a matter of fact, she turned out to be very helpful.

An oncologist was conducting a study, and he wanted me to participate. He had three protocols—three types of chemotherapy treatments—and the treatment I would get would be determined by random selection. If I participated, I would get the drugs free. Also, I probably would get much more attention, and he said it would all be carefully monitored. It was kind of appealing, but he drove me nuts in the hospital sending people up to try to convince me to participate. I didn't think I knew enough or had read enough, and I didn't want to be a guinea pig. At that point I didn't care if I helped anybody else or not. I was feeling very unsure and totally confused. The counselor told me to tell him that I wasn't ready to make any decision and that when I was I would let him know. So I wiped my tears and thanked her. I was very emotional about anything that had to do with the surgery.

How did you feel about your surgeon after the surgery?
Well, when you decide on a surgeon you do begin to think he is
practically God. I did kind of fall in love with him, and I thought
he was really attractive and brilliant. But now I'm beginning to
think maybe he didn't get me back together too well. He did say
when they have to take out all these lymph nodes that it's hard
to get the skin back together under your arm. But sometimes I
wonder if he was the best. I guess I'm not sure what doctors
really know. You really want to believe they know everything.

How long was your stay in the hospital?
Eleven days including the biopsy and the mastectomy and the
recovery from the surgery. And then I drove home sixty-five miles
an hour. My town is seventy miles from Oklahoma City. The
doctor's attitude was I should do everything I can for myself, and
I'm all for that.

Did you have any problems during your recovery at home?
I was very sore. The worst was in the morning. I like to sleep on
my side. I can't do that anymore. There are lots of adjustments
to make, but I think I've adjusted to everything. The doctor didn't
want me to go back to work for a month. In the beginning I didn't
have any energy, and I thought, I should have gotten somebody
to take care of me, but then in about a week I started feeling
really good. I went back to work about a month after surgery.

How was it going back to work?
Naturally, at first, I didn't have as much energy as I used to. I
thought, God, it's hard to get through the day. I went half days
for the first week, then worked myself up to a full schedule. The
worst part of going back to work is that you think everybody's
looking at your breasts. Of course they aren't, but I remember
going to the post office to mail some letters knowing there were
two really nosy women working there. I thought, This is the acid
test. If I can go down there and do this business with them and
nothing is said, then I'm fine. I was fine.

*Are you concerned that the cancer might turn up in the
other breast?*
No. I don't think it will. The only thing I'm worried about is that
it might turn up in my brain or my kidneys. That's the reason you
go for the chemotherapy, so that microscopic cells won't turn up
somewhere else. The doctors are always concerned about the
liver. In the hospital after the surgery, they would wake me up
about 5:30 A.M. to do a liver scan, and I'd say, "Where's the can-

cer?" They'd say, "It's not in your liver." They would do a bone scan and tell it wasn't there, either. They also gave me an extensive gynecological examination, and I was totally clean there as well.

What did you decide to do about participating in the chemotherapy study?

After my initial reaction I decided to read about the study a little more, and my attitude changed. I felt it was something I should do. My protocol lasted a year. They picked me up twice a month and drove me to the city. They administered three drugs intravenously—1,000 milligrams of Cytoxan, 26 to 100 milligrams of 5-Fluorouracil, and 26 to 100 milligrams of Methotrexate. A saline solution was given at the same time to cut the drugs. The process took about forty-five minutes every time. I was also given drugs to counteract the nausea, but none of the stuff helped, so I stopped taking everything except for Benadryl [diphenhydramine]—an antinausea drug which knocked me out—and prednisone, a steroid that made me gain a lot of weight.

How did you feel during the chemotherapy?

The first time is hard because you don't know what to expect and you really feel frightened. But then you get to know the routine. I would ride the sixty-five miles from the city back home after the treatment, take Benadryl, and simply go to bed. I knew I would feel terrible the morning after the treatment—generally sick and very nauseated. By mid-afternoon—twenty-four hours after the treatment—I'd feel better, and I'd be back to work the next day. But the effects of the chemo are cumulative, and by January, six months after I began treatment, I would throw up from seven in the morning until seven at night for two days. I couldn't keep anything down, not even water. I was so dehydrated I sucked on ice cubes. I was exhausted from throwing up—it really does things to your muscles. I told the doctor I wouldn't be able to go through that again. He recommended tetrahydrocannabinol, a marijuana derivative, to prevent vomiting, and that really helped a lot. But two days out of every month I was more or less out of commission, and the rest of the time I went on with my normal life.

The interesting thing was that as the time for my treatment was approaching I would get very upset because I knew how I was going to feel afterward. Just walking into the doctor's office would make my stomach turn over. I've heard about people who throw up when they just see the nurse who administers the treatment.

What kind of medical care are you getting now?

I get a mammogram once a year, but I see the doctor every three months for an examination. I am on tamoxifen, an estrogen blocker, because it's been determined that my tumor was heavily related to estrogen. I will take tamoxifen for five years.

Are you on any diet or nutrition plan?

Yes. My doctor recommended I go on a structured program of diet and exercise because I was one hundred pounds over my ideal weight. The program is based on general health principles, and following it helps keep down the swelling in my arm. Removal of the lymph nodes reduces the body's ability to drain fluids; the less weight a woman carries, the lower the level of fluid retention. My diet consists of lots of fish, vegetables, and fruit. I take calcium supplements and occasionally have some plain yogurt. So far I've lost sixty-nine pounds, and I feel fine.

"THE PROBLEM WITH BOOKS IS THAT ANY BOOK WITH STATISTICS IS ALMOST OUT OF DATE BEFORE IT'S PRINTED—THINGS ARE CHANGING SO QUICKLY. I WOULD RECOMMEND SKIPPING THE STATISTICS AND READING ABOUT THE THINGS THAT YOU CAN DO TO HELP YOURSELF."

A lawyer who had a mastectomy when she was thirty-seven, three years before this interview.

How did you discover you had breast cancer?

I felt a lump. I always had lumps in my breast—I had cystic breasts—but this particular one bothered me, because it hurt. It hurt under pressure and during my periods. It was very large—cherry-tomato size. I just thought it was a cyst. And so did my internist, when I went for a checkup. This was in the fall.

He asked me to come back two months later. In the intervening time, my best friend had a mastectomy. It made me panic, so I went back to check it sooner than my doctor expected. It had grown. He said, "It's a cyst. Don't worry about it, but have a biopsy." So I went and had the biopsy, which was an office procedure, and the lump was removed. The surgeon said, again,

"Don't worry about it—it looks terrific." He sent it off to the lab, and it was malignant. Everyone was surprised.

Do you have breast cancer in your family?

No, nothing. Except my father died of pancreatic cancer.

Would you describe the biopsy?

I went to the surgeon my internist recommended. It was really very simple. Just a local anesthesia, in his office, with a nurse attending. There was very little blood. He stitched it closed. It was very fast—forty minutes at most. I didn't feel anything.

What was your emotional state?

I was pretty nervous after my internist told me to have it out, but that was a very short period of time—three or four days—because he said do it immediately. I went alone, I didn't ask anyone to go with me.

How long did you have to wait for the results?

Three days. The surgeon called to tell me. And then I had a weird reaction. I tend to space out during things like that, to disassociate from my body. When my friend called me from the hospital and told me she'd had a mastectomy, I burst into tears and cried and cried. And I didn't over mine. I didn't cry, I didn't go into despair. I was relieved in an odd way. I thought, Well, you wait all your life to get cancer; now I've got it. I can stop waiting. I thought, well now I really have to get on with my life. I've been given a choice. I've been shown that I am mortal, and who knows how long I have, but now I'll start living. I was always a very fearful person. I said, "I'm going to stop being afraid of things—because why be afraid?" So it was a liberating thing, oddly enough.

What did you do next?

The surgeon recommended surgery. I wanted a second opinion, and he said, "Fine." He told me I'd need a slide to show to other doctors and the lab report. As soon as I got the slide, I went racing around to doctors to find out what my options were. I went all over. I felt if you go to a surgeon, he'll recommend surgery. So I wanted to see an oncologist, who wouldn't necessarily be partial to surgery. A friend of mine was doing her residency at Harlem Hospital, and I went to the chief of oncology there. He looked at my slide and said, "Yes, it's definitely malignant, and you have to have a mastectomy."

I went to another friend's surgeon, and he concurred. Everyone said that I didn't have any choice—radiation simply wasn't an option for a woman my age. Since it was estrogen-positive, and I was still menstruating, it would continue to grow.

They also said that radiation affects the breast adversely—it hardens, and the tissue changes. If you have a lot of radiation treatments, your breast is not so terrific anyway. I don't know if that's true.

And when I asked if I could have a quadrantectomy, all three didn't think that was smart because, they said, you never know whether it's in the rest of the breast. The only way you know is to take the entire breast off.

How did you decide on the doctor?

I liked the biopsy doctor best. I didn't want a doctor who was into radical mastectomies—some of these doctors have reputations for lopping off your whole body. The surgeon was affiliated with the same hospital as my internist—that was part of the decision. I chose both the hospital and the surgeon. I knew this hospital was more prone to chemotherapy than the other doctor's.

Did you want chemotherapy?

I wanted the best option to live. At the other hospital, they didn't give you chemotherapy if you had fewer than three nodes. At mine, if you had any nodes, they recommended chemotherapy.

What did you like about the doctor you chose?

Oh, he was terrific. He's a typical surgeon in the sense that he has no bedside manner. He doesn't deal in a warm way with people. But he's very, very competent. And he has staffed his office with supportive women. It was really remarkable! The receptionist was *so* nice, and *so* warm, and *so* considerate. She called me before and after . . . she did all the human interface for him. His office was well organized, so you didn't have to wait a long time; the staff knew the patients' names. . . .

In the one conversation that I did have with him after the biopsy, face to face, where he gave me the options, he was very nice and answered everything—absolutely honest, no duplicity. He just wasn't the warmest person in the world.

And how soon after did you have surgery?

A matter of days. I was working for a judge who was very nice. She said, "Of course you have to do it," and she said she wouldn't talk about it, which I appreciated. I wanted to be secretive about it, for some reason.

Were you embarrassed?

I didn't want sympathy. I didn't want people to think of me as a cancer patient or a victim of cancer.

How long did you plan to be out of work?

He said I'd probably be in the hospital only four days and then home for three—which was right.

What happened the morning of the surgery?

They put me on a cart and wheeled me down—a bad thing, because there were rows and rows and rows of us on gurneys, waiting for surgery. I wasn't terribly agitated—I think I was having Valium intravenously—but I was there a long time. Then I remember being wheeled in, the anesthesiologist introducing himself, and the surgeon—and then I was out.

I woke up in the recovery room, and I was freezing cold and I lay there for what seemed like a long time. I felt like I was all alone in this big, freezing-cold room.

I don't know how I got back to the room. I woke up there, violently ill, with my head just throbbing and throbbing, all night.

And the next day?

I was still sort of out of it. But that night, I think I was all right again.

By the second day, I was fine. But by then it hurt. I couldn't move my arm. This is something you should note: you have to take a button-up nightgown, because you can't lift your arm. They make you start doing exercises, which are really hard. It's amazing—you can't do it: reaching up, crawling your fingers up the wall, just slightly swinging your arms.

All of the procedures having to do with it hurt. Having the bandage taken off hurt, because they had to rip it off. The tape is just horrible—it's waterproof, so it's real sticky. And I had some kind of tube that was draining it. They had to change that, and that hurt. And groups of students would come around and they'd have to untape it. And being a subject for the classes was a little bit of a drag—not so much having them look at me, because I'd space out—but the *tape* coming off.

I definitely didn't want to look at it when they changed the bandage, and I didn't look at the scar for a long, long time, and I didn't show it to anyone for a long time. Now, I'm perfectly comfortable with it, but it took a long time.

And you didn't feel that you could refuse to be a subject for these demonstrations?

No, I didn't. It didn't occur to me. It usually seemed to be in conjunction with some procedure that had to be done. An intern would take off the bandage and check the tube and change the tube; or maybe the nurse would change the tube and then close it up. Then a little later, either the resident or the surgeon would come in with a student or two and take it off and check it, put it back . . . maybe three times a day they did it.

My internist and the surgeon stopped by, and they didn't have the reports on the nodes until the third day. I think I had four or five nodes involved. Then I really got worried. Up to then, I felt, Well, this is like my appendectomy. After the report, I realized, Well, this really might be it, and I don't know what my odds are and I don't want to know what my odds are—but I'd better take myself in hand. Then I got some books . . . I can't remember the name of that positive-thinking guy.

Simonton?

Yes, I got his book, and I got the tape. I decided not to be licked by this thing, that I would do everything I could do. Getting the node report was very sobering.

I went back to work and started rushing around faster than I should have—I'd be running up and down stairs and get dizzy. I needed to take it a little easier than I did. And I started interviewing chemotherapists.

I went first to this hotshot guy, very high-tech, who came very highly recommended. He was terrible! He threw a chart at me, this complicated scientific chart. He was explaining that there's a national research program of chemotherapy, and if you participate, a computer decides what your regimen will be, rather than the doctor: six weeks on and off; or two and two. It's real complicated. He put so much pressure on me to participate, and I tend to be subject to guilt anyway, so I thought it was my obligation as a woman to participate for the good of women so they'll find out which treatment is better.

He also showed me, on this chart, the different kinds of drugs available. A very odd presentation, very technical, as if it were to a medical school class. And he did not administer the chemotherapy himself—his nurses did.

He didn't prescribe. He didn't administer it. He billed?

Actually, a computer billed.

So I didn't like him. Then I interviewed the doctor my internist recommended. And I just loved her. She does all the administering herself. She told me about the same program but didn't pressure me at all. She was much more human in presenting it and said, "There's no reason to feel an obligation to do it. If you don't want to do it, you don't have to. If you do, and the regimen you're on makes you sick or you're uncomfortable with it, you can get off at any time."

Her regimen began with six weeks on, then two weeks off and two on, and another cycle of two weeks off and on. The initial six weeks were very hard, because basically chemotherapy is poison; your body is getting poisoned. The more poison you get, the worse you feel.

And you were still going to work?
I never missed a day of work.
Did you have much nausea?
No, very little. I had nausea pills. I'd take Compazine before I went in there on injection days. And sometimes I could go home and eat, and other times I'd just have soup or go to bed.
How was the chemotherapy administered?
In the elbow of the nonmastectomy side. Nothing can be done to the mastectomy-side arm after this. You can't have blood pressure taken, you can't have shots—because the immune system is gone. So you're supposed to be very careful not to burn yourself, not to get hangnails, and you definitely can't get vaccinations.

But anyway, it's an injection that she does by hand—she doesn't do an IV bottle. It's big tubes of junk, and she just injects it. She puts the needle in, and then puts in one vial of stuff, and then switches to the second, and then a third. It's a bunch of mixtures. It's pretty yecchy.
Does it hurt?
It doesn't hurt. She was very good at it. And she scheduled the procedure around my needs. I'd go in early Friday mornings, on the way to work, for the blood test to see if my white count was high enough, and go back late in the afternoon for the injection —she'd stay late for me. And I took pills three times a day.
What were the pills?
Poison. All poison. Part of the Simonton method is to think positively about chemotherapy. To think of it running around your body killing all the bad things. But I had a hard time with that, because these pills looked like poison. They're white and have little blue crystals in them, and they're very big. I'd take them for two weeks, and then stop for two weeks. As time went on, I got

more and more tired. I never lost all my hair, because I have very thick hair. But the other women I was going through it with did lose all of their hair.

Did you get a wig?

I did, and I immediately got a prosthesis. So I was outfitted. I didn't have to wear the wig, thank heavens. The other thing with the chemotherapy is they give you a lot of prednisone to raise your blood count, so you get very fat. I gained about thirty pounds. And I was ravenously hungry all the time. I couldn't control it. Chemotherapy is physically discomfiting, I think, because you gain weight and you hold a lot of water—you get very bloated and constipated. Physically, you don't feel so good. You don't have any hair, and your sex drive is way down, and you get very tired. The doctor said I could either work or play but I couldn't do both. And that was true. I had no energy for evening things.

How did you get through that period?

I really consciously worked on it. I did the Simonton work. I learned to meditate. I completely changed my diet and cut out all carcinogenic foods. I started eating broccoli seventeen times a day! And I cut back drastically on meat and fats. I read a cancer book by some doctor who went into macrobiotics—that sounded too ghastly, but I really did try very hard to change my diet. And I'm still doing that, pretty much.

I also joined a group at a hospital near me; a social worker runs it, a postmastectomy group. I only stayed for a little while, because I found that I was the most positive person, so I wasn't getting much support. There was one terribly sad woman, twenty-five, who had just had a baby, and every woman in her family had died of breast cancer. So she was waiting. She was twenty-five and waiting. So despairing. A couple of older women were also very depressed. I felt like I was trying to hold up this group, and I couldn't do it.

Then I went to a Simonton therapist and did six weeks with her, trying to do positive thinking. I did the best I could in terms of getting through it.

What did you do about clothes? With thirty pounds extra, you can't wear the same size.

And I wasn't in the mood to shop—I didn't have the energy. I just bought two suits and wore them all the time. The doctor kept saying, "Don't worry, you'll lose the weight." It took a year, and I never did get back exactly to where I was, but I lost enough.

You said you were reluctant to show anyone the scar.

Well, I was involved with someone at the time. I suppose it's relevant that I'm gay. I always thought that I was lucky with that, because I felt women would be more understanding than men. I was involved with someone who was very wonderful, supportive, and helpful. I think she went out of her way to make me not feel self-conscious.

I have subsequently only been with one person, and I am very self-conscious. In fact, I think a lot about getting reconstructive surgery. Except that I don't think it's going to help that much.

What was difficult had less to do with feeling insecure about my femaleness than just the unattractiveness. I was getting so heavy, and my body was not performing right. Chemotherapy lasts one year, and it was a full second year before the consequences were over. I became almost arthritic from going off the prednisone and couldn't walk upstairs or sit down. It was at least eight months before my muscles got back to normal.

And one of the things that my doctor warned might happen has —as a result of the chemotherapy, I went through menopause. So while I was going through the chemotherapy, I was having hot flashes all the time. That was the final blow! I didn't have any emotional reactions, but the hot flashes were terrible. I was having twelve to fourteen a day, lasting five minutes each. It's almost over now—I have about one every two hours or so. But that didn't help my image as a woman, either. In fact, that's been the most damaging, I think. Here I'm forty, and I'm postmenopausal, and I haven't got a breast. Psychologically, I don't feel terrific.

What do you do about that?

I'm back in analysis. I haven't been doing as much positive thinking as I should be. As the fear of dying of cancer goes, you absorb the fact of having had cancer, and it becomes almost a past-tense thing, although it's present; it's not as imminent. I tend to think that stress is a lot more significant than diet in the business of cancer, and I am a highly stressed person. Every day I say I've got to go back to meditation, and I haven't.

But anyway, it has affected my view of myself as a woman. I definitely don't feel as attractive. I feel much older. I am working on that in analysis, but it's still there. I don't feel able to go out and look for a new lover. A friend of mine told me that her mother, after she had a mastectomy, came alive and began dating a lot of men and being much more sexually active than she had been. She found men very supportive and not at all turned off by it. I haven't had enough experience to know what the response of women would be.

Are you comfortable with the prosthesis?
Yes. It's a little bit of a nuisance, that's all. And again, everybody who does anything in relation to mastectomies is wonderful. There's a store run by two women, and they are so helpful. They have bras and bathing suits, and one of them is a young woman who got a degree at the Fashion Institute of Technology. She designs clothes that are great—negligees, nightgowns, everything. And the wig people are the same—absolutely the nicest people.

Did you find yourself wondering why this happened to you?
Yes, absolutely. I think cancer is sort of psychogenic, and I've always been a depressed person. I think when you're particularly depressed and particularly stressed, you're particularly vulnerable to it. The year before I got it, I'd broken up the most important relationship of my life and felt that I had lost a major part of myself. I had changed jobs, graduated from law school, moved— a lot of changes. But the breakup was the most devastating. That's why I think it's so important to be positive. I had no contributing factors other than stress and depression. That meant I had some control over it, that I could beat it. I didn't have to give in to it, which I finally believe: you don't have to give in to it, I hope.

Did you read anything particularly helpful?
I thought the Simonton book was helpful. Some people in my discussion group did not, because it lays a lot of the blame on the victim. I thought it gives you a lot of potential for making things better.

I read everything. And I skipped the statistics. The problem with books is that any book with statistics is almost out of date before it's printed, because things are changing so quickly. So I would recommend not reading a lot about statistics, but reading about the things that you can do to help yourself.

"A WOMAN WHO HAS NOT HAD A MASTECTOMY SAID
THE MOST TOUCHING THING. SHE SAID, 'YOU'VE
STRIPPED ME OF THE FEAR.' "

*Nancy Fried is a sculptor working and exhibiting in New
York City who had a mastectomy in 1986, when she was
forty, followed by abdominal surgery for an ovarian tumor
seven months later. Her sculpture is autobiographical,
dealing in themes of loss and regeneration.*

How did you find out you had breast cancer?
It began about three years ago. I had a little lump on my breast.
The doctor aspirated it and it seemed fine, but he said, "You
should have a mammogram." So for my fortieth birthday present
I had a mammogram. My father had been an obstetrician/gyne-
cologist and a breast surgeon, but being a feminist I wanted to
see a woman gynecologist. So I did, and she turned out to be
awful! She actually forgot to tell me that the mammogram was
irregular. Six months later her office called and said, "You
haven't had your second mammogram." I said, "Why would I?"
And her office said, "Well, your first mammogram was irregular."
Can you believe that? There were these gray areas on the mammogram, and apparently what I had were calcium deposits. I had
gone six months without treatment. The only good thing about
this woman is that she sent me to a wonderful breast specialist.
And what did the specialist say?
He confirmed that the gray areas were calcium deposits, but he
didn't think they were malignant because 90 percent of the time,
they're benign. But I was still nervous, going into biopsy. I knew
that he was going to biopsy two areas because my breasts are
large.
How was the biopsy?
It was done in the hospital. I went in only for the day, but for six
days after I was a zombie. I have no idea what the anesthetic
was, but it was strong, I guess, because they were going to take
a lot of tissue out. We took pictures of me naked after the surgery,
and the biopsied breast was really smaller and felt about two
inches shorter than the other breast. It was a needle-guided biopsy, and the technician was very rough with me. She had some

problems getting the pins or wires in to guide my doctor in the surgery. My doctor, on the other hand, was amazing and wonderful. It wasn't necessary, but he came up two flights of stairs from the operating room where he was prepping for my biopsy just to hold my hand. He was so considerate of me and so attentive to Chrissie, too—she is the woman I live with. He showed her the same respect he would have shown a husband.

When did you find out the results of the biopsy?
It took ten days. For some reason they couldn't decide on the diagnosis. It turned out I had a very small invasive ductal cancer near the lymph nodes, and I also had some very new cancer cells that weren't invasive but were all through my milk ducts. I was at home when the doctor called to tell me the news. I think I dealt with it incredibly well, but when you first hear the words "You have cancer, you need a mastectomy," all reality disappears. The doctor said there was no option. He said that they could have done a lumpectomy if I had just the invasive cancer. But I had all this intraductal cancer and those cells, like healthy cells, won't respond to radiation.

At the end of the call my doctor said, "Come in tomorrow and bring in every question you can think of, and you'll just sit and talk to me." So I brought in the list. My mother came up from Philadelphia, and she was with me. Again he was wonderful. Then my mother said to him—he's young, like forty-one—"Have you done a lot of operations?" It turns out he's this kind of famous breast surgeon.

I made the appointment for my operation, but he told me to go for other opinions. And I did because I wanted to see if there was someone that I might like more. I went to one very famous surgeon, and his attitude was just awful! He looked at the mammogram and said, "Well, it's got to come off. Make an appointment with my nurse." He didn't even know my name. It was appalling. I also saw another doctor—he was really warm, like my doctor. He was in his sixties. And he said, "Your doctor is your age, and he'll be with you the rest of your life." It was such a nice thing to say, and it's actually a very true concept because for the rest of my life I am going to be going for breast checkups. He also said, "You have the best young doctor in New York—once a month I go to lectures he gives—so don't change doctors." I also had the tissue retested at a cancer hospital. It confirmed the first pathology report, and then I knew it was accurate. It wasn't as if I was looking for one person to say I didn't have to have it done. I wanted to know that I had done everything I could so I would never look back and say, "I should have done one more thing."

*Did you discuss the diagnosis with your woman
gynecologist?*

Actually, ten minutes after I got the diagnosis from the breast surgeon, she called. And it was the only time I heard from her. She said, "I talked to the surgeon, and it's got to come off." I couldn't believe it. I hung up. It was shocking. She was supposed to be my doctor, but she had never once called to say, "How are you feeling?" or anything. On the other hand, I should have expected that. At the time of the original mammogram I also had a sonogram. That turned out to be irregular, too. There was some kind of mass on one of my ovaries. And she said to me, very casually, "Well, you might have a little cancer in there. We'll check it in three months."

What did you do about that?

At first I was really very upset, but I just sort of let it go because she didn't make it sound immediate, and I was trying to cope with the results of the mammogram. Eventually, I knew, I would have to deal with my ovary, too.

Is there any history of cancer in your family?

No. There is no cancer in my family, although two months after my operation my mother had a mammogram with a dark spot. When the doctor told her she needed a biopsy, he asked her if there was any cancer in her family. She said, "No." Ten minutes later, she said, tears started to fall down her face because she realized, yes, her daughter has cancer.

Did you go in for tests before the mastectomy?

Yes. A few days before—blood tests and the cardiogram and all of those things. And I was very sad. I mean, I remember lying there, and this jerk was pasting glue (to keep the electrodes for the cardiogram in place) over me, and I realized his would be one of the last hands that would touch my breast. Christmas carols were playing on his radio. There were other last times, too, and more of that sadness. Like the last time you take a shower with those breasts, the last time you make love with those breasts—I cried afterward for those times. But I am happy that they were such specific events because I will always remember them.

What do you recall about the hospital experience?

My mother and I went up to the room about four in the afternoon.

The hospital was small and lovely, and they let Chrissie stay in the room with me until midnight. And she probably could have slept over. If it happened again, I would just have her stay there. The doctor came in that night and sat with me for about an hour. I think this is rare. I talked to him about a lot of very personal things including my father's death. What was so amazing about this man was that he knew I needed to talk, that I needed him to know me because he was going to do such a personal, intimate operation. He didn't say, "I have to get home for dinner." He was just so wonderful. And he gave me sweet little hints. He said, "You know, you're going to be tired. You're going to be frightened. You don't have to talk to anybody on the phone. You can take the phone off the hook." And I did. It was a real gift, because I wouldn't have thought of doing that. I would have thought I'm supposed to talk to people who call.

The next morning he came to see me before I went to the operating room. My mother and sister and Chrissie were with me. I remember lying in the room where you're lined up before surgery. Everyone was aware that I was losing my breast. At forty-one, at *any age,* it's hard to lose your breast! It's hard to have cancer.

I remember coming out of the anesthesia. I actually remember being brought back to my room, and I remember all these young doctors sitting me up in bed right away and me letting out this blood curdling scream because it hurt so much—it was like my breast was being *ripped* out. It's the most horrible feeling! I remember my mother running out of the room to the nurse's station to say, "Get her twenty-four-hour nurses!" I just can't even imagine what it must have been like for my family, watching someone they love go through this.

Why did they sit you up like that?
I don't know. I guess it was their way of getting me into the bed. Anyway, for days, when they would come in to check me, they would make me sit up, and it hurt. My surgeon said, "It will hurt less if you keep your bed angled." So I got into a habit of sleeping almost sitting up for months because the process of coming up from lying down was so terrible for me.

How many lymph nodes did the doctor remove, and what did he find?
They took all the lymph nodes, and they were all clean. So that was wonderful, but I have numb spots in the skin under my arm, at the back of my arm, and behind the shoulder. If I tickle the

skin, it has no feeling. If someone leans up against me, I can't feel it, and that's almost nauseating. It's like not knowing my body in a certain way. I don't like to wash under my arm because I can't feel it.

When did you begin doing arm exercises?
The Reach to Recovery people came in right away, on the first or second day after surgery, and I started my exercises. The women were very sweet, but they both had on their perfect fake breasts, and that turned me off. In the beginning, for about three months, I wore a prosthesis, too. Then I went to Cape Cod. I had this three-pound, silicone, ugly breast, and I thought, I can't wear this in the heat. Everybody I know knows I don't have a breast. What is the secret? Who am I hiding this from? That polyester fill hangs down to your stomach when it gets wet and you have to pull it up and squeeze it out. I certainly wasn't going to lie on the beach with it on, so I gave it up there. God, it felt so good not having it on! But these women do push you to wear it. I think it's about keeping the secret—women are supposed to have breasts. My doctor says the only problem with not wearing the prosthesis is you sit off balance. Eventually, I guess my back will hurt. I try to sit straight, but I have noticed in the Polaroids of me that I use for my work that I lean toward the breast side. But I just can't imagine wearing the prosthesis again. This is who I am.

Did you have pain after the surgery?
Apparently the pain after a mastectomy is different for everybody. It was very painful for me. I had to stay in the hospital for two or three days extra because they discovered I was bleeding internally. I was swollen and the area under my arm turned colors, so I had to be aspirated every other day for about three weeks after I got out of the hospital. And I had the most excruciating pain in my right arm. While the nerve endings were healing I couldn't be in a car, I couldn't be on the subway. I could barely walk for months because the pain in the arm was so severe. It was unbelievable. I was very athletic before the operation, and I had been swimming about a mile every day and running five miles every day. I was strong! And yet recovering from the mastectomy was incredibly difficult for me. Chrissie asked my doctor, "When will the pain stop?"—thinking he'd say, "A week or two weeks." And he said, "Ten years. Maybe never."

Apparently, with this surgery you're going to have pain sometimes. The skin stretches. Right now, if I reach to turn off the light, it feels like the skin is being pulled. There's a tightness across the area where the breast was. Here it is, a year and a half later, and when I touch my chest, it's tender underneath. And then it itches at night, viciously, but it's too sensitive to scratch directly, so I use my clothes as a buffer to scratch it. With all the lymph nodes removed under my arm, the nerve endings are really sensitive, too.

But for all that, I'm back to swimming. As wonderful as my doctor is, he said things that turned out not to be true. He said, "You'll probably never be able to do the kind of swimming you did before." But now I do a mile. It took me a little time to build up. Yes, my arm is weaker at night. I mean, there are times when I think I can't lift it, I have to push it up. But the fact is, if you push and decide you're going to do something, you can do it.

Was it difficult for you to look at your incision?
I am very fortunate that the woman I live with has been so supportive. I mean, after the operation, it was not pretty. I was black and blue because of the internal bleeding. I was swollen. And she told me that I looked sexy, that the scar looked sexy. It was great. It really changed how I saw myself. I don't think she really thought it looked sexy. I think she was terrified, but the fact that she said that meant a lot.

How long have you lived together?
Seven years. I don't know if it's different being with a woman than being with a man when it comes to dealing with a mastectomy. It was a woman who said, "I could never look at her again if I lived with her." And another woman said to me, "The idea of looking into the mirror at that body . . ." I know women who have had mastectomies who feel like that.

Did having your work help you get through this time?
I've been through a lot of hard things in my life, so I'm strong, but, yes, because immediately I did a very small piece when I was really too sore to work. It was my body—just a torso that had the little stitches across the chest. The next piece I made was a woman, and it's called *Mourning*. It's my favorite piece. About eight inches high, it's also a torso, but she has a head. She has the scar, and she is holding the remaining left breast in her right hand, and the two breasts are touching. It's like they're saying good-bye. Her head is tucked into her shoulder and she is weeping. It was the beginning of the process of my saying good-bye and really acknowledging that the breast was gone, but also of

loving it. When I made the scar I worked from Polaroids, and I made it look like it looks—I have a little fleshy area at the underarm. I did it in clay, and I smoothed it lovingly.

There is a piece I made called *The Flirt*. It's about a ten-inch-high torso—no head, but she's wearing a skirt. She doesn't have a top on and the breast is hanging. It's not a beautiful young breast. It's the hanging breast of a forty-two-year-old woman who has gained and lost weight, and there is the scar. But she's hot! She's pulling her skirt out the way little girls do, and she's flirting. That's the one my doctor bought.

Did you show your doctor the work you were doing?
He was totally involved in my work. I think it's because I dealt with my mastectomy so differently from other women. By making pieces celebrating my body, I really made what my doctor does more okay. The very early pieces are mourning the breast, but they aren't angry. They are about the anger and the fear and the nightmares. But the pieces focused on the body are really saying, This body is beautiful. I think that must be very special for him. His office is very involved in my case because of my art. And when I panic and I call the office, they say, "Just come over." They know who I am, and every time I get reviewed positively, the office is thrilled.

What kind of sculpture did you do before the mastectomy?
My work has always been very autobiographical. I did a series of twelve pieces which were little settings about my childhood and my relationship to my father. One about being an abused child—a woman cowering in a corner and a belt on the floor. And another one called *Waiting for His Footsteps*. It's frightening.

I always did women in a very low-cut top, like a slip, and because I have big breasts, the women's breasts were kind of ample.

Then I had the operation. You know, as long as my arm hurts, I'm going to be aware that I don't have a breast. My work will never have two breasts in it—well, I shouldn't say "never," but I work from Polaroids of me, and I don't have two breasts. People do self-portraits; and that's my self-portrait—one breast and a scar.

Has the response to your recent work been different from the reaction to your earlier work?
I was doing well before—I sold ten of the twelve pieces from my childhood show. But the recent show was something completely

different. My dealer, who had taken some of my earlier work, made no commitments for another show when I left in June. And when I let her see the new body of work in October, at first she said, "Nobody is going to show this." But she stayed for three hours, and by the time she left I was scheduled for a show in two months. What she said was, "This work won't sell, but it's very important to have seen it." She didn't mean it was important because of the cancer; it was important as sculpture.

The response to the work both from women who have breast cancer and those who don't has been touching. I have letters from women who walked past the gallery on Madison Avenue—I'm with Graham Modern—and saw one of my biggest pieces in the window. It was a torso called *Tribute to Dr. Cody*. A seventy-year-old woman thanked me for doing what she could never do—be open. She said she used to think she was the cat's pajamas in the fifties—even walking around the beach naked. Then she had a double mastectomy when she was fifty, and not only did she stop being naked on the beach, she never walks naked in her house. She never looks at herself in the mirror. And her husband never looks at her. After seeing my work, she told me, she and her husband went home and she took her clothes off and they looked at her. It was amazing! Another woman who has not had a mastectomy said the most touching thing. She said, "You've stripped me of the fear." You know, when everything's kept a secret, it's more scary. The mother of a student of mine had a mastectomy two years ago and then had a breakdown and was institutionalized. My student said, "I've got to get my mother to see this." The mother came the last day of the exhibit—this Sutton Place matron, totally formal, and she ended up sitting in the corner, weeping and saying to me, "Thank you. No one knows. No one knows. They think I went to a fat farm."

Earlier in the interview you mentioned you had a mass on your ovaries. Did you deal with that after your mastectomy?

I went for sonograms every three months like the gynecologist said I should. I remember doing one sonogram, about two months after my mastectomy, the radiologist was telling what he saw, using these big words that terrified me, and I started to cry. I said to him, "It's too much. It's just too much." I was so strong, but every once in a while I'd think, I just lost my breast. And every three months there was another sonogram.

Finally, on June 1, I was on my way to the Cape. The cats were in the car, Chrissie was in the car. I felt strange about leaving for three months because we were still watching the mass. Before I left, I went to see the oncologist and he'd said, "You really need an operation." They knew it was a tumor on the right ovary, the same side as the mastectomy. So we'd decided we would do an exploratory operation at the end of August because I really needed to recuperate from the mastectomy. But the waiting turned out to be really hard. A part of me would say, "Nothing could be wrong." And another part of me now knew something could be wrong. I felt fragile. I had a different kind of summer than I ever had. I knew life was precious in a different way, so my work just took off.

How was the exploratory operation?

I had a laparoscopy, and the mass was huge. He said he didn't think it was malignant, but he must have been a little worried because he scheduled the surgery for four days later. I had a barium enema, and the resident made a mistake. He gave me too much barium, so from six o'clock at night until eleven o'clock the next morning when I had the operation, I had eleven enemas to clean me out.

What were the results of the surgery?

The ovarian tumor wasn't malignant, so I kept my ovaries and everything. But my appendix was taken out because it *did* have a malignant tumor on it. That was really frightening for me to think about because it meant my body had produced cancer in another place. He did a vertical incision, and at first I was furious because everyone I talked to had a bikini cut. I thought, What a rat! He must think because I have one scar, Oh, so what. Just give her another one. But when they think you might have cancer, they want the incision that lets them see the most.

How long was your recovery?

After I left the hospital I stayed at a friend's apartment for a week and then took a four-hour car trip to get to an artists' colony. I probably should have stayed in New York for a few more days, but I felt I needed to start working, which I did. I left the artists' colony at the end of September last year. And now there was a new scar I had to deal with, which was really kind of wonderful. You can tell right when I had the ovary operation because I did a piece called *The Belly Mask: Dr. Smith's Concept of Beauty*. I first did a small one with a huge vertical scar. Then I made a life-size one. It's very powerful. It's like my standing naked in front of you: This is who I am. Between October and January—my show was in January—I did some of my most important work. One night I looked at a sculpture I'd made of my body, showing all the scars of my surgeries, and thought, My God, it's an abstract pattern. A scar comes from the pubic hair to the navel, and then a scar goes from under my arm pointing to my breast to the nipple, so there are all these lines going into circles. It's really kind of wonderful. And when I realized how beautiful the work was, I knew my body was beautiful.

Are you going for regular checkups and mammograms?
In the beginning I was checked every month, and now it's every three months. I'm supposed to have a mammogram every year. But I'm going to have one in the fall, because I have a lump under my arm and it's made me nervous.

When did you find this lump?
I started feeling it three months ago. I've gone once a month to have it checked. It seems to go up and down with my periods, so he thinks it may be breast tissue. It doesn't feel that way to me. To me, it feels like a ball. My ovary doctor also thinks it's extended breast tissue. If they do exploratory surgery, that will mean even more scar tissue, which then makes it harder to feel what's going on. And on top of it all, I have cystic breasts, which makes examination difficult. After the recent *New York Times* articles [recommending chemotherapy for all women diagnosed with malignant breast cancer], I've been having a hard time. I think I should have had chemotherapy. And my doctor said that if all of this were happening now, we probably would have done it, but the longer you wait, the less effective it is. You know, at the time I was thrilled that I didn't need it. But now I wish I had done it, because it would be over and I would feel safer.

"I DON'T KNOW WHY GRASS WORKS, BUT I KNOW THAT HARVARD RECOMMENDED IT FOR CHEMOTHERAPY, AND THE DIFFERENCE WAS NIGHT AND DAY."
A senior writer for a national magazine, fifty-eight at the time of this interview. She had had a radical mastectomy

fourteen years before and a lumpectomy two years ago. She is divorced, the mother of two sons.

I really consider a doctor no different from a plumber or an electrician. I have no patience with the American myth that doctors are God or that the statement "He came very well recommended" resolves all questions. So what? A plumber can come well recommended, but if he suggests something that doesn't make sense, then you get a second plumber in. You do absolutely the same thing with a doctor. They are not gods—they are very much human beings. Obviously there will be a point where you must yield to their judgment, but you must understand fully why.

Would you start at the beginning? What happened?

My mother had had breast cancer when she was well into her sixties. She had a mastectomy. I always had checkups, but to tell you the truth, I never really thought about it in terms of myself. I was, I guess, forty-three, taking a shower one Sunday night, and just happened to be stretching out and thought, Oh, dear. I felt a lump and really went into sort of shock.

What did it feel like?

Not even as large as a walnut. Almost an acorn. It didn't hurt. But it was definitely there. So I went to my gynecologist, who was a wonderful man, and he said, "Look, obviously our next step is a surgeon, and I'm going to get you there immediately." He said, "If you feel you have to be spoon-fed through this, I will get you someone who has a perfectly wonderful bedside manner." I said, "Come on, you've delivered two of my children. Cut that crap right now." He said, "Okay, I'm going to send you to the one surgeon who is merely considered the surgeon's surgeon here. If I ever had to have anything done, he's the one I'd call. He's rather shy and reserved, but he is top-drawer." I said, "That's the one I want."

So I saw him, and he described the alternatives if the lump was malignant. He said, "We can do a modified or we can do a radical." Lumpectomy wasn't even a possibility—this was fourteen years ago. He said, "I am conservative, but you are young, you have children: I would recommend a radical at this point. We feel that's the safest thing to do." I said fine.

But from this point on, there are certain things you have to do for yourself. I've gone to Cape Cod all my life. There's one beach where I think things out. I thought, I've got to just walk that beach and decide what to do. Which I did. Then I really was fine. I said to myself: "First of all, there's no point in saying you're not going to be mutilated—you are going to be mutilated. How do you deal with this? Are you going to be able to look in a mirror? You can't hide under a rug: it's there, it's a fact of life."

So I went in, and I was due for surgery at one o'clock. They rolled me into the operating room, and the clock said five after one. I said, "Okay, when I wake up in recovery, if it's about three, it was benign. Fine. If it's about six or seven, that's it." In the recovery room, I looked at the clock and it said ten of seven. I thought, Okay, that's it: we are not going backward!

The next morning, by God, I got up, I brushed my teeth, I combed my hair. I don't know how I did it. I put makeup on and said, "All right, I'm ready for the day. That's the way it's going to be." I still had the intravenous in, and I said, "I want to take a walk now." The nurses said, "Oh, no," and I said, "I am going to take a walk around." I was staggering around the halls, and I came around a corner and I hit, stretched out on a stretcher, the biggest, blackest man I have seen. It was Matt Snell, the football player, who was in for therapy for a shoulder separation. I must have gone, "Acckkk!!" because he started to laugh, and I started to laugh. You have to do that—you have to have a sense of humor. It's like combat humor. You can't withdraw. Mutilation produces anger, but you can't let anger take over because it is just counterproductive. You have to replace anger with humor.

I had a young intern and a young resident who were superb, very supportive. After ten days, I said to these two guys, "I really feel fine and the hospital routine drives me nuts and the food is awful. I'd like to go home." I had gone in wearing a silk shirt and a pair of slacks. I said, "Listen, I came in this way and I'd like to go out this way." They said, "Sure, get the lamb's wool." They made this artistic creation, with me in the bra I wore in—the whole thing was humorous.

The other thing that several doctors at the hospital did was refer you to a special nurse. My surgeon said, "I don't know what it means to lose a breast. It's not the same as losing a testicle. So we have a gal who works with a group of us, and you should talk to her."

She's wonderful. She was there the first night, she explained what a prosthesis was, she explained the whole process. She isn't equipped, I'm sure, to deal with extreme anger, but she gives total support. So even before you're out of the anesthesia, people are saying, "Let's go!"

I kept thinking, Well, I guess I'm going to go into a depression. I never did. That high kept going.

You're saying you were on a high after the surgery?

It's a sense of survival and a sense of disciplining yourself to go for it. This is not the end of the world. One interesting thing that I did do a few months after the operation—I'm not saying it's commendable, but perhaps it's understandable: my marriage was really breaking up at this point, and I started a very casual love affair. If I was going to be rejected, I wanted it not to matter. I found that it made absolutely no difference sexually: it's simply that the breast isn't there now. There is no distortion, there is no ugliness. Which is great—I have seen some radicals that have been hacked.

So this was all happening while you were in the middle of a divorce?

Yes. I'm sure it was stress-related.

Who was helping you during your recovery?

My two sons were very good, even though they were young— eleven and nine. And friends were marvelous. Nobody should try to go through this alone.

Did the doctors tell you whether any nodes were involved?

They were clean both times.

Was there a Reach to Recovery program at that time?

This girl was sort of the same thing.

The differences between then and now are interesting: no preliminary biopsy, a hospital stay of ten days instead of four or five, the staff discouraging you from taking a walk. . . .

Exactly. I noticed all that the second time, two years ago. I had gone for a routine gynecological checkup, and my doctor said, "There's something here I don't like." In retrospect, I remember that there'd been a little bit of soreness on that side, but I thought I had probably pulled a muscle.

I went for a mammogram, and they said, "Yeah, it doesn't look good. There seems to be a thickening of the tissue," and I thought, Oh, you do think of the cleverest lines. My doctor said, "We'll do the biopsy." I said, "I'm having trouble with this." He said, "Why? You did so well the first time." I said, "There's a big difference between having one breast and having no breasts at all. This is really castration, and I want to think about it just a little bit."

Then, oddly enough, my oldest son, who was then twenty-three, said, "Boy, you're some kind of journalist, Mom. Would you please look at your own magazine's article on lumpectomy and the Pittsburgh study?"

I said, "The what?" So I went running upstairs and pulled the breast cancer file. Meanwhile, a friend of mine dates a lawyer. He called me and said, "Listen, don't let them talk you into anything."

So I went back to my doctor with the lumpectomy information and said, "I really want to try this." He said, "Okay. But I have to do the biopsy first. If it's over 5 centimeters, we can't do a lumpectomy. And you know that it will require follow-up radiation." I said, "Okay, I'll take my chances." He did the biopsy next day, then the lumpectomy, and I was out of the hospital in five days.

Can you describe the procedures?
You're awake during the biopsy—it's done under a local, in the hospital. My doctor came down within half an hour afterward and said, "It is malignant. All I have to do tomorrow is go back in and widen the incision a little bit more and you're done." The next morning, under general anesthesia, they simply enlarged that area.

Did the biopsy hurt?
Not bad. It stung. I think they put an ice pack on it. I didn't feel the need to take a painkiller.

When did they start the radiation?
About two and a half weeks later. I had a lot of trouble with it. My doctor selected a radiologist who has an excellent reputation, a private doctor who worked out of his office rather than in a hospital—my doctor said it can be a zoo at a hospital. This guy had four assistants. The first day he kept me waiting three hours and hadn't read my files. Then I had to meet all the assistants. The first bell in my head was, "Oh, God, this is like Rembrandt's *Anatomy Lesson,* and it's going to cost me an arm and a leg, and I'll never see any of these bastards again." He worked up a plan, and a technician gave me the treatments.

Here's where you have to be prepared for a little problem. The radiation: it's a machine and it burns you, and you get an anger reaction. You sit there for three minutes, with red markings on you, and somebody zaps you with a machine. You get cross. I didn't like these guys. Their bill, incidentally, was higher than the surgeon's.

You're supposed to have twenty—three or four a week—and then they give you high intensity for five treatments. I got to the seventeenth treatment. I was planning to go away for Memorial Day weekend. I had already said to myself, "No way am I doing five more. I don't like these guys, I don't like this, I've had enough."

After the seventeenth treatment I got home about ten o'clock and went to bed, because I was tired. Radiation makes you terribly tired. I woke up at ten of twelve, with terrible muscle spasms from my waist to my shoulder, and I couldn't breathe. To make a long story short, I sat on the edge of a chair 'til nine o'clock the next morning. I couldn't breathe. I didn't know which doctor to call. So I called the radiologist. He said, "Well, it wouldn't have anything to do with the treatments, but why don't you come in." He was rude. He did a lung X-ray and thought there was a blood clot. He handed me the X-rays and said, "Go see your own doctor immediately."

I was turned out onto Fifth Avenue in ninety-degree heat. My own doctor said, "There's fluid in the lungs. Get over to the hospital. We're doing a lung scan." They did what's called a lung biopsy, where they inject a needle in and take tissue from it. It sounds horrible, but it didn't bother me because the doctor was good and told me exactly what he was going to do. If someone tells you what he's doing, you don't panic.

They finally determined that there was tumorous tissue present and put me on chemo immediately.

Are you saying they found cancer in your lungs?

Yes. And I think there was a direct relationship between too much radiation and this traumatic situation of the lungs filling with fluid. In my X-ray before I started the radiation, the lung was absolutely clear. I've since discussed this with my onocologist, who will go as far as to say, "Yes, I think you were overradiated." And it is still sore—the whole area that was irradiated. I cannot be in the sun without using a total screen.

Is the skin red?

No, I was lucky. My skin did not discolor, but it can happen.

Who managed your chemotherapy?

My doctor got me a very good oncologist—I love him. He will answer every question. But he, too, did the standard procedure: when they start out, they zap you for the first two weeks. Very often, your blood count goes way, way, way down, and you're subject to infection. That wasn't explained to me. At the end of the zapping, I picked up some sort of virus. I was sick as a dog. I finally went in and asked to see him. He said, "Why aren't you undressed for examination?" I said, "I don't want to be examined. I want to talk to you." I said, "No son of a bitch makes me that sick without telling me about it." I said, "How dare you not explain to me that there was a danger of this reaction? We either play ball with each other or screw it. I don't care." He said, "Why are you so angry?" I said, "Doc, this is my third time around. What do you want, Rebecca of Sunnybrook Farm?"

From then on, we worked very well together. The chemo should be two weeks on, two weeks off, two on, two off. I explained to him that I don't tolerate drugs well. He said, "Okay, we'll cut it back a little bit." At the end of nine months, he took me off and —knock on wood—it's been fine. I have X-rays every three months, scan tests every six months. The last time I had a reaction—I was having a fever that went from 99 degrees to 102—he said, "Back in the hospital." I said, "No, no, back to Cape Cod." He insisted I take a friend, which I did. On the fifth day, the fever went right through the roof to 105. I called him and he said, "Okay, start two Tylenols fast." And it broke.

I was very lucky with the chemo. I did not lose my hair. I have a very good guy who cut it very short. He said, "It's getting brittle —you're just going to look like Rod Stewart for a year." And I kept working—that's the best discipline in the world.

I should have been told more about radiation, what to expect and why. There's a big school that says preventive radiation is a lot of crap. If I'd been given the choice, I would have said chemo is absolutely essential, but radiation? No—I should have quit after four or five times. I should have used my own judgment and said, "I don't like these people." You try to be a good patient, but when you don't like them, that's creating stress within yourself.

My chemo guy is very cautious. He wants you to call him with the slightest symptom of anything wrong. He says, "I know what I'm doing, you don't. No call is unimportant. I don't care if you bumped your toe: you call me, and I'll tell you what's wrong."

He'll call you back immediately, which is important. He's terribly good.

How did you react to the chemo, other than the fever?

You get very spacey because of the steroid. You're going to gain weight, that's just inevitable. I would go out to a business lunch, and if they put down three baskets of bread, I can assure you I would eat all three baskets of bread. You're so hyped up. And I was not running the schedule of an East German swimmer, so I was not burning it off. But it was really not bad. I said, "Now, doctor, will it be okay if I go home after work and have my cocktail?" He said, "I'm not telling you that you can't, but I don't think you're going to want it." I said, "I'll just make it weaker." And I did! I was determined I would keep as much of my life in place as I could. He agrees with that very strongly. No calcium, no vitamins. He said, "I want you to eat the way you've always eaten, live the way you've always lived." Of course, if you have bad habits, you can correct them, but he said, "We can't spot a change if you go screwing around with your intake and outtake."

What kind of change?

He meant if you're suddenly tired, they can't tell what it means if you've changed your diet and you're taking eight vitamin pills and four iron pills and whatever else.

A friend of mine, a woman who had a mastectomy and now is dying of bone cancer, tries everything to keep her spirits up, get her family's spirits up. She will go in to her doctor and say, "What about the macrobiotic diet?" Her doctor said, "We're not sure it's going to help, but it won't hurt you." And she's sticking to it. I had dinner with her the other night, and I've got to tell you, I've never eaten so many twigs—God, it's unappetizing! But she said it's sort of a discipline. Now, see, if it were me, I would be having avocados and lobster and saying, "The hell with it." It's a different approach. For her, it's the discipline of optimism.

Did you have much nausea from the chemo?

Funny . . . I just remembered this: The head nurse came in at two o'clock in the morning once and said, "Are you awake?' I said, "Yeah, I am." She said, "I just wanted to talk to you. They are going to give you a stomach tranquilizer for nausea, and it's going to knock you out." I said, "I know, and I hate that stuff." She said, "Why don't you ask your doctor about smoking grass?" Well, I thought that was the most intriguing thing in the world!

So, the next time I saw my doctor, I'm saying in my best low-register, professional voice, "Doctor, I was just wondering—how about grass?" And he said, "Gee, I didn't think you were the type." I said, "I can learn anything. I don't want to take those pills." So, having screamed at my two boys about the dangers of drug addiction, there I sit in my living room with them teaching me how to smoke marijuana.

My sons decided that the water pipe would be the best method. My son offered to get me his old pipe from prep school, and I said, "Do you mean . . . ?" He said, "Mom, for chrissake, it's eight years ago. You're not going to yell at me now." And I was trying to learn how to exhale and not cough. It was one of the more hysterical evenings. I never got stoned, because I never could swallow that much, but my nausea was no more awful than car sickness.

So I had the pipe, and a friend of mine from work arrived one day with a large bag of the best Acapulco gold and said, "This is from your friends at the magazine." She was the most prim and proper of all of our saleswomen, and I have often thought of how management would have reacted if they could have seen this act of kindness. But I only had to use it about nine times.

What was the chemo regimen?
It's a four-week cycle. The first week, you get a shot which is comprised of three drugs, and you get the same thing the next week. Then you have two weeks off. While you're taking the shots, you're also taking two other drugs by mouth, Cytoxan and the steroid prednisone. Now they can vary this, depending on what your reaction is. You are most apt to feel very, very nauseated in the first two weeks while they are introducing you to it. That's when I'd smoke grass more. I used to carry the equipment around in a Crown Royal bag. This one guy I was dating was terrified that he was going to get caught in the car with me.

And the grass really helped?
It was absolutely amazing. I kept choking, trying to swallow it—I would blow it out my nose instead of my mouth—but honestly, it was amazing. I don't know why it works, but I know that Harvard has recommended it for chemotherapy. The difference was night and day, really, with just two drags.

Did you notice any other changes in approach between your first and second operations?
People are much more up-front now about breast cancer and

mastectomy. Women aren't so traumatized by it. It's more acceptable. When I was in the hospital the first time, two women pointed me out. "That's the one, that's the one who had the breast removed." For a moment, I started to shake. Now you suddenly find that an amazing number of people have them. It's easier on the patient.

Are you glad you chose the lumpectomy rather than
another mastectomy?

Oh, yes. Because this was very small. It was on the outside of the breast, lower down. The incision is about three inches. I don't think I was ever particularly vain about my bosom—I didn't go around in décolletage. But two—I really, really balked at that. I thought, Well, if it recurs and I eventually have to have a mastectomy, fine. But I'd rather try this.

"A LOT OF OLDER, TRADITIONAL WOMEN DON'T WANT TO KNOW MORE THAN IS NECESSARY. MANY YOUNGER WOMEN WANT TO KNOW EVERYTHING. BY RESEARCHING, *I* FELT EMPOWERED."

A single, forty-five-year-old art director who had a lumpectomy in 1986, followed by a mastectomy on August 6, three weeks before this interview.

How did you discover your lump?

Eight months ago, during a routine exam, my gynecologist found what he said was a lump and said I should have a mammogram. I must say I never could find the lump, but he sent me to a clinic that specializes in mammograms to be on the safe side. There was a six-week wait at the clinic for an appointment, so I made one with a private doctor where I only had to wait two weeks. But during those two weeks I decided to go to a psychic healer two or three times to see if we could get rid of whatever was there, and I worked on visualizing a benign cyst being aspirated successfully.

Had you ever been to this healer before?

Yes. I'd read his book about a year before my surgery, and I was impressed because he said he was able to kill cancer cells, although at the time cancer was something I never worried about.

In my family, we have a history of heart disease. My father and uncle both died of heart attacks.

When you finally had your mammogram, what did it show? The mammogram was negative. The doctor who examined me couldn't find any lump. I said, "Well, what about this little thickness here?" He said, "It's just normal breast tissue. Don't worry about that." Then about six months later the doctor sends me a little announcement to come back for another mammogram. I thought, I'm not going back there. He was too expensive. I'll go to the clinic. So I make an appointment for about a month later. When I went in, the doctor palpated me and said, "Oh, there's a lump here." I said, "Oh, I had that before. It goes away." She said, "Well, probably it's nothing, but better come back next week to see our surgeon." When I went back, there were sixteen women waiting for the surgeon. Everyone was very nervous. I was pretty sure when I went in that she would say it was nothing. But instead she said, "It's just a little thick, and you should really go to your doctor and have him recommend a surgeon and have a biopsy." Now *biopsy* is a really frightening word. So I call my gynecologist and go to see him immediately. He says, "Hmmm, well, there's something there. It feels like the same lump as before, but it is a little bigger." Then he says, "Quite frankly, it doesn't feel malignant. Your tumor moves around. There's a little tenderness there. It's not irregularly shaped. It just doesn't have any of the characteristics of a malignancy." But he recommended a surgeon—just to be on the safe side—who turned out to be the same woman who examined me at the clinic.

Did the doctor recognize you? I don't think she quite recognized me—she sees virtually hundreds of women. Besides having her own practice, she works at the clinic once a week—and that's sort of wonderful. So she examined me and felt the lump and then tried to aspirate it. Nothing came out, so that was the first sort of warning. She said, "It feels like nothing, but there are a few nasty kinds of cancer that you can't really tell about unless you take them out. But 95 percent of these lumps are not malignant, so it probably isn't serious." She made an appointment for me to have it removed in the hospital on an outpatient basis. She was going on vacation, and then there would be another two weeks to wait, so I said, "Before you do the biopsy, don't you think I should make an appointment to see you just to make sure the lump is still there?" I was sure I was going to get rid of that lump. She said, "I have no problem with that."

What did you do during those weeks before the biopsy?
I listened to a healing tape, I visualized the lump disappearing again, and I went to the psychic healer again. He is only in town every two weeks out of the month, so the weekend he was in I saw him three times. The biopsy was scheduled for a Thursday. The Tuesday before, I went back to see my doctor, hoping the lump had disappeared. But it was still there.

What was the biopsy like?
The idea of being awake in an operating room was really very frightening. There were quite a lot of folks there, and my doctor was very nice. We chatted and made jokes through the whole thing. She took the whole lump out—it was 1.5 centimeters, small enough for a lumpectomy. She said, "I really can't tell anything," and sent it off to the lab so they could do a frozen section. I got dressed, and five minutes later she came back. I could tell from her face that something was wrong. I said, "Oh, not good." She said, "Not good." Well, I felt I had been hit on the head with a mallet—I was stunned. I had fully expected to be okay. She was as stunned as I was. I said, "What does this mean? What's the next step?" She said, "We have to wait for the pathology report." This was Thursday, and the report wouldn't be ready before Monday or Tuesday, so I would have to wait over the weekend. She said, "Here's what we're going to do. We're going to assume everything is fine. Come in Tuesday and you'll have all the tests necessary to let me go in and cut a wider margin around the area where the lump was, and we'll go in and check the nodes. If the pathology report indicates you have to have a mastectomy, we'll cancel the operating room and you'll get second opinions."

And what were the results from pathology?
I had two kinds of malignancies. One was intraductal, a more localized, less serious cancer. The radiologist said intraductal cells were like a precancerous condition. The second type was an infiltrative duct carcinoma. Studies show that the survival rate with Stage I cancers, which mine was, is the same with mastectomy or lumpectomy, so we decided to go ahead and do what we planned to do. But my doctor did say, "You have to understand that if the margin isn't clean, and we find node involvement, you may have to have another operation." But I still assumed they wouldn't find anything. They were all sure, too.

How was this surgery?

Coming out of the anesthesia was nothing. They gave me some Demerol in the recovery room, which made me very nauseated so I thought I'd rather have the pain, but there really wasn't any pain. The IV was out as soon as I could hold something down, and that was almost immediately. I felt very good in the hospital. There was only a little discomfort from the drain, and I took some Tylenol for it. My surgeon said they didn't find any more tumors and that everything looked good—by eye and by feel—without a report. In fact, I met with the radiologist, and we were beginning to plan when my treatments would begin.

When did you find out the results from this surgery?

I went home from the hospital on a Sunday—I was only in for four days. That was the hardest time, because I didn't know. We were praying that the lymph nodes would be clean. I had everyone sending me energy. The psychic healer had been trying to clear out my lymph nodes and my whole system. The waiting and the not knowing were terrible for me. I was doing Camille and *Swan Lake,* feeling I was going to die. I called all my friends. On Monday the lab report still wasn't in. Then Monday night, there was a phone call on the machine. I recognized my gynecologist's voice, but the message wasn't clear. I figured he must have the report. The next morning about seven o'clock he called me again and said that yes, he did get the pathology report. There wasn't any node involvement, but one of the margins was not clean. I didn't know what that meant. He said, "I don't know what that means, either." I said, "Well, maybe that's not so bad. Maybe they just have to go in and take a little more."

So I called my surgeon and said "What are margins? What does it mean that they're not clean?" She said, "I wish he hadn't told you this. We need to talk about it. It isn't simply that the margins aren't clean. There was a large mass of tissue on one of the margins that was *all* tumor. But it looked and felt like normal tissue." It's what they call an occult tumor because you can't see it or feel it. This was a much larger mass. She said, "We have to recommend a mastectomy because we don't know what else is in the breast. It is very largely involved, and we can't be sure the radiation will get the stray microscopic cells. And we are concerned about recurrence when more of the breast is involved. Recurrence is also more difficult to track with cystic breasts. And if you're thinking of reconstruction, it's harder to reconstruct once you've had the radiation. But mainly we are concerned about saving your life."

What did you do with this information?
I immediately took the slides up to one of the best pathologists at a specialized cancer hospital. He read them, and he was a little more sanguine. But he said even though there was a clean margin around the tumor, "We would recommend a mastectomy in your case." So I had two opinions, both for mastectomy, from a pathologist and a surgeon.

I decided I would go to an oncologist for a third opinion. He was very nice. He talked to me on the phone, and then he met with me. He said, "I don't feel it's life-threatening at this point. You can be treated with radiation. If you decide on radiation, I would also recommend a couple of weeks of chemo. However, you should know that if you take the breast off, there's that much less chance of recurrence." Then he said that most physicians would probably recommend a mastectomy because with the kind of tumor I had they couldn't be certain the cancer was contained. But he said, "As far as I'm concerned you have a choice." That made all the difference to me. He also said, "Before making the decision you have to know two things. One, whether you can live with losing a breast at this point in your life. And two, whether or not you can live with the uncertainty of *not* having a mastectomy."

That made sense to me. I had walked in there with great wide eyes like a ninety-pound ballerina doing the dying swan, resigned to the inevitable. But when I walked out of there I was myself again, just because I had a choice. I then had the courage to start doing more research—calling up other doctors I had heard of to get their opinions. I called one cancer specialist, foremost in his field, and he said with no hesitation, "You'd better get that cancer out of your body. If you were my wife, I would just have you take it off." I told this to the oncologist, and he said, "Don't go to him." And I know why. Because this guy was a big advocate of the Halsted radical mastectomy for a long time, although I think now he's less adamant about it. My oncologist knew he wouldn't offer me an option to mastectomy, and he wanted me to talk with people who would be open to options so I could make a decision I felt comfortable with. I even talked with a macrobiotic counselor. He said, "Take these next two weeks before the mastectomy to follow a macrobiotic diet, and then make the decision." Now that's not such a terrible thing to do, and it was a rational approach. But curiously enough, by that time I had the *will* to have a mastectomy. I felt as if I were driven to have one. I felt there were dues I had to pay in order to insure that the rest of my life would be okay. I know it sounds very convoluted, but seeing the macrobiotic counselor was just going through the motions of getting alternative opinions, because I was bound and determined to have a mastectomy.

What was the diet?

I really disliked the food so much. The macrobiotic breast cancer diet consists of grains—mainly brown rice, with pearl barley and millet twice a week—seaweed and certain vegetables. None of the vegetables I really love, either. No potatoes. No tomatoes. No yams. No eggplant, peppers, avocado. Winter squash, but not summer or acorn squash. A few seeds, like pumpkin seeds. No fruit, except every ten days I could have stewed peaches, apples, and apricots if I wanted. No nuts. No oils, period. No animal products. No eggs. No dairy. No fish or chicken.

So you didn't even want to try the diet for two weeks to see
if it made any difference?

Well, I was kind of on the diet from the time the lump was diagnosed as malignant, but I was eating potatoes and yams because I liked them, and that sort of defeated the purity they emphasized. The counselor said, "You can cure this cancer, but you have to stick to the diet strictly." He also said that if I had the surgery, I shouldn't go off the diet at all because there would be even more of a chance of recurrence. He gave me some stuff about how losing a part of your body makes it even more necessary to balance your body through the food you eat. It sounded like scare tactics. He may have believed it, and maybe I did, too, but I guess the bottom line was that I was unwilling to stay on the diet. Other people told me about some woman who went on a macrobiotic diet and used all the traditional medical methods and died. This just supported my decision to have a mastectomy as scheduled.

Did you consider having reconstruction?

Yes. And I knew I had to decide by the time I had the mastectomy because it would make a difference in the surgical process. So I was faced with having to make some important decisions at the same time—was I going to have a mastectomy, and was I going to have reconstruction? If I was going to have reconstruction, should I have it simultaneously with the mastectomy or later? I visited with four plastic surgeons in the same two-week period I was getting second opinions about a mastectomy. One doctor who shares an office with my surgeon said they could do the reconstruction at the same time as the mastectomy. He said, "You may not have enough skin, so I'll probably have to put in an expander." That's a silicone implant that's placed under the muscle and has a little tube attached that leads outside your body. Every week for three months they expand the implant by adding a little more saline, so the skin and muscle stretches. When it gets to be the right size they do another operation and put in the final implant. He seems to use what a lot of plastic surgeons are using these days. The implant is called a double lumen—one part silicone with an outer part containing saline to give the breast a more natural feeling. But there are problems with saline. One out of every four hundred of these implants leak and your breast suddenly deflates. So everyone has their own methods.

Why did he think you might not have enough skin? Are you very small?

The amount of skin they have to work with is determined by where they have to do the cut. The lump was rather high, so when they took it I lost a lot of skin. If I hadn't had the extensive margin surgery, they could have made the incision around the nipple. Then there would be all that skin to work with, and the implant could have been done with no problems.

Did you like this plastic surgeon?

I liked him, but I didn't care much for the pictures of his work. And I actually saw a woman whose breast he had reconstructed, and it looked awfully lumpy to me.

Did you see anybody whose work you really liked?

Yes. I walked into one doctor's office and said, "I'm thinking of having a mastectomy," and I started to cry—that was the only time I cried. It was strange, but I knew why I cried. He was the first doctor I had seen who looked like a doctor. He was a man in his sixties, with white hair and glasses—he was Central Casting. The other doctors were young, and peers, and they talked to me very directly, whereas he didn't quite know how to talk to me. I would keep asking these questions that he wasn't quite sure how to answer. But when he showed me the pictures of his surgeries, he realized by the way I responded that I was the kind of person he could talk directly and honestly to, and although he wasn't comfortable with it, he did it. He was a nice man, and his work was quite good. And he could do it immediately. He believed in doing breast reconstruction only under the muscle, but I really wasn't sure I wanted it under the muscle even though it seems to be the new, improved method of reconstruction. You see, those in favor of it feel it protects the implant—there's more flesh over the implant—and they feel it's easier to detect a recurrence of cancer if it happens because they don't have to feel underneath the implant. But then I saw another plastic surgeon who had been doing breast reconstruction for ten years—he was one of the first—and he would not do it under the muscle. He does it under the skin and uses only silicone. He'll consider doing it under the muscle only if the woman has had radiation and there is not enough skin. He feels that if you place the implant under the muscle, then scar tissue forms and the muscle can't slide freely over the ribs the way muscle is supposed to. He feels this could lead to the muscle tearing later on from activity.

Is there a difference cosmetically between reconstruction done under the muscle and under the skin?

Well, I must say that the most natural-looking reconstructed breast I saw was under the skin. It was done without an expander. She looked smaller than me—I'm a 34B—but not by much. But because it was the first reconstructed breast I had seen, I said to myself, "I don't want to walk around with *that* breast for the rest of my life." In retrospect, though, that was the best, except for one woman who had a bilateral by the Central Casting doctor. The bilateral is a very different story. If you have a bilateral, they can match the breasts perfectly. This woman had been very tiny, and her breasts were now spectacular. She didn't even want nipples put on because her breasts looked so good without them. She had this honey skin, and the scars matched. She said her breasts were better than they had been since she had her babies, so she was thrilled to pieces. But I knew I was in a different situation. I had to match one to another, and I had discovered too late that I had nice breasts. You know, I never thought about my breasts at all before this, and then all of a sudden I find myself saying, "My God, they'll never be as nice again, and they'll never match." *That* was depressing! The most successful reconstructions are done on women who are smaller than me, who have one breast reconstructed and the other breast augmented.

What did you decide to do about reconstruction?
I decided to wait and make all decisions about reconstruction later.

*Having the mastectomy was your third surgery in a
month. Was the recovery any different?*
This time, when I came out of anesthesia there was a taste of chemicals in my throat, a feeling of not being well, but I was up the same evening and I was eating. The IV was out sooner than the last time because I knew I could get it out sooner. I immediately took some miso soup so I could prove to them that I could keep something down. The operation was Wednesday, but by Thursday night the incision under the bandages was itching. And all of a sudden I felt where my breast was—in fact, part of it is still there, this fatty tissue at the sternum and this little indentation—and I almost fainted. It was my first realization that I had had a mastectomy. I got very nauseated and dizzy. I knew then that my emotions about this were really much greater than I had been showing. I thought, God! You haven't dealt with this. This is really much deeper than you think. I mentioned it to my doctor, and I also mentioned it to my internist, who is male. He talked to me for about forty-five minutes and was very sensitive and understanding and sympathetic. I also mentioned it to an Israeli doctor who had assisted my surgeon. He couldn't deal with it—I could see from his reaction. He said, "Well, it's just temporary. You're going to get reconstruction."

When did you actually see the incision?
On Friday my surgeon asked me if I wanted to see it, and I already had that feeling of "Oh, God," so I said, "Not today. I just can't quite look at it." But later on that day, or maybe it was Saturday, I thought, You have to look at it. And it was okay. I mean, it didn't look so bad. She left me a little cleavage, which is wonderful. It looks very natural.

*How do you feel about the scar now that you've had some
time to get used to it?*
I've been home two weeks, and yesterday I looked at myself and was angry. I really looked and said, "This is a mutilation." I could say "mutilation" from the beginning, but I couldn't acknowledge it as being part of my life. It's ugly! It really looks like someone took a bite out of my arm—it's all sort of chewed away. I'm so angry about that! And I'm also getting angrier when I think about the pathology department at the hospital. Who

knows how good they are? Once they take it off, it's off. They only analyze a piece from each quadrant. You just don't know if that's thorough. I know there's one terrific guy in the department, someone everybody talks about, but he doesn't analyze every case. There's another pathologist who tends to be very sloppy.

When you're under such stress isn't it hard to analyze
every procedure and figure out every step?

It is. But I am angry that there's no way of knowing what's what without taking the breast off, and that's too late. The doctors mean well, but they don't know. There's no way of keeping people healthy in this whole medical establishment that costs millions and billions of dollars. My doctor is thirty-seven years old. She's a good surgeon. She must make close to a million dollars a year. Top doctors make over a million dollars, and they only know how to deal with crises. It makes me furious. An oncologist I spoke with said they're working on finding the antibodies they can tag radioactively which will go immediately to any cancer cells in the body, but that may take ten years. I read about a surgeon in Washington who has been working to build up the individual's immune system and has been having a great deal of success. I'm going to see him and find out if he will work on someone who is not actively diagnosed as having cancer. Because I don't think my immune system is up to par yet.

But how are you feeling now?

I think I'm feeling better because my diet has changed. I felt best when I was on the really pure macrobiotic plan, eating steamed vegetables and rice and miso soup every night. I think the diet not only makes a difference in one's general health, but I also believe it would cure cancer. I just . . .

Can't do it?

I won't do it. Won't. I'm having trouble now. I have cookies occasionally. I want ice cream and I had some two weeks ago and I feel guilty when I do that. I tell myself that I cheat very little, but the strict macrobiotic menu is very restricting and I feel very deprived.

Does living with someone make following the diet more
difficult?

Yes. Not the diet particularly, but I really was worried about him and how he was going to deal with what was happening to me even though we've lived together a long time. I've said to people recently, "You know, if a friend of mine were going through this, I would have fallen apart." So I know how hard it's going to be. But on the surface he seems to be able to handle it very well. He was there. He was very supportive. He let me make all the decisions. Sometimes I wished he had been more involved. I really wanted him to discuss the issues with me. I wished he had more advice to give me, that it had been more of a joint process. On the other hand, by doing it by myself, I got the sense of my own strength.

What was his reaction to seeing the incision for the first time?

I think he was a little shocked, but he didn't mind. And he has been very loving. As a matter of fact, the entire experience from the diagnosis of cancer through the mastectomy has been very positive. It was quite a wonderful experience, if you can think of anything being wonderful under such terrible circumstances. I mean, everyone was generous and supportive, from the doctors who didn't know me who squeezed me in, to the nurse who took care of me the day of the mastectomy. The people on the floor, the doctors, my friends—such an outpouring of support. It was wonderful!

Do you think that your reaction to the cancer, the way you handled it, was partially responsible for the support you received?

I think yes. And people have said that. One friend called me up and said, "I've been terrified of getting breast cancer all my life. My mother had it. And the way you've handled it makes me not so afraid." It was very touching. I needed to talk about it openly, otherwise I couldn't deal with it. I think it helped people around me. They could ask questions. They could be as candid as they wanted. What really helped me was the humor. One friend said, "See, God found a way to put you on a diet." I told another friend I had lost fourteen pounds. She said, "That was a heavy breast." And even my mother. I said, "I'm afraid of going under anesthesia." Mother said, "Well, you won't feel anything." My surgeon was the only one who didn't think any of it was funny.

Do you need radiation or chemo?

They say they've gotten rid of the cancer, and there's no recommendation for any further treatment. My surgeon said she's spoken to several people and no one feels I need anything at this moment.

*When you feel up to it, will you begin considering
reconstruction?*

Yes. Whether I want it. Who to do it. And how to do it. Whether
under the muscle or under the skin. And the real consideration is
what to do about the rest of my body. The fear of cancer is an
ongoing concern. I mean, is there some condition in my body that
allowed this cancer to happen? I know that condition has not
gone away. So, I keep coming back to diet. I knew I couldn't avoid
the surgery by going on the diet because I wasn't strong enough
to do it perfectly as is required. I want to find a diet I can live
with, but I feel so deprived if I can't have a tasty meal. I just
haven't solved the issue.

MASTECTOMY AND RECONSTRUCTION

"MY MOTHER WAS THE SECOND OF SEVEN SISTERS, AND AFTER SHE DEVELOPED BREAST CANCER, EVERY SINGLE SISTER DIED OF THE DISEASE."

A forty-two-year-old physician practicing in California. She had breast reconstruction following a prophylactic double mastectomy when she was twenty-eight. She is married.

Why did you decide to have such radical surgery when you were so young, especially with no indication of cancer?

It was my strong family history of breast cancer. My mother had fibrocystic breast lumps while in her twenties—this was twenty-five to thirty years ago—which she had biopsied five different times, and each time the lumps were diagnosed as benign. Then she discovered a sixth lump at age thirty, and it was an aggressive malignancy. The nodes were high-percentage positive, and she had a bilateral mastectomy. She went through cobalt radiation therapy. She prayed and prayed that she would live at least five more years to teach her kids—we were age four, five, six, and seven—how to take care of ourselves. She did live five years, and then there was a recurrence. My mother lived just two more years. We were very young, but she trained us to take good care of ourselves. We could all cook, clean, and do what we needed to do by the time she died. My mother was the second oldest of seven sisters, and subsequently every single sister died of breast cancer with the exception of one who had ovarian cancer as well as breast cancer, and I think she died of metastic ovarian cancer. But that's not all. *Their* mother, our grandmother, as well as her only sister, also died of breast cancer.

Now, many of these women died when they were older, but

179

since my mother was so young when she developed her cancer, the prognosis was not good. With that as a family history—chiefs of oncology departments at Harvard and UCLA have said it's the worst history they've ever heard of—I was more inclined to consider prophylactic mastectomy than other women. Also, by age twenty-eight I had been in medicine for seven years. I'd gone to medical school and finished my first-year residency in pediatrics, but I always made it a point to follow the literature on breast cancer. I talked to experts, the heads of oncology services at the major universities in the country, about my situation. Perhaps if I'd been living a different kind of a life, outside the university medical environment, I wouldn't have chosen to have the surgery. But I couldn't deny the medical facts—that with my mother's history, even if I had regular mammograms and biopsies, there was a very good chance I could develop breast cancer and would have to have a mastectomy anyway.

Did you have a history of breast lumps like your mother?
I had slightly lumpy breasts and always had regular exams— yearly mammograms were not recommended then, particularly, because I was only in my twenties—but I never had suspicious lumps or really significant dysplasia.

But you had some dysplasia?
I had a biopsy on a lump not long before the surgery, and the diagnosis was "mild dysplasia." But you couldn't hang a diagnosis of cancer on that. No, my surgery was a prophylactic subcutaneous mastectomy.

Was it difficult for you to find the right surgeon?
In 1974, the year I had my surgery, a new chief of plastic surgery came to UCLA where I was doing my residency, and his forte was subcutaneous mastectomies and reconstructions. He had successfully done two hundred or three hundred at a time when very few had been done. So I thought, If I'm going to do it, I might as well go to someone who is one of maybe three people in the world who has done that many. Also, I had insurance at UCLA, and because I was affiliated with the hospital I could schedule my work and life around it.

What was your emotional state as you faced surgery?
I was in an emotionally stable time. I don't think I suppressed my emotions because I really did some work on my feelings with some friends. They said, "You really ought to seek counseling with someone before you do it—not about the medical aspects,

but about how you're going to feel as a woman." I never did that because I had such a cadre of close women friends who helped me work it through.

How did your family feel about your having the surgery?
They were surprised. I didn't tell them until right before surgery because I didn't want anyone to worry, and I wanted to make the decision myself without a lot of family input. But they felt fine about it. They have the same family history, and they understood. We are all real loving and real close even though they live pretty far away.

Was your surgeon sympathetic to your situation?
Surgeons are seldom noted for talking you out of any surgery. Their classic position is: Cutting is healing. But I have to give him credit because he really did go through all the pros and cons and discussed the losses I might suffer mentally and physically. He was very explicit about the potential risks involved in the reconstruction—loss of blood supply to the area, scarring, my body rejecting implants. He was very good about showing me pictures and discussing all aspects of them. I can't say he was deeply insightful about emotional issues—not like the counselors you meet today in some of the many programs offered to women with breast cancer. But I felt he was very good and professional, and I give him credit for saying to me, "It's not an urgent problem, and maybe you'd rather marry and nurse a few kids first." He even said, "We could plan to do this three years from now, if you like." I was going with someone at the time, but I thought, If I'm going to do this, it seems like I should do it now. And it's worked out, because I got married five years ago and we still don't have any kids. I'm glad I didn't wait and worry about the cancer all those years.

Because you are a doctor, did the surgeon discuss the actual surgery with you?
Yes. I knew a lot about the procedure, though no one can really tell you about pain levels or how you might respond to anesthesia. He was very explicit about saying, "There's a lot of blood loss in this. You're probably going to need transfusions. Do you want to consider autologous transfusions?" So I did. That was fourteen years ago, but I'm very glad I did it.

What procedure did the surgeon recommend?
He recommended removing as much of the subcutaneous breast tissue as he could but leaving the nipples and skin intact. He

said, "We're basically shelling out the breast from the inside. Once the drainage is done, you'll be left with a thin layer of skin over your ribs with the nipples still there. Then you'll have three months to heal after which we'll insert an implant. It will be covered over with your own skin and nipples." So I agreed.

The doctor also said, "Remember this doesn't mean you can rule out having breast cancer because you can never totally get all the tissue out." It's a real double-edged sword: you're in there trying to shell out as much tissue as you can close to the skin, but not so much that you're going to devitalize the skin because that would interfere with a nice result in the reconstruction.

Was there anything particular that you remember about the evening before surgery?

The thing I really didn't appreciate was lying on a bed and having these five male doctors standing at the foot of the bed, then surrounding me. I felt I was on display, and I understood something I've suspected for a long time—that being a woman on the receiving end of treatment in a man's realm of medicine isn't fun. It taught me a lot. I felt good about the surgeon, but I really didn't like two of the residents—very L.A., money-aimed plastic surgeon types—and I did not like having them as part of my care. I also didn't like being in the recumbent position with no control. It was a weird feeling.

How did you react to the anesthesia?

I didn't *love* it, but I'd been there when it was being administered to other people so many times that it wasn't frightening for me. The anesthesiologist was a very sweet man, and I remember him gently telling me how I would be falling off to sleep now. He really made it a fine experience for me.

Was your breast tissue biopsied?

Oh, yes. That's always done—we have to. My results read out as "mild dysplasia of the breast tissue."

Did you have any node excision?

No.

Did you need drains?

Yes, because the surgery was all through the breast area. I had four drains, two on each side. Two were pulled out after a few days. I think it was four or five days before the other two came out. I have a clear memory of the drains being pulled out. The nurse said, "Okay, this is going to hurt!" And it did.

Were you in any pain after the surgery?

It hurt afterward, and I was feeling a little nauseated.

Were the bandages uncomfortable?

It was like swaddling clothes. My torso was wrapped down to my waist, and they made me do lots of breathing exercises. I was a good patient. I didn't have any postoperative problems.

Was your doctor pleased with the results of the surgery?

He said it had gone fine and that he knew the final result would be good. But he was amazed at how much I bled. He couldn't understand it. He asked me what I thought was a curious question: "Are you having your period now?" And I said, "Yes, I am." Then he said something very interesting: "I've operated on two other women who bled more than usual, and they, too, were menstruating. I've never researched it or read anything about it, but having recently seen the two was enough to make me ask you the question." He had anticipated that I wouldn't need more than two units of blood—that's why I put two units of blood aside. In fact, he said, I probably should have had three or four units. But because I was young and healthy, they felt I could build my blood back up with just two units. He said, "You're going to feel weak because your post-op hematocrit is 27 to 28." A normal hematocrit is 37 to 45. And I was tired for a while and significantly anemic for a couple of months, but then I was fine.

Were you prepared to see the incision when the bandages came off?

When he was explaining the procedure to me, I, being very smart, medical, and pragmatic, said, "It's not my idea of fun, but of course I can handle it." But what I saw was shocking! It was really something to see! I looked like I was just out of Auschwitz —my skin was real thin and draped over my ribs, the tissue having been removed, with these little nipples hanging there. It was actually very funny looking but different from what I was mentally prepared to see. He didn't show me what I would look like for those three months of healing. After the pain was gone and I got used to looking at myself, it was humorous. But I really had to deal with my own feminine image. That was harder for me than dealing with the fact that I no longer had the ability to nurse a baby. That loss never felt heavy to me because I had been a pediatrician and knew that kids could do fine without nursing. But I was very conscious of how I looked. I wanted to go to the gym and work out and be able to change my clothes in the locker room without somebody . . . it's real heavy to be noticed.

Did you heal well?

Yes. I never had keloids. I was young, and the younger you are, the better it heals.

Did you wear a prosthesis?

No. I had this thick Ace wrap around me—that was my under-wear. It was a time when there were all these loose blouses, and I always wore clothes like that, anyway. So it worked out fine.

Did you discuss the reconstruction with your surgeon before the surgery?

Yes, in several private sessions. Whether you know it or not, UCLA is breast-augmentation city. So the surgeon asked, "Do you want to be larger or smaller? I always ask people." I said, "I'll be happy if I can be about like I was. I don't think I want to be Dolly Parton." He said, "Well, good, because actually it's ideal that you're rather small-breasted. Putting in a small implant is a lot easier for me, and I think it will be easier for you afterward."

But the guy I was seeing at the time—he was an internist—said, "Well, you *could* go a little bigger." He was generally won-derful and supportive about everything else. I mean, I wasn't asking him for an opinion, just telling him what the surgeon had said. I knew he was a little immature, but I remember being furious at him and thinking, You shmuck! This is not why I'm doing this. I think it was at this point that I decided this wasn't really the guy for me. At that time my priorities weren't about the size of my breasts. I was just hoping I wasn't going to have an indented nipple or something worse. I was just hoping to look fairly normal. I wasn't thinking about whether I was going to look better in a strapless gown.

And when it was time to have the reconstruction, were you ready?

I was actually looking forward to the second surgery when the time came around. But when I was half under the anesthesia, the chief resident, a guy I didn't like very much, said something like "Oh, go ahead, give her a thrill. Boost it up one size anyway. She'll like it." I remember thinking, You bastard! Dealing with so many starlets, he just assumed I'd want larger breasts. But other than that, the surgery went well. The first surgery had been much more extensive, and harder, with all that blood loss and pain. The reconstruction was an easier surgery. I still had to recover from general anesthesia, and of course, you're kind of debilitated and wrapped up again, and you have to have the surgical drains in again and all that stuff. But I really did fine. You can still see the scars. They're about three inches, and they come up over the sides of my breasts. But I hardly notice them now, and if I'm changing in the gym most people never notice, or if they do they're too polite to say anything to me. I don't think it looks as good as the real thing, but it looks fine enough so I can wear normal clothes. I took less that three weeks off before going back to work. And when I did go back, of course, I wasn't lifting babies for a while—I would ask the moms to do that.

Was there any feeling in your breasts after reconstruction?

The sensation is irregular. Some people get full sensation back after this surgery, but mine was partial. I could feel skin everywhere, but erogenous sensation is erratic—I feel it in some areas but not in others. So I just try to make the most of what I do feel! You can really learn to adapt, I've discovered.

Do you continue to have regular mammograms and checkups?

I have to be honest. I'm not very good about that. I left the L.A. area. I did go back for my follow-up after the reconstruction, but since then I've had zero trouble with it. So, although I have Pap smears and I've had three or four mammograms since that time, I don't go regularly. I'm due for a mammogram, and I'm dragging my feet, like avoiding the dentist. But I'll get to it. I've actually never written or called the surgeon to see what kind of follow-up he recommends. Fortunately, I've never had any problems.

Are you concerned about breast cancer?

Actually, I am not at all concerned. I don't think about it and I don't feel I'm repressing it. I think about it a lot less than I would have if I hadn't had surgery.

"THE RECONSTRUCTION WAS SO SIMPLE I COULD HAVE KICKED MYSELF FOR WAITING SO LONG. EVER SINCE, I'VE PRACTICALLY GONE AROUND BARING MY BREASTS TO PROSELYTIZE."

A wife, mother, grandmother who had a double mastectomy when she was fifty-four, eight years before this interview, followed by reconstruction two years later.

How did this begin for you?

I'd dealt for many, many years with lumps—a fibrocystic condition—and every time I would find a cyst, I would call the doctor, make an appointment, and they would aspirate. What threw me for a loop was realizing how inadequate I was in self-exam. Because I'd go in for one so-called lump and come out with thirteen, fifteen aspirations. I'd come home with a bunch of little Band-Aids all over me.

Was the aspiration painful?

No, not at all. I dreaded the thought of the needle going in, but I'd close my eyes. This particular August day, I remember feeling the needle coming out a little bit differently. And I said to him, "This is it." I made an appointment to have a mammogram immediately. I liked this surgeon enormously, but I wanted to be at the hospital where my physician was affiliated. My physician suggested the general surgeon who had taken out my husband's gall bladder. I thought one should have a specialist, but my physician convinced me. He told me a simple standard doctors use: "Who would you choose if it was your own wife or mother?"—not your mother-in-law, I noticed—and this surgeon had, in fact, done breast surgery for my physician's mother.

So I went to see this surgeon, and we talked about doing a biopsy. He called immediately for a hospital bed. The hospital couldn't accommodate me for a week. He tried to pull strings, but it was impossible. We then settled on doing the biopsy in his office.

I went alone. I wanted to handle this all by myself. And when I walked into the surgeon's office, there was my daughter-in-law, who is a resident at the hospital. I was absolutely furious. And the next thing I knew, in walked my husband. He was going to respect my wishes, but my son called him and said, "I can't believe that you're not going with Mother." As it turned out, I was totally off-track to try to face this thing by myself. I thought I was in control, but I really couldn't hear everything, and I didn't get all the nuances of what was involved. I had never faced breast cancer with a friend—I was sort of the first of my crowd.

In the discussion, the surgeon was so sure that it was malignant that he was convinced it was foolish to put me through this routine of biopsy and then, a week later, mastectomy. We decided

I would just wait the week out and have a good time in the meantime.

Did you discuss the possibility of a lumpectomy?

No. First of all, I don't think that they were doing lumpectomies in New York eight years ago. I did a lot of consulting with other doctors, friends of ours, reading—it was a week of inquiry. We found out that in other cities, they were doing lumpectomies—at Harvard and in New Haven. We asked lots of questions, but the fact of the matter is that the tumor was dead center—it was right behind the nipple. Strangely enough—and every doctor I went to see thought this was just totally fascinating—I had been radiated at that particular spot after the birth of my second child twenty-odd years ago. I'd had an infection, and they treated it with radiation. The memory of being left under that machine and feeling totally trapped in this room—I just dreaded the thought of radiation. I don't think I would have considered a lumpectomy even if I had been a candidate for it.

Is there breast cancer in your family?

No. There is colon cancer—my father died of it.

How did you spend that week?

I had a great week. Totally unreal, spaced-out. We went to a lot of movies. I got my husband to go out to Jones Beach. I had one fight with him. We had agreed that we would tell each other everything, we were going to share everything. And one day he said something in the car, and I knew . . . I said, "Have you spoken to the surgeon?" He said no, no, but finally he said, "Well, to tell you the truth, I have. I've been going through the steps of the operation as it's been explained to us, and I am very worried about what they do with the frozen section because there are all these mistakes in hospitals. How do you know if they did the frozen section on your tissue?" So I called the surgeon and told him that I was really very worried, that you hear about people having the wrong leg amputated, and he said, "You have every right to be concerned, but the fact of the matter is I have nothing to do after I've done the first incision, so I personally take the tissue down to the pathology lab and stay with it."

And I had the operation. I'd given them permission to do the mastectomy if the frozen section was malignant, and that's what they did.

How did your recovery go?

This operation really is nothing, except for the drainage. Psychologically, it's something else again, but physically, it's just not that huge.

After the surgery, I was told that the oncologist was going to see me. I was told I had six malignant nodes. I was told, when he came, that they were doing this test to see whether I was positive or negative for estrogen receptors, and the oncologist's advice was that I should start taking tamoxifen immediately, even before the results were in, because the side effects were negligible. I've since discussed this with many people—other doctors don't seem to do that—but at any rate, I started on it. And it did turn out to be estrogen-receptor positive—the prescription turned out to be correct. That was an educated guess on his part.

Did you also discuss chemotherapy?

Yes. By that time we knew that my hospital was using a five-drug therapy and another hospital was using a three-drug therapy. It was a problem. It was very confusing to know that two good hospitals were at odds with each other. I listened to what all the doctors here had to say, and in the end, we went to see a French chemotherapist I'd met a year before. I'd read his book, too, and resolved that if I ever got cancer, I'd want him to treat me. His mode of therapy was much more aggressive than the American oncologists, and he was terribly critical of the medical profession in New York.

My husband and I talked about my taking a flat in Paris, and we could fly back and forth. Then my husband looked at me and said, "Listen, he's very convincing, but I can't handle it—I'm not intelligent enough to evaluate what he's saying." We decided to wait and thrash it out with our doctors in New York.

But of course it has nothing to do with intelligence: you
were dealing with controversial material.

Yes, and when I discussed the French doctor with my doctors here, we decided his treatment was much too aggressive. I learned a lot about the immunological system—it's a very delicate balance between fighting the cancer and destroying your resistance completely.

So you decided to go with the American oncologist. Which
drug protocol were you on—the three or the five?

The three. I kept notes. [She opens a small calendar.] I had the stitches removed, went to Nantucket, went swimming. Two days after returning home—two weeks after the surgery—I had my first treatment: 500 milligrams of 5-Fluorouracil daily; 50 milligrams Cytoxan every day for fourteen days; tamoxifen, 110 milligrams, twice daily.

Everything seems to have gone along very well. The second month was when I went to Paris to consult with the French oncologist. Gradual hair loss recorded toward the end of that month. Tired. Watering in both eyes for about one week. November, the third month, was just fine, until I got the flu and was totally zonked. Loss of hair continues. Practically all underarm numbness [from the node excision] has disappeared. By the end of the month, I seem to have a sinus infection. Sinus X-ray, tetracycline, liver scan. A cyst removed in office.

A breast cyst?

Yes, in the beginning of December, and another chemotherapy treatment. I was going once a week for chemotherapy. Then a week in Puerto Rico after a treatment. My husband wouldn't go to a sales meeting and leave me here, so I said, Okay I'll come. I was sick for a day or two, and then I recovered and had a great time. Halfway through December I took Compazine, with good results. Right eye tearing and cruddy. I had a lot of eye problems —it must have been some low-grade infection. Headache. Not as tired as previously. Another sinus infection. Tetracycline for ten days. I went to an ear, nose, and throat doctor—I was kind of doing badly in December. January: treatments on the second and ninth. Compazine for two days. Felt pretty good.

Did you take the Compazine before or after treatment?

Before. I also remember someone slipping me a joint at some point. I think it helped. [She continues reading from the calendar.] April. Felt terrible at the end of week. I had a very low blood count. Treatment on the sixth. Cytoxan dosage cut in half. Felt better on night of seventh. Another cyst on the left breast. On April 28, I had a mammogram. On April 29, I scheduled surgery for May 17.

That was when I decided to have the prophylactic mastectomy. Because I had two cysts in the same breast. They were both benign, but it was psychologically very upsetting, not only to myself, but to the doctors, thinking of my getting these cysts while I was under chemo.

I continued with the treatments but stopped the Cytoxan because I felt so awful. I don't remember exactly how I felt—probably nauseated and dragged out. If I didn't have these notes, I wouldn't admit to feeling that awful. Checked into the hospital May 16. Surgery 1 P.M. on May 17. Went home on May 19. On May 26 I had a treatment and the staples removed. May 28, I played tennis—I can't believe that! In June I had a treatment . . . and I have nothing after that. I may not have recorded the last treatment or two.

Tell us about the decision to have the second mastectomy.
Well, if you want to hear a little humor . . . I remember the surgeon saying to me, "Would you consider having a second mastectomy, rather than putting yourself through this all the time?" Because the anxiety level was tremendous. I found one cyst right before my son's wedding but didn't tell anyone until after.

I went home and must have discussed it with my husband. He said, "What's so good about one breast, anyway?" And that sort of amused me. Because actually, it was a problem with the prosthesis, taking it out, putting it in, changing it. And all of a sudden I thought, Oh, my goodness, I could be flat-chested—which I have sort of always wanted. I finally decided, Why not do it and get rid of the anxiety? And I think there is a certain amount of anxiety when you have one mastectomy that you might have to have a second, particularly, I think, if you have a history of cysts.

Did you discuss reconstruction at this point?
No. I knew I could have reconstruction because I had the flaps—there was a lot of talk about the flaps. But at that point, I was looking at myself and saying, "I'm fifty-four years old, I'm married, I have three children . . . " I went through the whole list. And I said, "What do I need elective surgery for?" Of course, if I had been younger, I might have considered it then.

One day, several years later, sort of out of the blue, I started to think, You know, I am really being very unintelligent. I have ruled out reconstruction, and I know very little about it. So I started to make a few inquiries.

Were you bothered by the prosthesis?
No, not particularly. I know exactly what it was that prompted me. My first grandchild was getting a little bit older, and I remember thinking that if she was around, I'd sort of have to quickly cross my arms over my breasts if she came into the room, and what if she wanted to snuggle in the middle of the night when she had a sleepover here?

How did you choose a surgeon?
I did my usual asking a lot of questions. My doctor recommended

one, saying he was kind of kooky and not to be put off by it. I went to see him, thinking I was going to research it even further, but then he examined me, and before he could ask me what I wanted to do, I said, "When can we schedule it?" He showed me pictures. He described the operation, which was so simple that I couldn't believe it. I could have kicked myself for taking so long to reach that decision. And that's why ever since I've had it, I've practically gone around baring my breasts to proselytize. I met Nancy Reagan last night, and I really had to hold myself back because I had this urge to say, "I hope you've considered reconstruction." I decided it was not the proper time to do it, but I really think every woman should consider it. And every person that I've spoken to about it has gone and done it.

What did the plastic surgeon tell you?

He told me that it was really a simple thing if you do two because you don't have to match one, that it could even be done on an outpatient basis if I went to one of the hospitals he's affiliated with—and that's what I should have done. There was no reason to spend that stupid night in the hospital presurgery. It was easy —done under local, and we were having a very zippy, funny conversation throughout the whole thing. He is an eccentric— charming. I was told that every two years he learns a different language so he can travel to another far-off spot.

What kind of an implant did he use?

Saline. I started to panic, thinking, What would I do if I were in China and the implant leaked? He said, "You'll just take it out and refill it." I figured I'd just take a little cotton or a sock and stuff it in.

I had the surgery, came home, and went to the movies. I was a little uncomfortable, but my theory is you have to distract yourself. I had to go back a few weeks later. One implant was a little higher than the other. The way I describe it, it was like going to the dressmaker to have a little alteration. I went down there, they gave me a little local anesthetic, and that was that. I think I had another readjustment since, but the way this particular doctor handled it, he made light of it. You know, "You win some, you lose some." I know someone else who went to him who was very upset and had good reason to be upset, because she was very small to begin with and said she'd like to be very small, and then he made her a little bit too big. But he fixed it up, and she couldn't be happier now.

Did you have the nipple reconstruction?
No. He described the operation to me. You're supposed to be un-comfortable with this one, so I decided I didn't care. I suspect that if I'd had a single reconstruction, I'd have done the nipple. Somehow you think of breasts in pairs. I was very self-conscious at first. I discussed it with friends: "Tell me if you think this T-shirt is a little too tight or it looks odd because I don't have nipples." But for me, I don't really think it matters. My attitude since having it done is that it's just fantastic. You're reminding me of how I first described it: "Look, Ma, no hands!" It's the most convenient thing. No prosthesis, no bra. I wear undershirts or teddies, which almost make me feel like a young girl.

A lot of women say they feel tightness or pulling around
the implant. Was that true for you?
I think there was a little in the very beginning, but it let up. I certainly don't feel it now—I feel nothing. Now, the one thing I have to admit to you is that I do not look in the mirror a lot. I don't think I ever really did, but I find that if I'm in a motel room, where there tend to be lots of mirrors, I am not really too happy. I mean, why confront it—it is a distortion. I never think about it in clothes. But if I'm naked . . .

Have you had any problem with leaks?
Never, and I'm delighted that I have the saline every time I read there is a problem with silicone. We did discuss the tummy tuck* procedure at length—it was really kind of a funny, wonderful thing—but he felt why have that kind of complicated surgery when you can have it done in such a simple way?

What's striking is that you haven't talked at all about fear.
At the time, I wouldn't let my thoughts focus on fear. Looking back, I see that I had this new grandchild, and she was tremen-dous. I thought, Oh, my God, I've just got to get through this! She was the goal for me. I mean, this was the most delicious, delight-ful little relationship. And I couldn't let on to the fear.

A couple of weeks ago, she and I were having a little conver-sation. She's going to be nine soon. She was saying that she met a few kids who were sick, who had cancer, and it's such a terrible thing. And I thought, When am I going to tell her? Is she going to feel that we deceived her? I decided that it's not for me to tell her,

---

* The tummy tuck creates a "breast mound" by transplanting tissue from the abdomen. See interview with David Hidalgo, M.D., p. 251.

but my instinct was to say, "It really isn't that awful. I had it, and I'm doing fine." It was tempting to tell her because we're all so fearful, and here you see a little girl starting to be fearful. She should know the success stories. I can prepare her for the next time the subject comes up: "But my grandmother had cancer and she's fine!"

But to get back to the fear . . . my husband was just a basket case, and my boys, too, and because of that, I sort of had to carry all of them.

Did "carrying them" help you get through it, or did you resent it?

I thought it was kind of tender that they were so concerned. You know, I had lunch with a friend I hadn't seen since grade school, and we asked each other what were the best and worst things that had happened to us since then. I said that my son's divorce was the worst thing. Sometime later I was discussing this with my son, and he said, "Mom, what about your operation?" I said, "No, that I could handle. I could do something about it. Your divorce I couldn't do anything about. With the operation, I felt that I was doing all that I could do. I was being constructive about it."

"YOU KNOW WHAT I THINK? SOMETIMES YOU HAVE TO TELL YOUR DOCTOR WHAT TO DO."

A woman who became very active in breast cancer research when her sister died from the disease. She herself had a mastectomy when she was thirty-eight years old, and reconstruction surgery a year and a half later. She is an exceptionally well-informed patient.

How did you discover you had breast cancer?
I had three benign tumors, right in a row, one more frightening than the other because no one knew what they were. Then I didn't have any problem for a couple of years until four years after my sister died. In 1984 I discovered a lump one night in bed —I was just brushing my hand over the sheet and I ran over this hard lump and jumped up. Fortunately I was married at the time —we had just gotten married. The next morning I went immedi-

ately to my doctor in the city—I was part of a study there because of my sister's death. And I was frightened.

Did this lump feel different from the three that you'd had biopsied?

Yes, it was harder. But my surgeon said that he didn't feel it was anything more than another benign problem, and he didn't want to biopsy me again because I had already had three biopsies on this side, and if you have too many, the scar tissue is so dense that they can't read it. He said, "Let's wait a few weeks. We'll see if there is any change, and if there is, then we'll do something."

In the meantime, I happened to attend a breast cancer symposium. One of the exhibits was Mammacare—they have these breast forms with lumps in them so you can learn to self-exam. I was standing there, and I just sort of felt one, and I thought, It sure feels like what I have.

A couple of weeks passed, and I kept thinking there was some kind of change, that it was getting a little larger. I went to see a friend of mine who's a surgeon, and we did a transillumination procedure on it, which they don't use anymore, and we did an ultrasound, and a clear little lump showed up, about a centimeter, with very concise borders. It looked very much like a little benign tumor—on many, many malignant tumors, the borders are not as clear. This surgeon friend of mine said, "I don't know what it is, but if I were you, I'd get that thing out of there."

I suppose this is an example of being assertive about your health care: I went back to my doctor a couple of days later, and I said, "Look, I want this thing out of here. I don't care if it causes scar tissue, I want it out." So he took it out, under a local. I was, of course, awake when he was doing it, and I kept talking to him and saying, "What does it look like?" He said, "Well, it looks benign, but I . . . " He didn't give anything away in his voice, but I had to wait an awfully long time in the recovery room, and I started getting suspicious after about ten minutes. They do a frozen section, and generally they can tell right away if it's just a benign dysplasia.

When he came back, I was kind of joking and said, "Well, is it bad? Is that why you were gone so long?" And there was this long pause, and he said, "Yeah, it *is* bad." Then it was . . . your whole life flashes in front of you. My husband wasn't with me, and my mother wasn't with me. We didn't expect this to be bad news. I had a friend with me. I think it's helpful to be with people you really love and feel very comfortable with. Not that I didn't feel comfortable with my friend, but when you have to strip away everything, you want to be either with yourself or with people who love you unconditionally. I had just watched my sister die from this a few years before, and it was frightening.

How did you decide what to do next?

He said to me, "You have several choices. You can have a double mastectomy and get rid of the whole thing. You can have a modified radical, or you can have a lumpectomy." And of course, the patient always has the opportunity to say, "Do nothing." There are a lot of people who say, "Do nothing. Just take the lump out." Which is a very dangerous kind of attitude, but some people survive that way. We all have choices.

But my decision was driven largely by what had happened to my sister and also by what I had studied about the disease. Because, don't forget, I'd had two and a half years of baptism by fire preceding my sister's death, and I had really gone into the science of it. So I already knew a whole lot. And I knew I wasn't going to take any chances. I could have had a lumpectomy, but I just wasn't into having six weeks of radiation at the time. And I really wanted to get rid of it. So I decided to have a modified radical mastectomy and to wait and make sure that I didn't have any recurrence before I had reconstruction.

I had the surgery the next morning, and then I was one of those patients who fell in the category of needing additional therapy. So I chose to have four courses of really aggressive chemotherapy. That's less than they used to do. Today, there are studies that indicate that as little as one course is a very effective dose.

The rest of it was getting fitted for a wig, spending a year without any hair, and going through the physical travails of chemotherapy—but I've been through worse things than that.

What's worse?

Oh, a divorce. Or getting a spinal anesthetic for some minor knee surgery and ending up with one of those spinal headaches—that's the worst thing I've ever had in my life. Five days of agony. At least with chemotherapy you feel sick for only maybe a day or two, like a mild flu. There's a period of six or eight hours of extreme nausea, but I just had them drug me so heavily that I'd fall asleep.

Were you in a lot of pain after the surgery?

No. The only pain I've had is, my chest has been tight, the muscle. And now, with reconstruction, you feel like there's a vise on your chest all the time—the implant's under the chest wall, the chest muscle. But it's nothing you can't cope with. It's not excruciating pain. Having grown up as a tomboy, I have a fairly high pain threshold, so . . . I don't know, but it seems to me there are a lot worse things.

I'll tell you, I feel sorry for women who are delicate creatures, because it is much harder on them. Much. You have to be a little bit tough, I'm very involved in sports, and one thing sports does for you is, you develop a certain strength and you realize there are lots of things you can overcome. In fact, maybe every woman who has breast surgery ought to go on an Outward Bound program. Maybe she'd feel better about the whole thing. I mean, there are things that are a lot worse than this! They ought to go out in the streets and look at these people lying down without anything to eat. That's a hell of a lot worse than losing a breast or having surgery. I don't have any truck with whiners at all!

How soon after surgery did you start chemo?

Right away. In fact, today they're doing studies where you start chemo before the surgery, to see if the tumor can be shrunk.

And when did you decide to have the reconstructive surgery?

About a year and a half later. I just wanted it to be easier to buy clothes and *feel* better about how I looked. I hated looking at myself. I looked horrible, I thought. I have an eye for symmetry. I like beauty. I like fashion. I like looking good, feeling good about myself. I'm thrilled I had it done.

I wanted the most minimal thing. I had the choice of doing that flap deal, where they swing the skin and muscle around from the back, but I think that's overdoing a good thing—I agree that you get a more pendulous look and all that, but I know women who had painful scars on their back. I didn't care about being a busty brunette. I just wanted to look good, to fill a bra, look evenly matched, and go on. None of this is perfect! We're not talking here about ending up with something you're born with! I had enough tissue left to do the simple implant—some people don't, and they have to use the expander. And then six months later, I had the nipple reconstruction, which is easy. They take the skin from the top or inside of your thigh. And then he had to replace the original prosthesis. They do that sometimes because it gives you a better shape. I haven't had any problems, knock wood. I know that there are many botched cases, but the advice is to go to a good comprehensive cancer center, study your plastic surgeons, and don't do it unless you've seen their work. You ask them not only for pictures, but you say, "I want to see a couple of patients you've done." And if they won't show them to you, then don't use them. You wouldn't buy a car without driving it.

After a positive biopsy, most women usually spend two weeks racing around trying to figure out what to do. You didn't feel the need to do that.

Most women have to race around because they haven't been educated about the disease. So they have to get several opinions. I knew enough then to make up my mind. I also had people I trusted around me. They have a team approach at my hospital—most good cancer centers have a program where you have people working in tandem. The reason a woman has to race around a lot of times is because she's got to go somewhere for the surgeon, somewhere to see her pathology, somewhere else to see an oncologist. And it's true: she is ragged by the end of two weeks.

Don't forget, I was unusual. My sister had died of this three years before. I did not want to have chemotherapy. I saw what it did to her and how horrible it was—because it was unsuccessful in her case. But I also saw what happened when you wait too long, and how aggressive cancer can be from the very earliest stages. I wasn't about to fool around with anybody telling me it was a minor problem. My advice is at the complete opposite end of the spectrum from Rose Kushner and any of those people who say, "Minimal, keep it minimal." Cancer is not a minimal disease. When he told me I should have chemotherapy, I didn't jump up and down with joy, but I thought it was right. We still are in a very crude stage with chemo. We're not sure exactly which drugs work on which type of disease—it's always a roll of the dice. And a few scientists say chemotherapy can do more harm than good because you can develop leukemia from it later on in life. My feeling about that is, if I develop leukemia at sixty-five, I'll worry about it then, but I would like to have the opportunity to live to sixty-five. I believe the only way to battle cancer is to be very aggressive right at the beginning.

What kind of cancer did you have?

I had a medullary tumor, which in many cases isn't as aggressive perhaps as intraductal, but nonetheless, the histopathology was estrogen-negative. That was enough to convince me to do the chemo. I'm glad I did it. I never really minded any of this. I did for a while. You know, I mourn losing my breast because it was a sensitive part of my body, and the loss of it alters your responses, your sexual response—when you lose a part of your body, I don't care what it is, you have to readjust. I didn't like that. But I wouldn't want to live with a breast, thinking cancer could come back. I know a lot of women do—I just didn't want that. Right now, in fact, I'm considering doing a subcutaneous on the other side and getting it all over with. I'm tired of thinking about it. I don't want to worry about it anymore. I don't care about it anymore.

For me, the surgery and the chemotherapy wasn't as frightening as the aftermath. Somehow, after you get off the chemo you sort of feel like there's nothing there to protect you. It could recur. And if you recur within two to two and a half years, you've really got a problem. Only 5 percent of those patients survive—there's no successful treatment for advanced breast cancer. Anyway, I was scared to death from the horror of it. Dealing with it afterward was as difficult as anything. You deal with an altered body state. Your cleavage is gone—not that it mattered, not that my breasts were ever my big attribute, but, you know, you still feel . . . altered. Asymmetrical.

What chemotherapy did you receive?

Adriamycin, 5-Fu, and Cytoxan, which are three very powerful drugs. I had it administered through a catheter, which is another thing I would recommend. Most people still get chemotherapy by injection in the arm, which I think is barbaric. I realize there are lots of thing about catheterization that can be dangerous, but I loved it. They put a subclavical catheter in your vena cava artery [a tube is inserted near the collarbone and left there for the duration], and I loved it because I didn't have to be stuck all the time—I didn't get my veins all burned up.

Were your nodes clear?

Yes, but that isn't always an indicator of metastasis. We're finding more and more that there are micrometastases in early breast cancer patients that have nothing to do with nodes. It's already spread. Yes, nodal status is a great indicator, because once it's invaded the nodes, then it really has advanced, in one way. But in Stage I breast cancer—in all breast cancer—it's extremely important to study the histopathology of the tumor, and particularly the S-phase [stage in cell life preparing it to divide; an index of how aggressive the tumor is]. We want to see how fast the DNA is dividing. And I think in the next few years we'll have some good new prognostic factors.

It's surprising to us how many doctors will tell a woman that the lump she's found "looks fine," and she shouldn't worry about it.

You know what I think? Sometimes you have to tell your doctor what to do. That's a horrible way to think about it, but you have to take the offensive many times. *Most* times. It's a very complicated disease, and it's a very complicated treatment. And a lot of it you have to take in your own hands, with an educated opinion.

After hearing the stories we've heard, if we discovered a lump, we'd want it aspirated immediately or, at most, in a week or two to allow for changes in the cycle.

Yes! And I'll tell you something else I'd do. This is going to upset every doctor's office in America if people really start doing this, but I would refuse to wait for my test results: when I have a lung X-ray, I want to know within an hour what it looks like. I'm not going to sit and agonize. I want to know! I want to know right now! Don't tell me you're going to do a biopsy and the results are going to come back in ten days. I want to know now! I have a right. It's my body.

Do you go along with the Simontons' work?

A little bit. Yes, I think it's very important. And we do know that the patients who are fighters do better—patients who have that "you're not going to get me down" attitude do better. But at the same time, it's not enough.

Do you think that stress can trigger the onset of cancer?

I think there's something to that. Listen: I went through a period of losing my sister, a terrible divorce with real financial problems, I had a little child to raise, my family lived in another city and I had no one to help me with my child, and his baby-sitter died six weeks after my sister did. And my job was ending, and my boyfriend took a flyer. Well, I gave him the flyer, but that's a lot to go through.

You've been studying cancer treatment for years. Where do you think a woman should go for the best care?

I'd go to Sloan-Kettering and UCLA. Craig Henderson at Dana Farber in Massachusetts has a very good program. Mark Lippman, who is going to be at Georgetown [Washington, D.C.], is going to have probably one of the best programs in the world when he gets done building that center—the Lombardi Cancer Center, which is affiliated with the National Cancer Institute. I would certainly consult with the NCI—with 1-800-CANCER.

Are there any guidelines women should follow—this
treatment for this kind of tumor?

It's not that simple. But I would say that if you're Stage I breast cancer, consult an oncologist—a surgeon is not enough—and possibly a radiotherapist. Ask for a team opinion. It doesn't matter what it costs. It's important that you educate yourself—what you do in the beginning could possibly alter your life and the course of the disease. The second thing I would say is, if you are premenopausal, have an estrogen-negative tumor, and the histopathology appears to be fairly aggressive, you are more than likely a candidate for chemotherapy even if there's no node involvement. If you are postmenopausal, have an estrogen-positive tumor, and there is node involvement, you are probably a candidate for hormonal therapy or one of the antiestrogen drugs.

That's about all I can tell you for sure. There are lots and lots of areas of gray, particularly with the early stage breast cancer. We're more in a muddle about that than anything.

What if you have nodal involvement and you're
premenopausal?

Boy, I'd get myself to a comprehensive cancer center or a teaching hospital immediately, for a second opinion, anyway. There are some wonderful people in private practice—don't get me wrong. But I would always get a second opinion from a comprehensive cancer center or a teaching hospital, where there is research going on and they are extremely up to date. You can still go to your own doctor, but he can get referral or advice from the center.

And if you had your choice between the most aggressive
treatment or a moderate one, you would choose the most
aggressive?

Oh, boy, yes. At the very beginning. Chemotherapy works best the first time.

"LOSING THE BREAST DIDN'T BOTHER ME. I WAS FOCUSING ON A FIGHT AGAINST CANCER. AND I WAS FOCUSING ON THE FACT THAT CANCER IS NOT A DISEASE TO BE

MINIMIZED. SO I WENT FOR THE LIMIT. THAT'S WHAT MADE ME COMFORTABLE."

A sales director, divorced, with one child, who had a modified radical mastectomy in 1982, when she was thirty-four, and a few months later—too quickly, she thinks now—reconstructive surgery.

When did you first notice something wrong?
I felt the lump about eight weeks before I had the surgery. It was like a pearl, a marble, very distinct.
Did you do regular breast self-exams?
Umm-hmm—I found it.
Any breast cancer in your family?
No, and they didn't expect it to be malignant.
How did you react?
I like to take care of things. I felt something I didn't think should be there. I wondered what it was. I made an appointment to see my gynecologist immediately. He'd been my doctor even before I gave birth, for about eighteen years. He felt it and said he wanted to wait a little bit because I was close to my period. I came back after my period. It was still there. He said he wanted it removed. No mammography. He wasn't interested in mammography: it would show a lump, but it wouldn't show what it was. He just wanted it out.

I went to see a breast surgeon recommended by my doctor. He told me the lump was absolutely benign. I said to him, "Why don't you take it out and look at it under a microscope, and then when you tell me it's benign, I'll believe you."
Was he suggesting that you didn't need surgery?
No, because my gynecologist had already told him he was going to take it out. He wasn't given an option—I was going with my doctor's decision.
You didn't feel you needed a second opinion?
I wanted it out. That's how I am. I would go crackers if I had to walk around with a lump in my breast. Having it taken out was what was comfortable for me. It's no big deal. All it is is an incision about an inch and a half long. You do it on an outpatient basis. You go in in the morning, and you're out in three hours. You go into a little locker room and take off your clothes and put on a gown. There's a nice volunteer to keep you company. Then your doctor comes in and says hi. You walk right into the operat-

ing room and sit down on the table. There's no pre-op. They give
you a minimal amount of general anesthesia—they want to be
able to move around, and if you're on local, they can't play with
you as much.

You wake up very soon after, with a little bandage. And when
I woke up, the doctor said—I'll never forget it—"This isn't what
we wanted to hear." And that was the end of that doctor. I mean,
I didn't like his attitude originally—telling me it's benign. You
can't tell something's benign by feeling it.

After the biopsy my mother went frantic-frantic, and we found
a doctor who came very highly recommended. He is not a breast
surgeon. He is a surgeon. But he has done a lot of surgery for
cancer. He gave me all my options, from lumpectomy plus radiation to modified radical mastectomy. I also went to an oncologist,
a chemotherapist. He, too, recommended a modified radical.
They are going for longevity—they want to give you as many
years as they can—and statistics then were still pointing to a
modified radical mastectomy, all lymph nodes out.

So, a month after the biopsy, I went with the modified radical.
The biggest surprise was that I had a positive lymph node, which
they did not expect.

Did you have chemo?

That was the most unpleasant part. That's tough. It's supposed
to be a year. It used to be for three years, but they cut it back to
nine months. After I started they had another convention, and
some doctors wanted to up the dosage and cut the time back to
six months and some doctors want to leave the dosage and drop
the time to nine months. My doctor didn't want to raise the dosage, but he did stop it after about nine and a half months.

So you have your surgery. In and out of the hospital in five days.
Great care, wonderful people, and I started my chemotherapy in
November. So you go and meet your chemotherapist. He explained what was going to happen to me, which is enough almost
to scare you out of it. But to me, there was no choice. You do what
you have to do. A lot of people did not want me to take chemotherapy. They said it was like shooting a cockroach with a can-
non. I didn't agree. To me, it just would make me feel better to
know that I had given it my best shot.

*What kind of research did you do before you made your
decision?*

I asked around. I spoke to some people, I did enough research to

know there were options. I went back to the surgeon. An old man
—lovely, gentle. I talked and talked and talked. My boyfriend,
whom I've been living with for some time, went with me and
wanted to know everything. He also had about an hour's discussion on his own with this surgeon about my options. The surgeon
was very impressed with that. He told me I was a very lucky
woman, because too many women make this decision by themselves. And I went to an oncologist, who also was into the sur-
gery/chemotherapy route.

*All your doctors, then, were pointing you toward surgery
and chemo.*

Yes, but a lot of people didn't want me to have the mastectomy.
They wanted me to go up to Boston, to Mass. General—just to
have the lump removed, have radiation. I was young, and there
was no cancer in my family. Also, my child had a lot to do with
this decision. When you have a child, your options aren't as vast
as they might be. My daughter is handicapped. And I went
through a lot with her and doctors. Ultimately, what you do is not
a doctor's decision. It's your decision. Everyone has to make a
decision that she can live with. And as it turned out, I was lucky.

Why?

In a lumpectomy, they don't take the lymph nodes out. [This is
not true: they always take some, between eighteen and twenty-
five.] Both the surgeon and the oncologist told me I probably had
no positive lymph nodes—but I did.

What were they basing this on?

The fact that the lump was so small, that I had no cancer in my
family, that I was in perfect health. Plus—they get thrown, too.
I'm attractive. I'm young, I'm energetic. I'm a lot of things. I
don't look sick. The last time I went to my chemotherapist for my
checkup, he said, "You look beautiful! The picture of health."
But I said, "I looked beautiful the last time, and I had cancer."
So you've got to be really careful! I like to be thorough. This
approach—the surgery plus the chemo—seemed thorough. Losing the breast didn't bother me. I was focusing on a fight against
cancer. And I was focusing on the fact that cancer is not a disease to be minimized. There's a lot we don't know. So I went for
the limit. That's what made me comfortable.

What kind of arrangements did you make for surgery?

The doctor said I'd be in the hospital maybe a week or less, and I
wouldn't need private nurses. He told me exactly what they were

going to do: they were going to cut me from under my arm to the middle of my chest. They fold back the skin like a book and then go in and sever practically all your nerves because they have to get your lymph nodes. I had twenty-seven. He told me the center of the chest would be the last part to heal and I might never get my feeling back—I would be numb. And under my arm, I am still numb. I do have all the movement back.

How did you feel after the operation?

You have a surgical bra on, and you're very padded. So when you wake up, you can't tell that you have lost a breast. They are very worried about you psychologically. From the residents to the nurses, they do almost anything so you won't be blue. Nobody pokes you. Nobody does anything if you don't want it. They're awfully gentle. It may have something to do with your doctor and what signals he sends out. Mine came every day. The first time he changed the dressing, he told me he did not want me to look. He was very worried about me. He said he worries about patients who don't get upset.

You're very groggy the first day. Groggy and nauseated. The nurse got me up to walk, and I threw up all over my boyfriend. And my daughter was there. She was a trooper. She said, "Mommy, they took your breast off." They gave me a shot for pain. The next morning, I was feeling much, much better. I was surprised that it didn't hurt more! The mastectomy really isn't a painful operation. I would say you're sore, that's all. And I wasn't depressed. I wasn't depressed until the fourth day when they told me I had one positive lymph node.

My doctor had already briefed me about lymph nodes, what the odds are. With less than four, and with chemotherapy, you still have a great chance of twenty-five-year survival.

They wanted me to stay in the hospital, to have a liver and bone scan, but they couldn't get the tests done the next day, so they wanted me to stay in over the weekend. I threw a tantrum and said "I'm going home. Call my doctor—I will not stay here." I'd had enough. I felt fine! I wasn't going to hang around the hospital for a weekend. And, of course, my daughter wanted me home!

What are the liver and bone scans like?

Like nothing. You go in, in the morning. For the liver scan, they give you an injection in the arm—the arm on the other side (you're not even supposed to cut your cuticles on the operated side). You wait half an hour, and then they lay you on a table and lower this thing over you and take pictures.

The bone scan, you come in again, take the shot, and then leave for three hours. You drink as many fluids as you can. If you don't, you don't, but it makes life easier for them. The bone scan takes about an hour. Psychologically it's very difficult because you lie under the machines while they do your whole body, and you worry about what they're going to find. But there's no pain.

When did you go back to work?

I went back after ten days. But I wouldn't recommend that to anyone. My daughter would say, "Mommy, when are you going to get out of bed?" I probably could have stayed home another week or ten days and just slept a little.

It was making her anxious for you to be in bed?

Yes. That's what got me up.

Did you have any help while you were recuperating at home?

Just my boyfriend.

Would you suggest having someone to take care of you?

Yes. You feel all right, you really feel good—except from here to here [she points from her shoulder to her waist]. You're sore, and you definitely cannot move that arm. You could use someone to help you in and out of the bathtub. You can't go reaching for things. My pots are above the stove. I couldn't get to them.

How did you heal?

Fine. The doctor said he wasn't too happy with it here [she points to a spot on her chest], but I've been reconstructed, so you can't tell—you absolutely cannot tell. I can wear strapless dresses and a bikini. You'd *really* have to look to see any difference. I have not had a nipple put on yet. I don't know if I will. They take the skin from the vagina, and I'm not in a big hurry.

How long after surgery did you start chemo?

About a month.

What happens in chemo?

You go to the hospital. You take an injection—they give it on the back of your hand. He gives it to you himself. One thing about this doctor, nobody touches you but him—not a nurse, not an assistant.

How often did you go?

It's three weeks on, two weeks off. So you go to the office twice a month, two shots a month. The injection part doesn't even take a minute. As soon as the needle is in, you taste it, you feel it. It's an incredible sensation. It's like you're being poisoned. And it's cold—they take it out of a refrigerator. You feel it going up your arm. He calls the taste "metal mouth." The best thing for it is grapes. I ate lots of grapes. And it's very nauseating. I smoked grass—he told me to smoke grass. He said it would alleviate the symptoms better than anything he could give me. He would give me a shot and I would take about three or four tokes of a joint, and then I'd go to work. I worked every day.

So you take the shots, and you have different pills. They get to know you real well at the pharmacy. Your doctor is on twenty-four-hour call to you. You're supposed to call him not for nausea or your hair falling out, but for anything else. Which I didn't do. I got reprimanded a couple of times.

When should you have called him?

Twice I was totally wiped out and couldn't get out of bed. I just slept. He said I wasn't aware of how dangerous these drugs were. And once, they had to lower a dose. You do get very tired. You're sick, you feel sick the whole time—it never stops. My body is still not over it. And you look terrible. My friends told me that my skin was gray. My hair was all gone.

That's a lot of hair to lose. [She has long thick hair.]

I didn't get bald, but close, real close. It looked matted. The chemotherapist told me that my hair would fall out, I'd gain about twenty pounds, and probably lose my period. And everything he said would happen did. My hair fell out, I gained about fifteen pounds, my period lasted until the very end and then it left. Now, I'm in and out of menopause symptoms.

Can you take estrogen?

They don't want to give it to me. It's not so terrible without it. The sweats are bad. When you have them, they last on and off during the whole day. But you can alleviate them by not wearing turtlenecks, by wearing lighter clothing, by being aware when one is coming on and maybe just sitting down and relaxing for a bit.

Someone described the warning feeling as a sense of almost suicidal depression. Is that true for you?

It signals a feeling that you wish wasn't happening, but suicidal, no. It's annoying, especially if you're with a client. It's a nuisance.

How long did it take for your hair to grow back?
A few months. My hairdresser told me not to get a wig. He said it's better for your scalp—your scalp can't breathe. I wasn't totally bald, and he cut and shaped what I had left.

Were you thinking about whether to have reconstructive surgery during this period?
Oh, that was always definite. There wasn't a doubt in my mind. I would definitely tell any woman to have it. Oh, I forgot to tell you: you must be cut in a certain way for reconstruction. And you must be very clear on that with your doctor—you better be very sure that your doctor is working with a reconstruction surgeon from the beginning. Another girl who was having a mastectomy asked her doctor if she was being cut to be reconstructed, and he said, Oh, yes, yes, yes—and then he cuts her straight across rather than on the diagonal. She's always going to have a scar. And they have to leave skin to pull down over the implant.

Why are you so in favor of reconstruction?
The prosthesis is heavy. I never had to wear a bra, and after you have your mastectomy, you're wearing this thing against your chest where that scar is, and it's heavy. I used to come home at night and take that thing out of my bra with a sigh of relief.

Reconstruction is more natural. If I were to put the nipple on and raise the other one a little, I'd be perfect. And if you're thirty-five or forty-five or fifty-two—why not? You're still a very vital lady. And the smaller you are, the simpler the operation is.

How long after the chemo did you have the reconstructive surgery?
Three months.

You researched it while you were in chemo?
Yes. Everybody recommended this one doctor. They said that he had done more breast reconstruction than anyone else in the country, and the more you do, the better you get. They gave him the highest recommendation that I had ever heard any doctor give another doctor. You go to him and he shows you pictures and tells you exactly what he's going to do. They have to build a pocket within your tissues—that's the difficult thing to do. Within that pocket, they are going to insert a bag of saline solution. He doesn't use silicone. You're awake when you go into OR, because you have to sit up on the table and press your hands together [as though praying] so they can draw lines on you. Then they put you to sleep.

How did the surgery go?

The first one didn't work. The tube backed up. I got all black and blue and started to swell. My mistake was not staying in the hospital. You go in the night before, they do you in the morning, and you're out in the evening or the next morning. My doctor's assistants removed the VAC and said I could go home. And they were wrong. I hadn't drained.

Reconstruction is not simple. I think any woman who has a mastectomy should get reconstructed—it makes a big difference. But I don't think it should be done in a one-day procedure. I think you should tell your doctor you would like to stay in the hospital three days. I definitely recommend that. It was more painful than the mastectomy. Even when it's done right, without a problem, it's more painful. You are very tender. And you have to be careful with yourself.

So I would tell people, Don't rush through this. And I would also say, Don't rush *into* this. If you have a modified radical mastectomy, and you're not taking chemotherapy, they will tell you that you can have your reconstruction immediately. I wouldn't. I'd take a breather. Because something could go wrong. And even when it goes well, it's more painful than you'd think. So I think that within six months is plenty of time; maybe four months if you're in an all-fired rush.

What happened when you left the hospital?

I went right to bed—the ride home from the hospital was agony. The next day, I was still in terrible pain. I couldn't move. Stupid me, I figured, Well, that's what it's supposed to be. The next day I slept. My boyfriend came home to make me lunch. He took the covers off and there was blood on the bed. We called the doctor; he was in court and couldn't be disturbed. I called my original breast surgeon and he said, "Get over here right away." He looked at me and got the reconstructive surgeon out of court— who said not to worry about it, to call him the next day. They wrapped me and sent me home. I had pain pills, and I was now black and blue all over.

The next day, I walked into the office of the reconstructive surgeon, and I'll never forget it. I sat down on the table. He comes in and goes, "Oh, this isn't right. Would you please come into the operating room." He lays me on the table and says, "I'm going to have to take the implant out."

He gives me shots of Novocain and proceeds to open my chest.

And I'm watching him! I don't feel a thing, but I was full of blood clots, which I could see because I had my contact lenses in. I wish he had told me—I could have taken my lenses out. And he dug it all out and holds it up and says, "All right, I'm going to close you up, and we'll have you back in after the new year."

How did the second operation go?

I went back to the hospital three weeks later, for five days. Again, I had extremely good care. The night before, I was very depressed. I had just about had my fill of surgery. When they wheeled me into OR, I was crying. They don't drug you for this. The doctor looked over at me and said, "Now, don't you worry. I had this gymnast once, and it took me three times before I got it right, but she got one of the best breasts I ever did."

So he did it, and I woke up and I was in pain. But this time the procedure worked beautifully. The breast was a little high—it had to drop—but in a bra it doesn't matter. And the nipple I can do at any time. Maybe if I were single—I mean, unattached—that would be the finishing touch. But it's a good breast. My gynecologist said he never saw a job this good ever, anywhere.

In the years since, have you changed your health habits at all, your diet or exercise regime?

I eat a very balanced, healthy diet. I always did. I went into this being very fit—I was a size 6—and I do a lot of walking now. But just as I don't go out and exercise as much as I should or eat everything that I should, I don't go the other way and worry about everything. I just go on with my life. I get a lot of rest, and I really do eat properly. If someone were to ask about the connection between cancer and diet—fats and caffeine—I would lean more toward stress as a factor. This came at the end of three terrible years in my life. I had just gone through a very bad divorce, a bad love affair, and a custody suit.

You said your doctor worried about patients who don't get upset. Did you ever get upset?

I cried to my boyfriend. Especially during the chemotherapy, when it hurt so much. There's a feeling you get sometimes as though the inside of your body is screaming to get out. That's the only way I can explain it. I would curl up in a fetal position. A horrible feeling through your whole body.

But still, you were able to go to work.

Yes, every day, and I made a lot of money that year. I will never forget one time—the chemotherapist missed a vein and had to try again and again. I was on my way to a client with three Band-Aids on the top of my wrist. I sat on the subway thinking, I look like a junkie!

Did your insurance cover everything?
Eighty percent, and then after a certain threshold, it flipped into 100 percent. I had Blue Cross/Blue Shield Major Medical. The breast reconstruction you have to pay up-front. That was $4,000. The insurance said they didn't allow that much for the surgery, but I should send the records. And they paid 100 percent of both procedures. Not a question asked.

And how are you now? Do you forget that you've been through this?
Not really, though I'm not conscious of it when I'm going about my business. I should see doctors every four months, but I go every six. I see the chemotherapist, and my surgeon, who examines the other breast. He says I'm supposed to be a patient for ten years. My chemotherapist told me that he had many patients who said this had given them a new feeling about life, or a new outlook, and he was interested to know how I felt about that. I told him that it really wasn't up there with having a handicapped child.

"BEFORE THE RECONSTRUCTION, I WAS AFRAID PEOPLE WOULD THINK, THIS STUPID OLD WOMAN—WHAT IN THE WORLD IS SHE DOING? BUT EVERYONE WAS SUPPORTIVE, SAYING, 'YOU'RE DOING THE RIGHT THING, YOU'RE GOING TO BE SO HAPPY.'"

A sixty-four-year-old woman who had a mastectomy four years before this interview, followed by reconstruction surgery a few years later.

How did you find out you had breast cancer?
I hadn't felt it myself—it was too soon. But I had just turned sixty and went in for my first mammogram—sixty is when you start doing that.* And I went right into a specialized cancer hospital.

---

* This is misinformation: the American Cancer Society recommends getting a baseline mammogram at age forty—not sixty—followed by a mammogram every two years in one's forties and every year after fifty.

My husband and I had called our friend who is head of our local hospital and asked him to recommend somebody. I wanted to go to someone considered the most experienced in this field.

I met the doctor our friend recommended, and I wasn't exactly smitten with him. He was too brusque. It's sort of an abattoir scene of women in stalls at this hospital. The doctor—I called him Dr. Central Casting—explained the options. I could have had the lumpectomy, but he wasn't particularly encouraging about it. And lumpectomy involved radiation; I wasn't terribly anxious to do radiation if I didn't have to. So I immediately scheduled surgery, and within two weeks I had a mastectomy. And it was more traumatic, I think, for the rest of my family than it was for me, maybe because of my age. It must be harder when you're younger. But my son, who was in college, just cracked. And it's been very hard for my two daughters.

Did you go for a second opinion?

No. I had seen the mammogram, and I trusted the doctor's recommendations. I knew I had the option of the lumpectomy, but I was at that point afraid: why take the more dangerous of the two options?

You felt that lumpectomy carried a greater chance of recurrence?

I had a friend who had a lumpectomy and the cancer recurred, and she ended up with a mastectomy anyway.

How was the surgery itself?

It was not a painful operation as operations go. But I had a lot of trouble with the draining. I think I went to the hospital every third day for six weeks to get sort of tapped out—drained. Some people are just what they call slow healers.

Did you have node dissection during the mastectomy?

Yes, and they were all clear. I was very lucky. They got it early. And I'm very careful now. I march myself in once a year for a mammogram, and in the middle of the year for a physical check.

When did you decide to have the reconstruction?

I waited three years because that was the folk wisdom. And because too much was going on in my life—I had too many other things to cope with. Now, I would have it done right away, immediately.

Did anyone try to discourage you from having the reconstruction?

No, but in fact that was one of the things that I was most nervous about. I thought, I'm going to go to the hospital and they're going to think, This stupid old woman—what in the world is she doing? But the nurses, the doctors, everyone was very supportive, saying, "You're doing the right thing, you're going to be so happy." And my family was wonderful.

What made you decide to have reconstruction?
I was very large—I was a 38D cup when I started. That huge rubber prosthesis was really a burden. I weighed it one day—it was three and a half pounds! You can imagine putting that in a bathing suit and trying to go in the water with it. You'd either float or sink—I'm not sure which. Finally, I decided to go and do the reconstruction. It was very involved, because they have to reduce the other breast first. But since that minute, I've never thought about my health again. I just don't think about it.

How did you choose the surgeon for this operation?
I got him from another friend of mine. I had very good care.

Tell us about the reconstruction surgery—you had two procedures?
I had the implant at the same time as they reduced the other breast—that wasn't a bad operation at all, really it isn't. The recovery is easy, painless. And three months later they put the nipple on. You're fortunate if you have large nipples so they can take some and save it, but if you don't, they have to take the tissue from your vagina area, and that was very uncomfortable for the longest time. The operation itself is easy, but getting over it . . . I guess it seemed longer than it was—it was actually only about three weeks—but the stitches are sticking out into you, and trying to sit through meetings, I'd bring my little pillow and put my leg up—people must have thought I had a social disease.

Did you need an expander?
No, they had left enough skin on the theory that I would probably someday consider reconstruction; and also, I was so much smaller now—I went down to a size 36, and I'd been one of these really imposing-looking DAR ladies.

Do you like being smaller?
No, I don't. I miss them. I miss them. My breasts had always been very important to me.

Do you feel that your husband has come to terms with this?
Oh, yes. He was terrific all the way through, even when I was so hideous-looking. He never faltered. He was very affectionate, very sexual, very supportive.

What do you mean—"hideous-looking"?

Well, you have this huge breast on one side and just nothing on the other. It's grotesque. And you just can't always wear that big heavy thing [the prosthesis].

Some of the women who've had reconstructive surgery describe a sensation of tightness in the chest from the implant, a stretching feeling. Do you have that?

Yes, you're conscious of it, but it's not painful, and it's just been a year since my surgery—they say it takes a while. The only time I think about it is sometimes at night—sometimes when you lie down, you feel that the implant has slipped to your side, and you can sort of "ooch" it around into place. It's not nearly as uncomfortable as it was early on, when the nerve ends were growing back and it burned. All that is over.

If you had to do the reconstruction over again, would you?

In a minute. First of all, I have a lot of grandchildren, and they used to just walk into the bathroom when I was in there. Now, people can walk in and they can see that I'm not perfect, but you'd really have to stop and look a long time to think, How strange that is. On first glance, I pass fine. The best thing is, I just don't worry about myself anymore—that's over for me. Maybe it's because it's not the worst thing that's ever happened to me. I have many friends who've had mastectomies—we call ourselves the bosom buddies—and we all handle it differently.

How did your friends handle their mastectomies?

Well, one friend had it in her nodes and much worse than I did. She went out and built a multimillion-dollar house and everything in the world, because, she said, "I'm owed this. Why me? What did I ever do?"

I've got a very different feeling. I feel I've got so little time left that I really want to make a difference. I really don't want to go up to St. Peter and hear him say that I shot an 82 in golf, I redecorated my house, I'm on the best-dressed list. I've just sort of thrown myself into volunteer work, particularly the mental health field. They don't need people for cancer—everybody in the world knows cancer isn't your fault. Nobody understands mental illness.

There are people who imply that cancer is your fault.

Oh, that dumb book—*Love, Medicine & Miracles,* or whatever it's called. A friend of mine who's a little mystical, a well-meaning friend, sent me the book, and I think it was supposed to be a comfort. It virtually says that if you get cancer, it's your fault because you didn't think positively, you didn't eat the right foods —a lot of people swear by this.

There's another theory that a certain kind of personality is associated with cancer—a "helpless and hopeless" personality.

If you could have seen my mother—my mother was about as helpless as a tarantula. She had a mastectomy when she was in her fifties.

How did your daughters react to your diagnosis?

My older daughter lives in California, and she is very California, very antidoctor. She thinks that doctors and hospitals often *create* the health problems. She's a very smart girl, and her husband is a very smart man, but they don't believe in doctors. She had her two little children in a birthing room, and her family eats rice and grains and nuts. I cannot get her to get a mammogram. She's thirty-five. I think when she's forty she'll come around. And my younger daughter has already had a mammogram. She and I are very close. She's much more East Coast about it.

Was there anything that surprised you about the surgery?

The psychological approaches at the hospital surprised me. They give you a lot of group therapy. And they scare you. They tell you you're supposed to wear gloves when you garden, and if you get an infection on this side, it will take forever to heal, and you must be careful all the time. The worst thing they did was to pass around a prosthesis, this pink breast. There were a lot of black women, and they would hardly touch this thing. I can't describe to you how strikingly insensitive the hospital people were. They really tried to toughen you up. They'd say, "If you've had cancer, you'll always have cancer, and you'll always be a cancer pa-tient." I came out feeling like a patient. My friends who went to other hospitals did not have that experience.

Do you now take great precautions with your arm?

Nothing. I'm frying chicken and the grease is spattering, and I've never had a problem. I assume I'm better. If I'm not, well, I'm sixty-four years old and I'm going to die of something. I hope it isn't cancer. I'd rather die of something else. I take very good care of myself, and that's about all you can do. Right after my mastectomy, I got hospitalized for a minor heart attack. They said that is a very common occurrence. From the stress, from the fear.

How would you rate the care your doctors gave you?
I had very good care from the plastic surgeon who did the reconstruction. The original surgeon was expert, but too busy. Nobody
should have that large a patient load, where you have fifty
women in your waiting room. Nobody has to make that much
money. You could wait two hours for your annual checkup. And
the women who were going to work were even more frantic than
I was. It's wrong.

   Did you feel that you could ask all the questions you had,
   or did you feel rushed by your awareness of the women out
   in the waiting room?
I was very aware of them, and one day I thought, Please, God, let
him have the right chart, because he doesn't know me. And one
day he came in and said, "Hello, Elaine." And I said, "Oh, God, I
knew it would happen sooner or later—you've got the wrong
chart."

   He called you by the wrong first name. Did it bother you
   that he called you by a first name at all?
Yes, and I have always said I'm going to go in and call him by his
first name before I finish. My other doctor and I both call each
other by our first names. But you know, the surgeons are the top
of the hierarchy of the medical profession—they are condescend-
ing to everybody. This man is very good looking. I'm sure he
thinks he's Mister Charm.

   Did he answer your questions?
Yes, but there was no question I hadn't read about. There was
nothing esoteric about it—it's a very simple thing.

   So the important issues for you were the risk of recurrence
   with a lumpectomy and avoiding chemotherapy?
Yes, and the other decision was whether or not to have the other
breast removed, the prophylactic surgery. And I did not do that,
because I hung on to what part of me I could. I am rather attached to myself.

   Is there anything you would tell women facing this
   surgery?
I'm sure the same thing that everybody has said to you: that life
just goes on. It isn't the end of the world. It just doesn't make
that much difference—at least it didn't to me. Maybe if I'd been
eighteen I would have felt differently.

THREE

Consultations with Specialists

ANESTHESIOLOGY

SURGERY AND ANESTHESIA CONSENT FORM

CHEMOTHERAPY

CHEMOTHERAPY CONSENT FORMS

ONCOLOGY NURSING

RADIATION THERAPY

BREAST RECONSTRUCTION

BREAST HEALTH NURSING

CANCER RISK ANALYSIS

SCRIPTS: QUESTIONS TO ASK YOUR DOCTOR

ANESTHESIOLOGY

MARILYN KRITCHMAN, M.D.

"DURING SURGERY WE'RE METERING IN THE ANESTHE-
SIA TO THE PROPER DEPTH OF RELAXATION."

*Marilyn Kritchman, M.D., is director of the residency train-
ing program in the Department of Anesthesiology and associate professor of clinical anesthesiology at New York
University Medical Center.*

*Anesthesia is a mystery to most people. Many don't know,
for instance, that anesthesiologists are doctors. Would you
tell us about the training of an anesthesiologist?*

After medical school, we encourage our residents to take a full
year of internal medicine because we function as the internist for
the patient in the operating room. Then, as residents, there is a
three-year postgraduate program in anesthesiology, which is the
same length as the programs for ophthalmologists, obstetricians,
gynecologists, urologists—many of the subspecialties.

Who chooses the anesthesiologist in any particular case?

In most instances, anesthesiologists practice in groups, with a
rotating schedule. But it is possible, always, for a patient to make
a request.

*Could you take us through the surgical process, focusing
on the anesthesia? Say I'm a woman who's just checked
into the hospital, scheduled for surgery the next day.*

Anesthesiologists will come to see you after reviewing your chart.
If there's anything on the chart that concerns them, they will
speak either to your surgeon or to a medical person who has been
taking care of you, as well as interview you intensively.

What are they looking for?

They're looking for significant disease, especially circulatory and
respiratory—heart disease, respiratory problems, smoking. People who smoke have irritated airways and reduced power to pick

219

up oxygen because they have a lot of carbon monoxide in their blood. It is also important to determine what specific medications patients are taking since many interact with anesthetic agents and drugs.

Is there a good reason to stop smoking before surgery?
It helps to stop two weeks or more before surgery. Some people say the anxiety associated with trying to give it up at that point is not worth it, but I would rather see them stop smoking and take Valium. It's my experience that general anesthesia is easier to induce and maintain if the patient reduces or desists completely for that period of time.

The night before surgery, what do you need to tell your anesthesiologist?
Ideally, anesthesiologists should ask you everything so you shouldn't need to add anything. They should know of any drugs that you've been taking, because there are interactions between drugs—even aspirin, which may have an effect on your blood's ability to clot. They should know about any untoward reaction you've had to a drug, any specific allergies, although allergies to drugs are a little less common than people think they are. Very important is a previous history of difficulty during anesthesia.

A woman who is in Alcoholics Anonymous suggested that anyone who is an alcoholic tell her anesthesiologist because she'll need more anesthesia. Is that accurate?
Alcoholics may need more if they're drinking up to the time of the surgery. Patients who come in drunk, however, need less because alcohol is a depressant. Patients who maintain a steady, continuous intake of alcohol often require larger doses of drugs to reach the same end point. In that respect one can consider them "more tolerant" to anesthetic medication.

Is there anything else the anesthesiologist and the patient should discuss the night before?
In the best of all practices the anesthesiologist will describe the kinds of anesthesia that are possible. That is how I practice. It's an opportunity for the patient, if she has a special request, to bring it up. Patients should ask for this discussion of their choices if the anesthesiologist doesn't initiate it. If a mastectomy is planned, there is no choice, but for hysterectomy or face lift procedures, the choice does exist for the healthy patient.

What would your choice be?
In the best of all worlds, I would have a regional—an epidural or

a spinal—for a hysterectomy. But if my anesthesiologist or surgeon was not comfortable with it, it wouldn't bother me to go to sleep. It *does* make a very big difference to me who my anesthesiologist is.

> *How can the ordinary patient judge the competence of her anesthesiologist?*

I admit that's a very difficult problem. You have to depend on your surgeon, I guess. But on the other hand, how does the woman know that her surgeon is the best?

> *You get to know your surgeon.*

Yes, in terms of personality. But you have no way of knowing about his surgical skills any more than you do about the anesthesiologist's.

> *What is the purpose of the tube inserted after you're under general anesthesia?*

You're thinking about endotracheal intubation, which means that a tube is placed in the trachea, the major air passage. We use that to ventilate the patient and also to keep fluids from the gastrointestinal tract from getting into the lungs. General anesthetics eliminate the gag reflex, so you have no protection against aspirating gastric juices into the respiratory tract. Intubation is customary practice for, say, a hysterectomy, as opposed to a D&C, because of the longer time, the greater depth of anesthesia and of muscular relaxation, and the position of the patient, all of which facilitate access of fluid from the stomach into the trachea.

> *What are anesthesiologists doing during surgery?*

They are monitoring your vital signs at all times, making sure they're physiologically normal. If the patient is under general anesthesia, anesthesiologists are maintaining a proper depth of anesthesia and relaxation by metering in, if you will, the anesthetics. They're administering fluids and blood, if necessary, to keep your circulation adequate. With the muscle relaxation, your breathing ceases, so they utilize a ventilator and assure its proper functioning, or they hand-ventilate the patient.

It's constant attendance, monitoring, and support of vital functions. And at the end, they want to wake you up, want you to breathe properly, so that they can take out the tube.

> *When does the anesthesiologist's job end?*

When you are transferred from the recovery room to another area of the hospital. They do, however, make postoperative rounds.

And, should you have any complications, they will attend to ame-liorate your discomfort. But their major work is over after the recovery room. In every hospital today, the anesthesiologists are in charge of the recovery room care.

Why are patients in the recovery room allowed only crushed ice or lemon soaked in water to appease their thirst?

After general anesthesia, your peristalsis tends to stop. Normal elimination is slowed, so volume tends to increase in the stom-ach. We could give you a teaspoon of liquid—the idea is just to keep a minimum volume of fluid in your stomach.

The most common complaint about general anesthesia is that is causes a loss of concentration. Is this a known side effect?

It has been shown that after general anesthesia, judgment is impaired for a few hours, and it is suggested that, besides not driving home from the procedure, you don't make any significant decisions about your stocks and bonds and that sort of thing.

But remember that the kinds of surgery you're dealing with are very emotional experiences, and when you're emotionally in-volved, I think, your concentration diminishes anyhow. Let's say that if you had a prolonged anesthesia—three to four hours—your concentration, or your ability to judge, would be affected until the next day. But after shorter surgical procedures, I think the larger cause for the loss of concentration is emotional.

Now, nobody suggests that anesthesia will *add* to your health. Our only idea is to try, as the expression goes, "to do no harm" in terms of the anesthesia.

What are the risks of anesthesia? Why are people so scared of it?

Statistically, we are safer than we've ever been. I always say it's more dangerous to go on the Long Island Expressway or the Los Angeles Freeway than it is to have an anesthetic. The risk of a problem occurring is something like one in two thousand, and most of those problems are minor.

The accidents that may occur under general anesthesia in a healthy patient are usually misadventures—a problem with the machine and oxygen deprivation. Vigilance overcomes these.

I think that the fear you're hearing is less related to the science of anesthesia than, say, to the women's fears of these particular surgeries, lumpectomy or mastectomy, where there are issues related to body image and disfigurement. Many people are afraid of going to sleep and having no contol or never waking up. There's no question that once you get the hospital gown on, you feel that you've lost your self, your image, your control. But as far as the anesthesia goes—maybe because I'm involved in the specialty—I've never been concerned about going to sleep. I've always picked my anesthesiologist, and when he said, "What do you want?" I've always said, "Whatever you want to give me." I have personally experienced both types of anesthesia without concern and, happily, without complications. As long as it's done well, what difference does it make?

SURGERY AND ANESTHESIA CONSENT FORM

PERMISSION FOR OPERATION AND/OR
PROCEDURE AND ANESTHESIA

1. I hereby authorize Dr. _____ (NAME) _____
or associates or assistants of his/her choice at _____
Hospital to perform upon me or the above-named patient the
following operations and/or procedures (please type or print):

_____

_____

2. Dr. _____ (NAME) _____ has fully ex-
plained to me the nature and purposes of the operation/proce-
dure and has also informed me of expected benefits and complications (from known and unknown causes), attendant
discomforts and risks that may arise, as well as possible alternatives to the proposed treatment. I have been given an opportunity to ask questions, and all my questions have been
answered fully and satisfactorily.

3. I understand that during the course of the operation or procedure unforeseen conditions may arise which necessitate procedures different from those contemplated. I therefore consent to
the performance of additional operations and procedures which
the above-named physician or his/her associates or assistants
may consider necessary.

4. I further consent to the administration of such anesthetics as
may be considered necessary. I recognize that there are always
risks to life and health associated with anesthesia and such
risks have been fully explained to me.

5. For the purpose of advancing medical knowledge and education,
I consent to the photographing, videotaping or televising of the

(continued)

224

operation or procedure to be performed, provided my/the patient's identity is not disclosed. I also consent to the admission of observers to the operating or treatment room.

6. Any organs or tissues surgically removed may be examined and retained by the Hospital for medical, scientific or educational purposes and such tissues or organs may be disposed of in accordance with accustomed practice.

7. I acknowledge that no guarantees or assurances have been made to me concerning the results intended from the operation or procedure.

8. I confirm that I have read and fully understand the above and that all the blank spaces have been completed prior to my signing. I have crossed out any paragraphs above which do not pertain to me.

Witness
(Optional): _____   Patient/Relative
                (SIGNATURE)   or Guardian*: _____
                                                   (SIGNATURE)

_____   _____
    (PRINT NAME)   (PRINT NAME)

Date: _____   _____
                                  (RELATIONSHIP, IF SIGNED BY
                                   PERSON OTHER THAN PATIENT)

I hereby certify that I have explained the nature, purpose, benefits, risks of, and alternatives to, the proposed procedure/operation, have offered to answer any questions and have fully answered all such questions. I believe that the patient/relative/guardian fully understands what I have explained and answered.

Date: _____   Physician: _____
                                               (SIGNATURE)

* The signature of the patient must be obtained unless the patient is under the age of 18 or incompetent.

NOTE: THIS DOCUMENT MUST BE MADE PART OF THE PATIENT'S MEDICAL RECORD.

CHEMOTHERAPY

WILLIAM GRACE, M.D.

"AMONG PATIENTS OF WORLD-CLASS ONCOLOGISTS, NAU-
SEA AND VOMITING FROM CHEMOTHERAPY HAVE ALMOST
TOTALLY DISAPPEARED."

*William Grace, M.D., is chief of medical oncology at St. Vin-
cent's Hospital in New York City. He is assistant professor
of medicine at New York Medical College and on the board
of directors of the American Cancer Society.*

How did chemotherapy evolve as a treatment for cancer?
It began back in the 1930s with the discovery of penicillin. Researchers found that penicillin stopped the uncontrolled growth
of bacteria by inhibiting the construction of the cell wall. It didn't
take a mental giant to hypothesize that if antibiotics worked to
stop bacteria growth, antibiotics might be effective in inhibiting
the growth of cancer cells—and that turned out to be a successful
exploration. In the early days, researchers called the use of antibiotics *chemotherapy*. And even today, in Europe, *chemotherapy*
means drug treatment for infection whereas in the United States
chemotherapy means the use of anticancer drugs.

The first step in the research process was an exploration of
what nutrients cancer cells needed to grow. Folic acid was one of
those nutrients, and they learned that it worked to inhibit the
growth of rapidly dividing cells. This discovery led to research
into the metabolic requirements of cancer cells. At the same time
researchers began experimenting with drugs that could cut off
the supply of what the cells needed. And as the research evolved,
the use of antibiotics against cancer cells increased outside the
realm of controlled studies. When I graduated from a cancer program in 1976, there were very few medical oncologists in the
country. There were physicians taking care of cancer patients
who knew very little about how to treat the disease, and there

were very few tools that could treat cancer successfully. Immunotherapy of cancer in the *classic* sense as physicians practiced it in the 1960s and 1970s didn't pan out.* Today, we're just beginning to have some success with immunologic therapies for cancer. Interleukin II and interferon have produced some anticancer activity by manipulating cancer cells in the patient's body, but they are still very expensive.

How does chemotherapy work?

Chemotherapy attacks cancer cells. When you treat breast cancer with chemotherapy, seven out of ten women respond. The 30 percent who do not respond to treatment are getting poisoned without benefit. It is important to understand that the drugs we use are systemic metabolic poisons which optimally eliminate the cancer without damaging the patient too severely. We have at least five different kinds of drug combinations for women with breast cancer. A woman could fail drug combination number one but respond to drug combination number three or number five. Certain breast cancers demand that we come up with new combinations of drugs, and I think in this area a medical oncologist's creative skills are tested.

When a patient is referred to you, how do you come up with a treatment program?

You need some basic information: What stage is her disease? Is there nodal involvement? How old is she—is she pre- or postmenopausal? What is her estrogen-receptor status? Has the cancer been removed? This is a big factor in how you stage a patient. Experiments on animals have demonstrated that chemotherapy is more likely to be successful when there are fewer cancer cells in the body. Has she been treated with chemotherapy in the past? What does the patient want to achieve? Does she want the possibility of complete remission regardless of possible side effects? Some patients want *quality of life* as a priority, not *quantity of life,* and might choose to forego aggressive, very toxic regimens.

---

* According to Fredrica Preston, clinical nurse specialist, University of Pennsylvania Cancer Center, it is felt that cancer patients have a decreased immune system. "The idea behind immunotherapy is finding a way to make the immune system more active so it can go after cancer cells." In the 1960s and 1970s immunotherapy of cancer was far more random in its methodology. "Researchers explored applying drugs directly on a section of malignant melanoma to see if the immune system could be increased. Today the methodology is more specific. A culture of a certain type of tumor is taken and grown in the lab, and its response to different drugs is noted."

Then, as the oncologist, you have to determine the reasonable objectives you can achieve with the drugs or the hormones you have to work with. A woman's age and her performance status* have a lot to do with how aggressively you can treat her disease. Age used to be a far greater factor in determining whether a woman could be treated aggressively—it is still an area of controversy among oncologists—but women sixty and sixty-five have been treated aggressively quite successfully.

The patient is involved in the treatment—it is a partnership—and it's important for me to understand what a particular woman is willing to go for when it comes to treatment. For example, if a young woman has a fairly advanced disease, we have to find out if she wants to have bone marrow transplant—a highly aggressive treatment—with the hope that she might have a complete remission, which might prolong her life for a significant period of time. Is she a woman who says, "Let's go for broke. Throw everything at me all at once. Maybe I'll pull the high card from the deck." That could mean a very aggressive regimen. Or maybe she wants to take a less aggressive, less toxic therapy, knowing she'll never be cured of the disease but will have a better quality of life for the rest of her life, however long that might be. I can give her my opinion, but she has to make the final decision.

Is there the absolute possibility of a medical cure with chemotherapy?

Yes. With very aggressive treatment of certain kinds of breast cancer, we can achieve cures—defined as a state free from symptoms or evidence of cancer for five years—in a fairly high percentage of women who are generally not thought of as being curable.

How do you feel about the National Cancer Institute's latest announcement that all women who have been diagnosed with breast cancer whether or not the disease is localized should consider chemotherapy or hormone treatment?

Let me clarify something. Vincent DeVita, M.D., who was the NCI's spokesman and who is going to be the new head of Sloan-

---

* Performance status is another way to stage a patient's disease: 0 means patient is normally active; 1, has symptoms but is ambulatory; 2, in bed less than 50 percent of time; 3, in bed more than 50 percent of time; 4, 100 percent bedridden.

Kettering Hospital in New York, was alerting all physicians in America not to dismiss chemotherapy as a treatment even for a small cancer. It was a very difficult and controversial statement to make because some physicians feel that chemotherapy is not an appropriate treatment for women with very small cancers. Personally, I feel every case needs to be assessed individually.

I try to inform my patients about the risks and the benefits of the treatments I recommend. I tell them if we do nothing now, then a certain percentage of them will be dead in ten years' time or have the disease again and be in chemotherapy. I say that if we give you chemotherapy now, then we know a smaller percentage will be dead or will have cancer again. They have to decide to which of those two groups they want to belong. If a patient wants to belong to the favored group, I tell her the potential side effects, which she may or may not have, and I tell her the short-range and long-range toxicities.

Are the side effects of chemotherapy like nausea and vomiting dependent on the individual woman?

No. Among patients of world-class oncologists, nausea and vomiting from chemotherapy have almost totally disappeared.

Why is it, then, that so many of the women we interviewed reported nausea and vomiting? Did they get the wrong treatment?

I don't play hockey as well as Wayne Gretzky, okay? There are differences among oncologists as there are among hockey players. I always use three classes of antinausea medicine on every patient. If you go to a large hospital specializing in cancer where sixteen people are in a room getting chemotherapy, it can be a horror show. One person vomits, and the smells get everyone going. When a new patient walks into a room like that, she thinks everyone who has chemotherapy is supposed to puke. It's not true. Here at St. Vincent's we always use individual treatment rooms. When the one patient in twenty in our hospital gets sick, nobody else knows about it, nobody else smells it, nobody else sees it. Many of our patients are given a Walkman and/or a TV to distract them. Our nurses are compassionate and hold patients' hands. You have to treat people with dignity.

What is the most common way of giving chemotherapy?

There is no one set pattern. Cancer is six hundred different diseases. There are many good chemotherapeutic regimens: some in which the medicines are taken orally, some where they're given intravenously. Cytoxan and Methotrexate can be given by mouth or taken through the vein. If a woman doesn't like swallowing pills, I think it's better to give it by vein. It's an area of controversy as to whether one is more effective than the other.

As a chemotherapist do you consult with surgeons and radiation oncologists?

I hate the term *chemotherapist*. I am a medical oncologist. My role is to integrate all the disciplines. To do that requires a complete understanding of cancer therapy whether it involves chemotherapy, hormones, radiation, or surgery. The oncologist is not there to push poisons—that is the definition of a chemotherapist. In the fifties, physicians were taught how to push poisons, but they didn't understand *why* they were pushing them. Oncologists are trained to provide total treatment. Before seeing a patient I see the records from every doctor she has consulted so I have as much information about the patient as possible. It's the only way to recommend the most appropriate options in therapy. I have to know the pathology. I have to know what the surgery entailed. I have to know how likely the failures are going to be. Will the failures be systemic with the possibility that the disease will return? Or is there a high probability of a local failure, in which case more local therapy is appropriate? Or maybe I might want to use some combination of different therapies.

You also have to know other things about a patient. Many of the drugs we use might be toxic to the heart, so it's important to know if a patient has good heart function. And then you have to assess psychological factors. A patient who is a famous movie star—very beautiful, very wealthy—was referred to me as a candidate for chemotherapy. She is basically a very unhappy person and has tried to commit suicide several times. Chemotherapy was out of the question for her because it was clear that anything that made her life one little bit more difficult would make her life not worth living. Basically, she said she didn't want curative management—very aggressive chemotherapy and radiotherapy —for her disease even though I can't imagine someone for whom it would have been more appropriate.

*How does a woman with breast cancer find a good
oncologist?*

It is very difficult because a woman feels very vulnerable at the moment she's looking. Not knowing anything about therapy, she generally has to trust her surgeon. And he may not know about every option in terms of therapy, nor all the different doctors who deliver it.

I think women may want to interview more than one specialist, so I suggest they ask their surgeon for a number of names. Also the recommendations of friends are very, very important.

Do you treat younger cases more aggressively?

We know that cancer in women under the age of thirty-five responds to aggressive hormonal treatment and aggressive chemotherapy. And that the more intensely we poison our young women, the greater will be the percentage of those women who are going to have long-term freedom from their cancer and the possibility of a cure. However, every new group of cancer trial reports confirms that no matter what the patient's age, the more a number of effective drugs are used together, and the earlier and more aggressively they're used, the greater the benefits. And that trend continues. A woman's age ultimately may be less a factor than the stage of her cancer in determining treatment.

The initial trials conducted with older women showed that most postmenopausal women with estrogen- and progesterone-receptor-positive disease seemed to be less advantaged by chemotherapy and have more to gain by hormone treatment. But that's changing now as more and more trials are being done. The recent trials show that some of the better chemotherapy drugs used in treating premenopausal women are actually producing good results in postmenopausal women. So it looks like an ever-growing percentage of older patients will also enjoy a better long-term outcome if we treat them aggressively and carefully.

*We've read that removal of the ovaries of premenopausal
women who have estrogen-receptor positive is effective.*

We don't know. There is a trial now being done to determine whether these young women will be benefited by surgical oophorectomy in addition to chemotherapy.

*What percentage of women go into menopause after
chemotherapy?*

The earliest trials have demonstrated that the great majority of

women over the age of thirty-five will have a premature menopause, whereas the great majority of women under the age of
thirty-five will not go into menopause with chemotherapy.

What makes the difference?

Chemotherapy is toxic to the stroma, the hormone-producing
cells of the ovaries. If menstruation returns, it means the therapy
did not affect those cells strongly, although it appears that the
menstrual life of these women is shorter than it might have been.

Do you adjust chemotherapy treatments for a woman over
thirty-five if she wants to conceive?

No. When you are treating a systemic disease there is no good
way of protecting a woman's cycle—nor should there be. And I'll
tell you why. When you start to protect one area of the body, often
that area is vulnerable to recurrence of cancer. For example,
when patients who are given postoperative chemotherapy for
breast cancer use hypothermia caps to help prevent hair loss,
quite often the site of the first recurrence is in the scalp. So we
have to be very careful. However, going back to your question,
there are reports of women in the older age group who have con-
ceived *on* chemotherapy. We warn all our patients, "This is not a
form of birth control."

What do you see as the future of chemotherapy?

Every year we're getting better at giving chemotherapy. We are
learning how to give it with less duration, more intensity, and
fewer side effects. Optimally, in a few years, we'll get the toxicities down to even more manageable levels and get the postoperative efficacy up to more acceptable levels. We are making
progress, and we continue to make progress. I don't think women
should be afraid of it. Chemotherapy is a growing and evolving
science. The new therapies will involve more drugs than we currently use—combinations of seven and eight instead of two or
three. In the future, chemotherapy will probably last only three
months instead of the six months or twelve months it does today.

The evolution of chemotherapy depends on patients' participation in cancer trials where standard therapy is compared with
possible new therapies. We ask women to participate in the exploration. The truth is, unless women agree to go into such trials,
we're not going to be able to answer the questions we need to
answer about the best possible way of treating breast cancer.

Do women need to fear that the treatment they receive in
trials is inferior to standard therapy?

Absolutely not. It is not an individual doctor's experiment. The National Cancer Institute and panels of cancer specialists establish the parameters of the trial. And, usually the new and experimental link of a new trial is a better therapy than standard therapy, but the trial is used to prove it.

If we never do clinical trials, we will never solve the problems remaining in breast cancer.

CHEMOTHERAPY CONSENT FORMS

THE STANDARD FORM

When a patient agrees to be treated by chemotherapy, she must sign a consent form. The following is an example of a standard form.

CONSENT FOR DRUG THERAPY

1. My doctor has informed me that I have a tumor or malignant disease which requires drug treatment. I, (NAME OF PATIENT) , willingly agree to participate in the described treatment explained to me by (NAME OF DOCTOR) .

2. I understand that my participation is voluntary, and this treatment directed toward cure or improvement may result in neither.

3. I have been informed that my doctor plans to treat me with one or more of the following drugs. He has explained fully how these drugs will be given and the known side effects as set forth below. Also, I have been informed that there may be potential side effects which are not yet known. I have been assured that every attempt will be made to minimize the possible risks or side effects through careful monitoring of blood counts and body chemistries.

(continued)

DRUG	METHOD OF ADMINISTRATION	POSSIBLE SIDE EFFECTS
_____	_____	_____
_____	_____	_____
_____	_____	_____

4. I understand that I am free to withdraw my consent to paticipate in this treatment program without prejudice to my subsequent care and to seek care from any physician of my choice at any time.

5. I understand that a record of my progress while on this treatment will be kept in a confidential form in this office.

6. I have read all of the above, asked questions, received answers concerning areas I did not understand and willingly give my consent in this program.

_____   _____
(PATIENT SIGNATURE)   (DATE)

_____   _____
(WITNESS SIGNATURE)   (DATE)

_____   _____
(PHYSICIAN SIGNATURE)   (DATE)

RESEARCH PROGRAM CONSENT FORM

Any patient who participates in an investigational study must sign a consent form similar to the one below. All such studies must be approved by the Food and Drug Administration and the institutional review board of the hospital.

PHASE II–III STUDY OF CHEMOTHERAPY OF
(Name of Disease)

RESEARCH STUDY

I, __(NAME OF PATIENT)__ , willingly agree to participate in this treatment which has been explained to me by __(NAME OF DOCTOR)__ . This research study is being conducted by __(NAME OF ONCOLOGY GROUP)__ and by __(NAME OF HOSPITAL)__ .

PURPOSE OF THE STUDY

IT HAS BEEN EXPLAINED TO ME THAT I HAVE __(NAME OF DISEASE)__ . I have been invited to participate in this study. This study involves treatment with antitumor drugs and in some cases X-ray therapy to the brain. The purpose of this study is to develop new treatments which will hopefully result in the relief of symptoms and prolongation of life. To do this, the standard drug regimen of __(NAME OF REGIMEN)__ will be compared to several new experimental agents. The effectiveness of the investigational drug I may receive is unknown.

DESCRIPTION OF PROCEDURES

This study involves initially the administration of __(NUMBER OF DRUGS)__ different chemotherapeutic treatments: __(NAMES OF DRUGS)__ .

Since it is not clear which of the drug combinations is better, the drug treatment plan which is to be offered to me will be determined by chance using a method of random selection called randomization. Randomization means that my physician will call a statistical

(continued)

office which will assign one of the drug therapies to me and that the chances of my receiving one of the offered treatments are approximately equal.

(The method of administration of each of the drugs to be tested, the amount of time it takes to administer each drug, the length of time it takes to complete the course of treatment is outlined. In addition to this, the form states what course of action is to be taken if there is a complete remission of the disease, if there is partial remission, or if the treatment is not effective.)

RISKS AND DISCOMFORTS

Drugs for chemotherapy often have side effects. The drugs used in this program may cause all, some, or none of the side effects listed. In addition, there is always the risk of very uncommon or previously unknown side effects occurring.

VP-16 may cause breathing difficulties, nausea, vomiting, a lowering of the blood cell and platelet counts (leading to an increased risk of infection, easy bruising and bleeding, and anemia), temporary hair loss, loss of appetite, headache, and mild low blood pressure.

CYTOXAN may cause temporary hair loss, bladder irritation with bloody urine, nausea, a lowering of the blood cell and platelet counts (leading to an increased risk of infection, and easy bruising and bleeding).

ADRIAMYCIN may cause a lowering of the blood cell and platelet counts (leading to an increased risk of infection, easy bruising, and bleeding), ulcerations of the mouth, temporary hair loss, and severe skin ulceration if the drug is leaked when it is being given. Adriamycin can also cause heart damage.

VINCRISTINE may cause damage to the nerves of the legs and arms, constipation, muscle weakness, and jaw pain.

CISPLATIN may cause nausea, vomiting, hair loss, lowering of the blood counts (which may lead to an increased risk of infection,

(continued)

bleeding or anemia), decreased hearing, numbness or decreased sensation in hands or feet, kidney abnormalities, and, rarely, decreased vision.

TENIPOSIDE frequently causes decreases in the white blood cell and platelet counts (which increase the risk of infection, bleeding, and bruising), nausea and vomiting, and temporary loss of hair. Less frequent side effects include low blood pressure, allergic reactions that can cause breathing difficulty, and skin rashes, damage to the liver, muscle soreness, and numbness and tingling in the hands and feet.

IFOSFAMIDE commonly causes lowering of the white blood count (which increases the risk of infection), loss of hair (which is not permanent), and nausea and vomiting. Less common side effects are damage to the liver, kidneys, or bladder. Central nervous system side effects such as confusion, weakness, drowsiness, and possible coma may occur.

MESNA usually causes no side effects, but nausea, vomiting, and diarrhea could occur.

WHOLE BRAIN RADIATION THERAPY may cause temporary hair loss, scalp irritation, and alteration in taste.

My doctors and nurses will be checking me often to see if any side effects or complications are occurring. Routine blood and urine tests will be performed to monitor side effects and results of therapy. Side effects usually disappear after the drug is stopped. However, my doctors may prescribe medications to keep those side effects under control. I understand that treatment to help control side effects could result in added costs. This institution is not financially responsible for treatments of side effects caused by the study drugs.

This protocol may or may not have harmful effects on pregnancy, but, as yet, the existence of any such harmful effects are not reasonably known. I am not pregnant at this time.

If I am not pregnant but decide in the future to attempt to become pregnant, or if there is even a slight possibility that I may be-

(continued)

come pregnant, intentionally or unintentionally, I agree to notify Dr. _____(NAME)_____ immediately so that the advisability of my continued participation in this study may be discussed.

CONTACT PERSONS

The physicians involved in my care have made themselves available to answer any questions I have concerning this program. In addition, I understand that I am free to ask my physician any questions concerning this program that I wish in the future. I have been assured that any procedures related solely to research which would not otherwise be necessary will be explained to me. Some of these research procedures may result in added costs which may not be covered by insurance. My doctor has discussed these with me. If physical injury is suffered in the course of this research or for more information, I can notify _____(NAME OF DOCTOR)_____ , the investigator in charge, at _____(PHONE NUMBER)_____ .

BENEFITS

It is not possible to predict whether or not any personal benefit will result from the use of the treatment program. Possible benefits are remission of tumor and prolonged survival. It is possible that the investigational drug may prove to be less effective than the standard regimen. I understand that if I receive treatment with the experimental drug and do not show any benefit from the treatment, I will receive treatment that has previously been shown to be effective. I have been told that if my disease becomes worse, if side effects become very severe, if my doctor feels that continued treatment is not in my best interest, or if new scientific developments occur that indicate the treatment is not in my best interest, I will be so informed and the treatment program will be stopped. Further treatment will be discussed.

ALTERNATIVES

Alternatives which could be advantageous in my case include treatment with different drugs, or radiotherapy. However, there is no clear evidence that other treatments would provide an increased chance of controlling my disease, and the side effects from other

(continued)

drugs may be similar to those from the drugs proposed in this study. I understand that my doctor can provide detailed information about my disease and the benefits of the various treatments available. Another alternative is no further therapy, which would probably result in continued growth of my disease. I have been told that I should feel free to discuss my disease and my prognosis with my doctor.

VOLUNTARY PARTICIPATION

Participation in this study is voluntary. No compensation for participation will be given. I understand that I am free to withdraw my consent to participate in this treatment program at any time without prejudice to my subsequent care. Refusing to participate will involve no penalty or loss of benefits. I am free to seek care from a physician of my choice at any time. If I do not take part in or withdraw from the study, I will continue to receive care. In the event that I withdraw from the study, I will continue to be followed and clinical data will continue to be collected from my medical records.

CONFIDENTIALITY

I understand that a record of my progress while on the study will be kept in a confidential form at ___(NAME OF INSTITUTION)___ and also in the computer file at the statistical headquarters of (NAME OF ONCOLOGY GROUP)___ . The confidentiality of the central computer record is carefully guarded, and no information by which I can be identified will be released or published. However, medical records which contain my identity may be examined by members of the Food and Drug Administration (FDA) and by the National Cancer Institute (NCI) during their required reviews. Histopathologic material, including slides, will be sent to a central office for review.

___(NAME OF HOSPITAL)___will provide immediate essential care for any physical injury resulting from my participation in this research protocol. However, neither long-term hospital treatment nor financial compensation will be available from the hospital.

(continued)

I have read all of the above, asked questions, received answers concerning areas I did not understand, and willingly give my consent to participate in this program.

_____   _____
(PATIENT SIGNATURE)   (DATE)

_____   _____
(WITNESS SIGNATURE)   (DATE)

_____   _____
(PHYSICIAN SIGNATURE)   (DATE)

ONCOLOGY NURSING

FREDRICA PRESTON, R.N., M.A., O.C.N.

"I WOULD STRONGLY ENCOURAGE A WOMAN CONSIDER-
ING ADJUVANT THERAPY TO USE THE ONCOLOGY NURSE
AS A RESOURCE PERSON, PARTICULARLY IF SHE IS CON-
FUSED BY THE INFORMATION SHE IS GETTING FROM
OTHER SOURCES."

*Fredrica Preston, R.N., M.A., O.C.N., is an oncological clin-
ical nurse specialist and assistant director of the Hospice/
Home Care Department of the University of Pennsylvania
Cancer Center. She received the 1989 American Cancer Society's Lane Adams Award for excellence in cancer nursing.*

What do oncology nurses do?
We work closely with medical and surgical oncologists providing
physical care—chemotherapy administration, wound management. We are very good at symptom management and at counseling and teaching patients with cancer. Oncology nurses
practice in a variety of settings, including hospitals, private of-
fices, clinics, and in patients' homes. We want to help. We're
well educated—master's degrees are very common, and many
nurses are taking Ph.D.s now—and we know the current cancer
research.

I think oncology nurses are the true patient advocates, with the
knowledge, skill, and authority to meet the needs of our patients.
We try to make the treatment fit the patient's life-style. For instance, if we know a patient works during the day or is in school,
we will try to schedule her treatment at night or on the weekend.
I would strongly encourage a woman considering adjuvant therapy to use the oncology nurse as a resource person, particularly
if she is confused by the information she is getting from other
sources. We have our own channels of information, and if one
nurse doesn't have an answer, a friend or colleague across

town can help. I think we are an untapped resource for cancer patients.

Is oncology a new specialization in nursing?

I started in 1975, and very few nurses specialized in oncology then. I became involved right from the start! It's a wonderful field for nursing—you work with patients long-term and get to know them very well. You work with their families. You're involved with research. It's a field oncology nurses have carved out for themselves. They have seen the needs and actively gone out to meet those needs. Also, the overwhelming majority of oncologists are more than receptive to our work—they're really enthusiastic about our contribution. Oncology is a field where nurses and physicians each acknowledge the contribution the other makes. The science of oncology is not as exact as perhaps some others, so the two disciplines work hand in hand to provide quality patient care.

As a medical professional, how do you feel about
alternative therapies for cancer, such as a macrobiotic
diet?

If we have nothing else to offer cancer patients and if the alternative therapy isn't harmful to them, then I think it's fine. If people feel their general sense of well-being is better on a macrobiotic diet, I say good for them. Do it. But I would strongly suggest they consult someone who really knows macrobiotic nutritional principles because the body is already compromised due to the cancer and the treatments. There are also treatments like biofeedback that emphasize relaxation, and I consider them very positive. The only problem I have with many of the alternative therapies is the subtle message they communicate to a cancer patient that she is in control of her disease and has the power to change the course of her illness. That's fine as long as she remains healthy, but if she has a relapse or something goes wrong, she blames herself: "If only I had tried harder." And that's not a positive state of mind! There are charlatans out there. Everyone is looking for a miracle—that's the problem. However, having said that, most alternative treatments are *not* toxic, and they can assist patients in developing a sense of inner peace. At the center we offer people relaxation tapes, and I think massage is wonderful relaxation.

I have patients who have read Bernie Siegel's *Love, Medicine & Miracles* and were helped by it. I really think that's great. But

I feel a patient has to consider the stage of her disease before turning to alternative treatment. If she is offered a multiple drug regimen when her cancer has metastasized to different parts of the body and the risks of treatment outweigh the potential benefits, and then she says, "No, I don't want this. I think I'm going to go to the mountains in Tibet," I'd say, "Go." But if she is in an early stage of breast cancer and she says, "No, I don't want surgery or radiation therapy, I'm leaving for Tibet," I'd say, "You're a fool." I would try to make sure she understands the ramifications of her decision to reject treatment of a potentially curable disease. But in my experience if a person gets strong emotional support and good medical care in managing her side effects from the professionals caring for her, she won't get to the point where she walks away from treatment that can cure her.

RADIATION THERAPY

MARK ROUNSAVILLE, M.D.

"A WOMAN WITH BREAST CANCER WILL LIVE JUST AS
LONG WHETHER HER BREAST IS REMOVED OR NOT."

Mark Rounsaville, M.D., is a board-certified radiation oncologist with Children's Hospital of San Francisco. He is an active proponent of patient involvement in health care decision making.

How is radiation therapy used in treating breast cancer?
It is often used in combination with lumpectomy. After the breast cancer lump is removed surgically, high-energy electromagnetic rays are carefully aimed at the breast. These rays are a form of radiation like light or sunshine, though they have much higher energy and are powerful enough to kill cancer cells. The treatments, which last approximately ten minutes, are given four to five times a week for about five weeks. Frequently this course of treatment is followed by a "boost" or additional radiation treatments to the original site of the tumor where residual cancer cells might remain. Many people, quite appropriately, wonder how this radiation could be effective in killing cancer cells. It can't be seen or felt. It doesn't leave a scar, and it isn't mutilating, yet modern-day radiation treatment has been shown in many studies to be just as effective as mastectomy in the treatment of breast cancer. X-rays kill cancer cells by disrupting their DNA or chromosomes. Normal cells are stronger, and that's why they are resistant to the effects of X-rays. Radiation treatment rids the breast of residual cancer cells and leaves the breast appearing much like it did before treatment.

*Are most women who are candidates for lumpectomy/
radiation offered that option?*
In California, Massachusetts, and I think several other states, it is a law that physicians treating breast cancer have to inform

245

patients of their options. However, even here in California we often find that many women don't receive the information they need or don't understand the information sufficiently to make a truly informed decision about mastectomy versus lumpectomy and radiation treatment.

A gynecologist or primary care physician usually refers a patient for a biopsy to a surgeon. In many cases, we find that a surgeon feels more comfortable with radical surgical treatment and will present treatment options with a strong bias toward mastectomy. Our patients have quoted some doctors as saying, "If you were my wife, I'd recommend a mastectomy," or, "If you're vain and really intent on keeping your breast, there is another procedure available, although I'm not confident about its effectiveness." Patients are then asked to make a decision to undergo mastectomy. Since many women are not referred to a radiation oncologist for consultation, they never learn about the effectiveness of radiation treatment. I don't believe surgeons intend to frighten their patients into a mastectomy, but sometimes that is the result. It's particularly frustrating for me when patients' evaluations show they are clear candidates for breast-conservation cancer treatment, yet they proceed to have a more radical surgical treatment without fully understanding the other options.

After a biopsy, does a woman with a breast cancer need immediate treatment to prevent the cancer from spreading?

There is no urgency to proceed within a day or two, or even within a week or two—after all, the tumor has been there for a while. But it shouldn't take longer than three to four weeks to get all the information you need to make a decision. When you're first told you have cancer you are in no position to make a rational decision. You owe it to yourself to wait until you have your questions answered and have the opportunity to think about the information you've gathered. The important thing to remember is to get at least two opinions. Make sure you get one from a surgeon and one from a radiation oncologist. If both opinions are from doctors in the same specialty, you will, of course, tend to get similar opinions. A woman should not be asked to make a decision to have a mastectomy without knowing and understanding her other, safe, less radical alternatives.

*Don't you think that, ideally, the surgeon and the
radiation oncologist should be working together on breast
conservation?*

Absolutely, but this frequently doesn't happen. Surgery is extremely important in breast-conservation cancer treatment. Unfortunately some surgeons act as if doing a good lumpectomy with minimal scarring is a less important function than doing a mastectomy. But there are others who realize that even though a lumpectomy requires less cutting, their role is even more important. Today both surgeons and radiation oncologists are becoming more involved in seeing to it that their patients achieve a good outcome emotionally and physically. Surgeons are being asked to remove the cancerous lump taking as little normal tissue around it as possible. This can be a difficult task and requires skill and experience because we don't want big, deforming scars on the breast. We've seen patients whose scars looked terrible after a lumpectomy, particularly when the surgeon is accustomed to doing only mastectomies. A good lumpectomy requires more skill in planning how and where the incision will be made to produce the least scarring. Women need to realize that, in most communities, the surgeons who perform breast surgery are general surgeons who might do very little breast-conserving cancer surgery. A woman would be wise to ask how much experience in breast surgery a given surgeon has had and how important he or she feels the cosmetic outcome is. Similar questions should, of course, be asked of the radiation oncologist.

*Can a patient determine on her own that a surgeon is
skillful in both the medical and aesthetic aspects of the
surgery?*

Yes, but it takes a willingness on the patient's part to become involved in her own health care. That means learning about her disease through books and articles written for the layperson. She must prepare and ask questions of her physicians and other health care workers so that she reaches some level of understanding about her cancer and the treatment options appropriate for her. The patient should talk to other women who had breast cancer treated by lumpectomy and radiation. Some breast cancer support groups will know of women who are eager to share their experiences. A few hospitals like ours have a breast health service where a woman can go for an independent consultation and guidance. A patient can judge the competence of her physicians only after she has some knowledge about her disease and after hearing what other women have experienced.

Are many of the women you see in your practice informed about breast cancer?

We are seeing more and more women who assert themselves, who ask questions and want answers. We don't want passive patients. We want the patient to be involved because there are decisions to make and we need her feedback. A physician cannot practice medicine well without the patient's help. She has to give us some idea about what her desires and expectations are, and the more she knows, the easier it is for her to communicate with all the medical professionals she has to deal with.

Are medical politics keeping women from understanding they have treatment options when they are diagnosed with breast cancer?

The medical politics in breast cancer are frequently connected to the doctor referral system. Let's say a patient has researched her case and realizes that she can keep her breast. What she needs is a lumpectomy, possibly an axillary sampling of her nodes or limited underarm surgery, and radiation therapy. She goes to her surgeon and asks about this less radical treatment. He or she may say, "It's very new. I don't happen to believe it is as effective as mastectomy in your case, but let me refer you to a colleague of mine for a second opinion." The surgeon may already know that his colleague shares his bias and will confirm his original opinion. Unfortunately the patient may feel that two expert physicians have come to the same conclusion independently, so it must be correct. This is why it is important for women to seek out other opinions from experts she has heard about from other patients, nurses, or doctors. This may mean a woman will see several consultants before she reaches a decision about treatment. She should not be concerned that her doctor may be offended if she gets other opinions. Breast cancer treatment philosophies vary from community to community and hospital to hospital. There are hospitals where 90 percent of women with breast cancer keep their breasts and other centers where 90 percent undergo mastectomy. Here, fortunately, most women keep their breasts. I personally think it's only a matter of time before mastectomy for most cases becomes obsolete—even in less progressive medical communities. I admit I have this bias—I don't understand why a woman wouldn't prefer spending five to seven weeks of undergoing relatively benign treatment to losing a body part, especially since the life expectancy is the same.

That's the question: Is lumpectomy/radiation therapy as
effective as mastectomy in managing breast cancer?

Yes. When you compare the results of different types of mastectomy—less radical to very radical—*without* radiation therapy to lumpectomy *with* radiation therapy, the survival rates are the same. In other words, a woman with breast cancer will live just as long whether her breast is removed or not. I want to say the same thing another way because it is so very important. Whether we do lesser or greater surgical procedures, we don't detect a difference in survival. Let's say we do both radical mastectomies and postoperation radiation therapy—the most radical treatment possible—on every woman with breast cancer, reducing the chance of cancer returning to the chest wall (where the breast was removed) down to 1 or 2 percent. Even then there is no evidence that we are improving survival or that these women will live longer than women who have had lumpectomy and radiation. Surgery for breast cancer during the past few decades is becoming less radical and deforming, simply because we can no longer justify mutilating procedures that add nothing to the patient's longevity. It is very hard for us to acknowledge to a woman that no matter what we do, the cancer may still return somewhere in her body. Perhaps that's why some physicians prefer to remove the breast, feeling then that they have done everything possible. But the point is, a woman can keep her breast, have radiation treatment, and live just as long as she would have if she had her breast removed. We've been comparing thousands of cases—more radical versus less radical breast treatment—and we've been doing it for two decades, and we have failed to come up with any difference in survival. We hope we are curing our patients, meaning they live their lives cancer free, but our realistic goal is to try to prevent the cancer from coming back in the breast area by radiation or surgery while at the same time providing an outcome a woman can live with that contributes to a better quality of life. It is normal for human beings to want to feel good about their bodies, and we encourage it in our patients. It's not vain to want to keep a breast. We don't want women to feel guilty because they want to keep their breasts. It is important for patients to understand that they will not live longer if they sacrifice their breast.

I want to point out that there are patients who are excessively concerned about radiation therapy. Usually we can show them those fears are unfounded. There probably is a small group that should have mastectomy because they cannot feel comfortable with radiation therapy. We don't want women thinking their breast is a time bomb. If a woman will have less anxiety by having her breast removed and a scar to remind her that her cancer has been treated, then radical surgery may be necessary for her. We know it's a false sense of security, but this conviction is difficult to overcome in some patients. Most women, regardless of their initial concerns and feelings about radiation therapy, become quite comfortable having this treatment—if we have the opportunity to explain the procedure and the issues. But it takes time. For the first week or two after being told she has breast cancer, it's not uncommon for a woman to feel that her breast must come off for safety's sake. We want to give women the time and information they must have to make informed decisions.

BREAST RECONSTRUCTION

DAVID HIDALGO, M.D.

———————

"BREAST RECONSTRUCTION ISN'T FOR EVERYONE. THE BEST CANDIDATES HAVE A VERY POSITIVE ATTITUDE AND REALISTIC EXPECTATIONS, ARE PSYCHOLOGICALLY STABLE, AND ARE NOT DOING IT FOR ULTERIOR MOTIVES —SUCH AS A FEAR THAT THEY'RE GOING TO LOSE THEIR SPOUSE UNLESS THEY GO THROUGH WITH IT OR ANY REASON OTHER THAN SIMPLY WANTING TO RESTORE THEIR APPEARANCE OR JUST BE MORE COMFORTABLE IN CLOTHES."

David A. Hidalgo, M.D., is a plastic and reconstructive surgeon affiliated with Cornell University Medical College, where he is an assistant professor of surgery. He is also an assistant attending surgeon, Division of Plastic and Reconstructive Surgery, Memorial Sloan-Kettering Cancer Center, and assistant attending surgeon at Manhattan Eye, Ear, and Throat Hospital.

What are the reasons women give you for wanting reconstruction?

The overriding concern is often a practical consideration, whether it's a problem with clothing and the inconvenience of an external prosthesis, or feeling unbalanced and asymmetric. Then there's the whole issue of body image, as you might expect. Many women feel that they aren't psychologically whole and can't put the cancer experience behind them until they have removed the deformity associated with the cancer—the physical defect is a constant reminder of the disease.

Many women report that their breast surgeon scheduled them for appointments with plastic surgeons so they could have reconstruction at the same time as the mastectomy. None of the women had asked for the appointment. Is that

*usual now—to presume not only that a woman wants
reconstruction, but that she's going to have it
immediately?*

We've come 180 degrees from the time, ten years ago, for example, when most breast surgeons were fixated on just the cancer
problem, and the disfigurement associated with it was given far
less importance. Although reconstruction may not be appropriate
in all cases, as a general rule I think it's better care to let someone
know that the option is available. It's really the patient's option
to pursue it or not to. She should not get the sense that she is
obligated to see a particular plastic surgeon, though the person
recommended is often a good place to start. A patient probably
should see several doctors. Very few plastic surgeons are well
versed in all techniques of breast reconstruction. Occasionally, a
woman's physical makeup suggests that she should have a particular type of reconstruction, but her plastic surgeon may prefer
to do a different type because he is more comfortable with it. So
multiple opinions is really the way to go, and if the research starts
with the urging of the breast surgeon, I think that's actually a
good thing.

*Once you've decided that you want reconstruction, the big
question is when to have it. What determines the timing?*

When I see a patient for the first time, I try to evaluate her as
much from an emotional and psychological standpoint as from
the physical to determine whether she should have reconstruction at the time she's being treated for the cancer or whether we
should let her sit for about three months and get used to the idea
of what she's going through and adjust to the cancer problem
before starting the breast reconstruction. Everyone comes to it in
her own way. Some women are ready for it right away, and some
have to wait a period of time, even years, until they are psychologically ready. It's overwhelming to most patients who want the
so-called immediate reconstruction (at the same time as the mastectomy) to try to deal with two problems at once—the breast
cancer issue and the options available for breast reconstruction.
I have to get a sense of the patient's support system—her spouse
and family. It's very difficult, for example, to treat someone who
is going through an emotional upheaval with her spouse—and I
see this with some frequency—at the same time as she's trying
to deal with the issue of reconstruction. It's better to delay reconstruction in patients who are not settled psychologically.

What determines which technique is appropriate?
In most cases the physical decision is very straightforward. The easiest patient to deal with from a technical standpoint is a small-breasted woman who doesn't have a lot of sagging to her breasts. That type of patient is usually best reconstructed with a silicone (or saline) implant. Many patients in this category present a problem in that they don't have a lot of skin left after the mastectomy to stretch over the implant. So I'll have to do a preliminary procedure whereby I'll put in a tissue expander, which is a device that will stretch the skin, and then about two months later there's enough skin on the chest so that I can put in the appropriate-size implant and achieve a more natural shape that will match the normal side.

Before we had tissue expanders, which was about ten years ago, we would just put an implant in. And it wouldn't be a very satisfactory result because there was not enough skin to drape underneath the implant, to make the crease below the breast. And we frequently would not be able to fit the size implant that we'd want and have to use something smaller, so there'd be a volume discrepancy between the two sides. This would dictate to us how much we had to reduce the opposite side. A tissue expander, although it's an additional step, gives us enough leeway so that we can do exactly what we need to do.

How much pain is associated with these procedures?
It hurts to have any surgery. But the level of discomfort is not that great, and it's not for that great a period of time. Breast surgery is surgery that in a sense is on the outside of the body, and most patients tolerate it very well. Tissue expanders also have some discomfort associated with the inflation process, because the body reacts to stretching with a certain amount of pressure and tightness that lasts for anywhere from twenty-four to forty-eight hours. Then the skin loosens up, the discomfort abates, and the body manufactures more skin. A week later, you go through the whole process again.

We gauge it individually to the patient. Some patients can tolerate a great amount of fluid being added each time, so the expansion process goes relatively quickly. With patients who have more discomfort, we tailor the process so that we're adding smaller amounts more frequently—maybe we'll see them twice a week. So we achieve the same result pretty much within the same period of time, but it's much more comfortable for them.

There is a common misperception that expanders and implants are a more simple type of reconstruction than tissue reconstruction. Actually they can be quite inconvenient and much more involved than a tissue reconstruction.

With this new interest in reconstruction among breast surgeons, are you finding that they're thinking ahead and as a matter of routine leaving enough tissue to make reconstruction easier or placing the incision with reconstruction in mind?

It works to the patient's advantage to have a plastic surgeon involved from the very beginning. I like to be in the operating room when the breast surgeon is going to start the procedure. He and I will get together, and he will draw an incision, and I'll make a suggestion if I think it's more advantageous for the reconstruction to do it another way. Then he'll tell me if that in any way compromises the cancer part of it. If you have two people working together, it's ideal. I can make just the smallest suggestion—to make the incision with a little bit less length or to orient it a little bit differently—and it makes a great difference in terms of the final result that we'll achieve.

The problems are when the incisions go in unfavorable directions, or when they're high, and sometimes when they're too long. I frequently urge the breast surgeon to try to keep the biopsy incision, which is usually about three inches in length, very close to the border of the areola. They no longer just cut where it's easy; they will struggle a bit, and that's an important consideration for reconstruction.

Other problems come from a kind of surgery that's less in favor now, the radical mastectomy.

Are you still seeing women who've had radical mastectomies?

I'm seeing older women who were treated that way twenty years ago, and something in their life has changed now—they're undergoing a separation or divorce, they're going back out into the world and feel that they have to be whole again.

Can a woman be too old for reconstruction?

I don't think there's an upper limit. Breast reconstruction can be tailored for the older patient—meaning sixty-five or higher—by doing it in a way that's not going to jeopardize her overall health and is perhaps a simpler type of reconstruction with a more limited expectation.

What kind of scar are you usually confronted with these
days?
Would you like to see some pictures? I am going to reconstruct
this woman.

[He brings out a front and side view of a torso—the head is
cropped—of a woman in her mid-thirties who had a mastectomy
eight months before. The left side of her chest is smooth and flat,
marked only by a horizontal scar at the level of her nipple. The
line starts about two inches from the sternum, runs right across
the middle of the breast, and goes around almost to the middle of
the underarm.]

These incisions are long because not only does the nipple and the
areola have to be removed, but exposure has to be gained into the
lymph node bearing area in the armpit.
    The nodes are scattered up the chest as well as under the
    arm. How does a surgeon get to those nodes?
Breast tissue goes all the way up to the collarbone. This can be
easily reached through a standard mastectomy incision.
    Is the mastectomy in this photograph really a typical case?
    It's so clean, so unwounded-looking—such a dramatic
    contrast to the old image of mastectomy as gory.
This is a typical mastectomy that's been done well. You can see
that, yes, the breast is missing, but there are no scars that will
show even in a low-cut dress. This incision is the best type to
have—it's low and horizontal or just slightly oblique as it approaches the armpit. Surgeons try to do that, but they do have
limitations—for example, if the tumor is in the upper part of the
breast, particularly the upper inner part near the center of the
chest, or if the tumor is quite large. But the most commonly found
tumor is in the lower and outer quadrant and in the central area,
right below the areola. This type of cancer can for the most part
be treated in this fashion. It's important to remember that everybody's scarring potential is different, and this influences one's
perception of how bad the scar is: some patients have very thick
red scars because that's the way they heal, but most women have
very good scars. Breast surgeons are leaving the pectoral muscle
behind now, so if you just expose the upper third of the chest, you
really wouldn't know the person had a mastectomy.
    So this is what patients can expect for the most part. During

the first week or two after surgery, many women are reluctant to look at the scar, but the overwhelming majority of patients say, once they finally do look, "It's not as bad as I thought," or "It's much better than I thought."

We've read about a new kind of tissue expander that becomes the permanent implant once it's reached the right size.

Yes, in plastic surgery the devices evolve very quickly. People are always introducing a new type. There's one out now that is a tissue expander with a silicone covering, so it feels soft. The proposed advantage is that you can put it in to stretch the skin and leave it in—you don't have to do another operation. The disadvantage is that breast surgery is frequently not precise. After the expansion process, you may want to change the position of the implant or put some stitches on the inside of the pocket to create a sharper fold under the breast. If you have the opportunity to go back and not only change the implant, but change the shape of the pocket and do some other maneuvers that make the two sides more even, you will, in fact, end up with a nicer result. I feel that the majority of patients today stand to get a nicer final result if they have the conventional tissue expander and then the implant placed as a second procedure.

Of all the implants, which do you think feels and looks the most natural?

The implants all feel the same, provided there is no scar tissue that makes them hard. You see, the implants themselves never get hard; it's the body's scar tissue formation around the implant that shrinks the space surrounding the implant and gives you the perception of its being hard. The implant itself remains as soft as the day you put it in. So the problem is to prevent the scar formation around the implant.

Comparing implants—nobody has been able to clearly show an advantage of one type over another. Here is a saline implant. It has an outer envelope of thin plastic, and inside is saline, a form of saltwater that has the same composition as found in the blood so if the implant accidentally burst, your body would absorb the fluid with no adverse effects.

Why would the implant burst?

It happens very rarely, but they can spontaneously deflate, either from a manufacturing defect or, conceivably, a blunt injury such as a car accident. If that happens, the implant has to be replaced.

The theoretical advantage is that the saline doesn't cause as much tissue reaction around the implant. Some studies suggest that there is less chance of thick scar formation around a saline implant than the silicone, but there are still problems with hardening, and I would say that most plastic surgeons still put in a silicone implant. I would recommend the saline implant to a woman who has a phobia about silicone. The fear is unwarranted, considering all the scientific evidence available, but nevertheless, saline is an alternative—with the understanding that if it deflates, it will have to be replaced.

The other and far more commonly used option is a conventional silicone implant, which is a silicone gel inside a thin plastic envelope. This device has been around in various forms for over twenty years. The main problem is that in as many as one out of three patients the scar tissue can make these feel hard. The hardness can be rock-hard, and that can be painful, and it can distort the shape of the breast, and then you have to replace the implant or do some procedure to break up the scar. But there's also a whole group of women whose breasts are firmer, but not objectionably so—the implant doesn't feel natural, but the patient doesn't feel that something needs to be done about it.

Another kind of implant has a polyurethane covering over the silicone. The covering has a texture [it feels like peach skin]. It has small interstices, or little holes, and tissue grows into those holes. The body seems to interact differently with this surface. With the usual, smooth covering, the body makes a sheet of scar; but here, the body forms a disorganized scar layer around the implant, and the cells that cause the contraction and hardening process can't function effectively. The end result is that these implants tend to feel softer. A couple of studies with large series of patients have reported results that are much superior to the conventional silicone implants. But this implant hasn't yet withstood the test of time. And many times a new product doesn't. We could find out that it hardens five years after it's put in as opposed to a few months. One disadvantage of the polyurethane implants we do know is that they are more prone to infection. When you get an infection, the implant has to be removed immediately, and sometimes it's technically difficult to do. So it's not all promise without disadvantages.

There's another type of silicone implant that gives a better shape to the breast; it has another area of silicone in the middle that's harder and gives a conical shape to the breast. The conventional silicone implants tend to be a little bit flatter across the front. This cannot be used in all cases, but it is ideal in properly selected patients.

Are these the same implants you'd use for breast augmentation?

Yes, exactly, and the same three options exist—the saline, the smooth silicone, and the polyurethane-covered silicone. Most plastic surgeons are leaning toward the polyurethane implant—the results seem to be better in terms of softness.

What happens to the implant as you age—do you have one breast sagging and the other remaining firm?

Yes, and that's one of the drawbacks of implant reconstruction. The implant tends to stay within its scar capsule, very high and conical like an eighteen-year-old breast, whereas the other breast continues to suffer the effects of gravity. What's necessary, if the patient wants to, is to tighten and lift the normal side.

This drawback is one of the reasons that there is a whole other school of thought favoring tissue reconstruction over implants.

Who is a good candidate for tissue reconstruction?

Let me show you another picture. This is an older patient, who is a little bit heavier. She has more mature breasts, and there is some sagging—the medical word for that is *ptosis*. But she also has enough excess abdominal tissue to make a breast. I take an elliptical piece of tissue from the abdomen—skin, fat, and muscle —and slide it under the skin up to the chest and shape it into the breast. That actually is the most challenging part of it—to get this piece of tissue to have the right shape, the right amount of hang; that's the true artistry of tissue reconstruction.

The advantage of this technique is that the tissue is her own, so she'll never have the problem of hardening of the breast. And once it's healed, it will be as if she were born with it there: it has a very soft feel; it can be folded to simulate the amount of sag that she has on the normal side. The disadvantage of tissue transplantation, of course, is that there is going to be a scar where you took the tissue, though the flattening of the abdomen may be a trade-off for the patient. With implant reconstruction, you just have the original mastectomy scar; all procedures are done through that same incision.

Another possible problem with tissue reconstruction, we have discovered, is that sometimes the blood supply from the belly is not adequate, and some of the skin dies. Some patients—very obese patients and smokers—are more prone to that than others. But there's another blood vessel that comes up from the groin, that can be hooked up to the blood vessels in the armpit with microsurgery, and that restores the circulation to this entire tissue.

In each case, it's a question of the patient's physical makeup— the size of her breast, the tone of the skin.

I can also transplant tissue from the buttock area—that's another option. I do that in very select cases. A rough estimate is that almost 75 percent of women have a tissue expander and implant reconstruction; maybe 23 to 24 percent will have the abdominal tissue reconstruction; and perhaps 1 to 2 percent will have a tissue reconstruction using the buttock area.

One reason women say they want reconstruction after mastectomy is that they're disturbed by being asymmetrical. If you take tissue from one buttock, don't you become asymmetrical?

Well, it's in an area that's not closely observed by the patient.

What happens when you sit?

The tissue comes from the upper portion of the buttock, so the lower buttock contour doesn't change. There is a little flattening to the area, but it is not that noticeable in clothing, even in very skimpy clothing. And we always have the option of matching the opposite buttock with liposuction. I have cautioned women against pursuing that, though. Should they have a problem in the future with the opposite breast, we would have lost a valuable donor site.

What about the back-flap reconstruction?

It's not used that much anymore. It leaves a scar on the back that's fairly significant. Sometimes you can place the scar so that it's in the bra line, but most of the time you can't. The reason that operation is done is to provide more skin—it was done very commonly before the advent of tissue expanders. The tissue from the back is not thick enough to use without an implant, however. So with the back-flap operation, you get the worst of two different techniques: you get a scar on the back, and you have all the possible problems with implants. There's also a mismatch in the color—the back skin is not the same as the chest skin, so it looks like a patch. But it does remain a very good operation for the reconstruction of radical mastectomy defects since it provides a lot of muscle tissue to reconstruct the armpit fold in the front.

Of all the reconstruction techniques, which do you prefer to do?

I divide the patients into two categories. The patients with the smaller breasts, or less sagging, who don't have a lot of abdominal tissue, I steer toward an implant reconstruction. The patients who have more sagging in their breasts, a good abdominal source of tissue, and a large opposite breast, I recommend the abdominal technique. I don't really push anybody in one way or the other. My job is to educate them, tell them what the drawbacks are of each technique, look at them physically, and make a recommendation. I let them decide. They may be a good candidate for implant reconstruction, but they are really opposed to having foreign material in their body. Or they are well suited to the abdominal operation, but they don't want all the extra surgery and the extra scar. The bottom line is it's all optional surgery. The patient, I feel, should have a lot of input into what's done and a sense of control in the whole process. That goes back to what you were asking before: they should have a plastic surgeon who is comfortable with all the different techniques, whether it's tissue expander and implant reconstruction or microsurgical transplantation of buttock tissue.

How often do you have to do a breast reduction on the normal side?

The majority of cases, I would say, with implant reconstruction, need to have alteration on the other side, either at the time of reconstruction or in later years when gravity has had a differential effect on the two sides. The breast can either be reduced, lifted, or both. It's easier to make a small breast mound than a large one, so we'll take a little bit of volume off the normal side and not put such a big implant on the reconstructed side, and end up with two sides that are then identical in volume.

What's much more difficult is to match the shape of the breasts. Most women will look fine in a bra, even if they don't have anything done on the opposite side. But without a bra, you tend to see a marked asymmetry. Even if you tighten the skin envelope on a normal breast, frequently it will still have a bit of sag to it, whereas the implant side usually does not.

Also, the reduction introduces scars on the normal side that can be quite significant. After you have removed the extra skin and breast tissue and brought the remaining portion of the breast together, you end up with one scar that goes all the way around the border of the areola, another in the crease under the breast, and one that connects the areola and the bottom crease scar.

The last stage in reconstruction is the nipple transplant.

Do most women take that final step?

I would say that at least 80 percent do. Breast reconstruction can never exactly duplicate the normal breast, but the nipple reconstruction gives the visual keys that, yes, this is a breast: it has a nipple, it has an areola. The reconstructed breast mound without a nipple and areola is still convenient for clothing reasons. It allows a woman to wear a swimsuit without the fear that the rubber or foam prosthesis is going to pop out of the suit. A breast mound is sort of an internal prosthesis.

We hear that the skin for the areola is taken from "the top of the thigh." Is that a euphemism for the vagina?

No. A portion of the labia, right outside the vagina, used to be selected for the areola, because it's a darker skin. But nipple reconstruction has also undergone an evolution. We've since found that we don't have to use the skin of the labia, and that the skin from the upper inner thigh, near the groin crease, is also a darker type of skin, and when you transplant it as a skin graft, it will frequently get even darker. We can also take the graft from behind the ear—it's no more noticeable than the scar from a face lift—or use the outer portion of the areola on the other breast if it's quite stretched out.

Where do you get the nipple?

The problem in nipple reconstruction is that it's hard to maintain the outward projection that a normal nipple has; so many tend to flatten out in time. The most common way to make the projection of tissue for the nipple is to bunch up the tissue. The other problem is with the color match. If you use the skin of the chest or transplanted abdominal or buttock tissue, the color is too light. I may have to tattoo the nipple or skin graft over the top to get the right color.

Another way to reconstruct the nipple is to borrow portions of the nipple from the normal side. If, for example, a woman has a very tall nipple, I can take off the top half and transplant it to the other side. The color match is ideal. The so-called nipple-sharing technique actually gives the nicest results, but you can't do it in everybody.

Is that a relatively simple operation?

I recommend general anesthesia, but the procedure frequently can be done as an outpatient procedure or as a one-day hospital stay. Some plastic surgeons will do this under local anesthesia if they are not doing any touch-up work on the shape of the breasts at the same time—which is often what I like to do.

How long, generally, does it take to heal?

It takes about a month to heal after a tissue reconstruction, and half that for an implant reconstruction, though the process is repeated if a tissue expander is needed first (there are usually two months between these two procedures). It will be about six months before the patient has a sense of the whole experience being behind her.

One of the fears of reconstruction is that an implant could obscure a recurrence of the cancer. Is that unfounded?

It has so rarely been the case that we are not overly concerned about it. What happens in other cases is something that's advantageous to the patient. The recurrences are frequently in the skin and just below the skin. I have seen patients whose implants prevented the cancer, when it recurred, from growing back into the ribs. This is never a reason to do a reconstruction, of course, but the point is, we've found that breast reconstruction does not really hinder the detection of a recurrence, so I don't think it's necessary to wait for two years to undergo reconstruction (statistically, if you're going to have a recurrence of breast cancer, it's more likely to happen within the first two years).

Is there any good reason to wait for reconstruction surgery?

Other than the psychological reasons we talked about earlier, for the small group of patients who present with advanced tumors, it may be better to wait. They will require postoperative chemotherapy and in some cases radiation, and chemotherapy can have adverse effects on healing: if you had a tissue expander in there, you could have a problem either with infection or the mastectomy incision opening, exposing the tissue expander, which then has to be removed. However, most types of chemotherapy do not prevent immediate reconstruction. Tissue reconstructions withstand the effects of chemotherapy and radiation therapy much better.

Which types of chemotherapy would give you trouble?
Some kinds of agents have been found to be more injurious than
others. Adriamycin is one such agent. But that's not a commonly
used chemotherapeutic agent in breast cancer; the usual medications—Cytoxan, Methotrexate, 5-fluorouracil—seem to be
okay.

*You mentioned earlier that a patient's emotional
"stability" could be a determining factor. A recent study
found that women who had immediate reconstruction were
happier.*

One of the most common arguments for waiting for breast reconstruction was that if a woman goes under anesthesia with two
normal breasts and wakes up with one that's not quite normal,
then she's going to be unhappy. The thought was that you should
let the person live with the deformity for a while. The actual
experience has been that most women are satisfied with the reconstructed breast and that a so-called mourning period for the
lost breast is not essential and not a prerequisite to getting a
happy patient.

*That suggests plastic surgeons were delaying
reconstruction to get better reviews.*

I don't think there's a plastic surgeon around today who would
delay a woman for that reason. And for a long time, breast reconstruction couldn't be done at the same time—we didn't have the
techniques. I find that the majority of women are very realistic
in their expectations. Very few are dissatisfied. I find, for me and
many of my colleagues, that the plastic surgeon tends to be unhappy more often than the patient is, because we like things to
look perfect. And it's not often the case that you get just a perfect
match.

*All of the women we interviewed would choose again to
have reconstruction, but from what we hear, there are lots
of complications—the implant's leaking, infections,
tightness across the chest even a year after surgery . . .*

Breast reconstruction does have a fair amount of problems associated with it because none of the techniques are perfect. There
are problems with implants getting hard, with poor symmetry.
There is a problem with tissue breast reconstruction causing additional unsightly scars, and sometimes there is weakness in the
abdominal muscles after the tissue is taken. I guess the bottom
line is, how many patients are unhappy a year later? How many

patients would say they wish they had never done it? That number is quite small. I've had patients in whom the reconstruction had to be abandoned for one reason or another, but they did not regret having tried.

I don't think that breast reconstruction is for everyone. Many patients have a very stable body image and do not have a need for reconstruction. The best candidates are the ones who have a very positive attitude and realistic expectations, who are psychologically stable and are not doing it for ulterior motives—such as a fear that they're going to lose their spouse unless they go through with it or any reason other than simply wanting to restore their appearance or just be more comfortable in clothes.

Can you give us an idea of the costs of the different procedures?

There's a perception that a simpler technical procedure, like an insertion of a silicone implant, is going to cost less than something that requires more operating time, such as a tissue transplantation approach. But the fact of the matter is that putting in an implant can involve first an operation for the tissue expander, than another to put in the implant, and then there's a fair chance that you may have to change that implant in the future. There's also the fact that you are likely to need surgery on the opposite breast. So the implant, which seems like a simple concept, is not really less involved than the tissue reconstruction; it just comes in smaller dosages, if you will.

A tissue reconstruction is one long operation that may go six to eight hours. But when you're done, the breast mound is there; very little needs to be done—just a nipple reconstruction in most cases, which is going to be the same for either type of reconstruction. Sometimes you touch up; many times you don't have to.

So I would say that the cost is pretty much the same, when everything is said and done, with either technique, and it's quite variable, depending on the geographic area of the country. A tissue reconstruction may range from $4,000 to $8,000. An implant reconstruction may be between $1,500 and $3,000 for each step.

Do you have a sense of the future of reconstruction, what kind of experimentation is going on?

I think we're not really headed for radically new techniques. The techniques we have today will continue to evolve so there will be fewer problems with them. I see a time when we will have the perfect implant, with no risk of hardening, which can be made in a variety of shapes that more closely simulate the shape of the breast. I think we are going to be more sophisticated in our tissue expanders, and we'll be able to stretch the skin so that the breast is not just a mound, but more of a cone. I think that is within our grasp within the next few years.

BREAST HEALTH NURSING

AMY CHOU, R.N., M.A.

"I REALIZED HOW DIFFICULT BREAST SURGERY CAN BE FOR PATIENTS. THIS ISN'T AN ORDINARY KIND OF OPERATION—THERE'S A LOT OF NEED FOR HELP."

Amy Chou, R.N., M.A., of Manhattan's New York Hospital, constitutes a one-woman support system for breast surgery patients. After mastectomy, Reach to Recovery sends out volunteers to educate and reassure women. Before surgery, the patient is on her own—unless she is at New York Hospital. There Ms. Chou created a specialty focused on the emotional care of women with breast disease, and her work is a model of what is possible. Born in China, she arrived in the United States in 1960, graduated from Cornell University-New York Hospital School of Nursing, and completed her master's degree in nursing at Teacher's College, Columbia University, in 1971. We talked with her in her office at the hospital to find out what she does for patients and how she does it.

How did you start this work?

I had a very dynamic department head, and all she said to me when I came back from school in 1971 was, "Amy, do whatever you can to improve patient care."

The first week back I saw two ladies before surgery. And I'll never forget them. One was told very distinctly that there was a strong possibility of malignancy and mastectomy, and the other was very distinctly told that it was probably benign and just a biopsy with local anesthesia. Both of them reacted so strongly! In fact, the one who was going in for the biopsy had more fear and emotions.

Somehow this hit me between the eyes for the first time, although I had been a surgical nurse for seven years. I was kind of shocked. I said, "Gee, Amy, where have you been? You didn't realize how difficult breast surgery can be for patients. This isn't just an ordinary kind of surgery—there's a lot of need for help."

But I didn't really know where or how. I couldn't say, "Well, I'll take a course and read up." I just sensed the need and said to myself, "I'll look into it and see what I can do."

As I learned and got more involved, I realized that my time was limited. So I began to drop other types of patients, until finally I decided I didn't have time for anything except breast.

How did you go about learning? There was nothing to read, as you said.

Mostly, I must say, I was learning from patients. Really by listening—learning their needs, how they react, what their fears are.

What are those needs, those fears?

We can group them into two main issues. One is cancer, and the other, of course, is the loss of the breast.

For most people in our society, cancer is a terrible word. It has the terrible connotation of dying. And it's not just death—it's how one dies. Many of my older patients will say, "I have lived my life, and I've been happy. I don't mind dying—but I don't want to die piece by piece, and I don't want to die painfully."

It's very frightening to think that one day you are going to be disabled or a vegetable. Lots of older patients in our society are alone. They have been independent for the last ten, twenty, thirty years. They do not want to become a burden to their children; or they know they can't count on anybody anymore. Some of them have seen breast cancer patients from years ago, and in those days there was a higher incidence of lymphedema. They worry if their shoulder is going to be frozen, if they'll have to rely on someone else to do things for them. It goes back to being independent —that's a big issue.

What do you tell them?

I can give them real reassurance—because nowadays, we don't see lymphedema that often. We're not doing the radical procedure, and the arm's not bound for ten days or two weeks—it's a big improvement. Most of my patients, by the time they leave the hospital, have 95 to 99 percent of their mobility. Even if they don't do the exercises we prescribe, if they're active, their arm comes back to 100 percent.

What else are patients afraid of?

The loss of a breast. Fortunately, we are doing more lumpectomy and radiation, for conservation of the breast. But the fear is there. And as a woman, you can understand. It involves a lot. Sometimes there's concern for how their sexual partner will react. He may have said, "It doesn't matter," but who knows what actually happens? And sometimes it's more the woman herself, her self-image. Is she able to feel complete? Can she have that confidence again even in daily business, never mind sexually?

How do you handle that fear?

First of all, I reassure them that they will be fitted with a temporary prosthesis for their own bra before they leave the hospital. And I must say that we probably are one of the very few hospitals, maybe the only one, that actually fits each patient before she leaves the hospital.

Maybe you would like to see it. I have this briefcase I carry with me. [She snaps open an attaché case and pulls out a beige, tear-shaped envelope of fabric.] A temporary prosthesis is really just a soft cover. And judging from a patient's breast size, I will pick the size of the pocket and fill it with this cottonlike material. [She deftly stuffs lamb's wool into the pocket, and instantly the pocket is breast-shaped.]

It works like a pillow sham.

Yes, and it can be worn immediately. A lot of women come in thinking that they're going to have to use a great, complicated piece of equipment—a "hammock," one woman said—or that they'll leave the hospital looking lopsided. But most of our patients, unless they are huge—like 44DD—are able to leave the hospital looking close to 100 percent normal. I try very hard to make sure that is done.

One woman complained that the temporary prosthesis slides up when she lifts her arm.

That's right—that's why it's only temporary. You can reduce that problem if the bra is well fitted around the back, and you can also get a lingerie strap, sew it into a V, and hook the two ends to the bottom of the bra and the other end to your panty or skirt. But most patients don't have to resort to that because the temporary is usually used for just a month or two, when they get fitted with the permanent, which has weight to keep the bra down.

[She unpacks three different styles of permanent prostheses, all made of silicone. Two are soft, breast-shaped sacs: one is covered in a beige fabric, the other coated in a rubbery, almost sticky surface that has the advantage of clinging to the chest (useful to women who are physically very active—who play tennis, for example). The third is denser, rubberlike, and hollowed out to reduce the weight, Chou explains, because "even if the weight of the prosthesis is exactly the same as the woman's breast, still the prosthesis will feel heavier. A breast is carried partially on the chest and partially on the shoulder, but the prosthesis is completely on the shoulder."]

I show these to patients so they know what I am talking about—temporary, permanent.

At what point do you show them to patients?
Usually a day or two before they leave the hospital. I don't feel it's appropriate or healthy to show them too early—it might be too shocking. And usually, that's the time we look at the incision for the first time. The temporary is as closely and nicely fitted as possible, and then I show them these. Very often, a well-adjusted patient will break down and cry, because this is the hit of reality: "Mine is gone, and now I have to use this."

How do you define "well-adjusted"?
The person can use the word *cancer* and talk about everything realistically. The so-called well-adjusted or very curious patients may look at the incision the day after surgery. They drop the bandage and peek, or when the doctors are changing the gauze, they'll look. I don't push the patients who are reluctant—and some of them are *very* reluctant. If they don't talk about it, I will try to bring up the issue a little bit at a time. And I make sure each patient takes a look before she goes home.

We hear a lot of stories from women about the bandages coming off for the first time when they're surrounded by a fleet of interns—which seems hard on the woman, we think.
Yes, and there usually are at least two or three of them. That's why I tell my patients, "If you'd like to look while they're doing it, it's fine. And if you don't want to, look away and let them do whatever they have to do, and when you are alone with a nurse or with me, we'll look together."

It's surprising to us that more women don't order those interns out of the room.
Well, in a teaching hospital like ours, that would be difficult. The residents and interns are here to learn and to take care of the

patients, and the dressing does have to be changed. I just think we need to educate the doctors to be more sensitive to the patients' needs: all patients have their need for privacy and to be considered a person rather than just an incision.

What makes you worry about a patient?
It may sound strange, but I don't worry about those who cry and talk and ask and repeat the same worry over and over. Because as long as the person can talk about it, she will eventually adjust.

I worry more about those who keep quiet and avoid the reality. Once in a while, I have a patient who has never learned how to verbalize, how to express herself, and you can see it's just inside, turning her upside-down. Or she has not learned to trust another person or relate to another person. Those people I worry about.

When do you meet the patient?
Usually on the night or the morning before surgery.

What do you do at that first meeting?
I introduce myself, saying that I am a nurse specialist and take care of all patients who have breast disease, and then ask what is she here for—because I like a patient to tell me herself. Once in a while, the patient will be confused, or say, "I don't know, my doctor is just going to do surgery." There's a reason that they're not telling me up-front what they're here for—they're frightened. With patients like that, it will take a lot more time to get them to talk about it. Usually I don't push them.

I ask if they've ever had surgery, if they've been in our hospital, and I explain the general procedure, like the NPO—nothing by mouth—from midnight on. I'm just trying to relax the patient.

Early in our conversation I reassure them that physically this is a very easy operation. You can start drinking fluid after surgery, and if you go early, you can even eat supper and get out of bed for a little walk the same night. And by the next morning, you'll be fine. The pain will be minimal, and the medication is always there—you can ask for it. By the way, I always include the family in the discussion, because I find they're sometimes more frightened and upset than the patient, and then the patient has to put up a brave front. Sometimes the family doesn't talk to each other, out of fear or worry. I try to get them all together so at least they can hear the same thing and, hopefully, start a conversation among themselves.

Once patients begin to relax and to see what I'm trying to do— that I am there to help them—they will start opening up. Then we'll go back to whatever they're avoiding. It may be several days later, maybe the day they leave, when they finally tell me all their concerns and fears. And some just pour it all right out at that first encounter. They will say they are petrified that the cancer has spread and it's all over their body, and if it's all over their body, will they have to have chemotherapy? That's another big fear. Chemotherapy has a horrible image: you think you're going to be sick, you'll vomit, you'll be zapped out, you'll be totally immobilized. And it's true that some types of chemotherapy can do that, but fortunately the chemotherapy for breast patients is not as toxic as other types of chemotherapy can be.

Most of the premenopausal women we've talked to go into menopause after chemotherapy.

Yes, but for some women it returns. Whether it returns or not, it's unpleasant. There is usually hair loss. That is terrible for a woman—just after losing her breast to become bald. And very often they gain weight and have that puffy look on their face. So there's a lot of real concern.

Anything else about the night before surgery?

I basically listen, and give them reassurance when it is appropriate. I check to see that they are aware of the possibility of reconstruction, and they may have questions about how bad that operation is. And of course, reconstruction surgery is rather simple—it's only about a one- or two-night stay. I'll give them hope in that sense.

Some of the women recall your leaving them a card for the wigmaker and the prosthesis person in their drawer that first night. Do you do that?

No. In fact, that's my biggest issue, and I do teach nurses—I tell them, "Anything you do has to be with a personal touch, with sensitivity." You don't just leave something in the patient's drawer. I do give patients a card for the prosthesis, but I would do it after I had fitted them and showed them what's available. *Then* I would say, "Would you like a reference?"

When do you next see the patient?

I see the patient after surgery. Very often I will go to the recovery room so they will wake up to a familiar face. And after I see the patient, I'll go back to the family. It's very interesting: the family has been told by the surgeon that "your wife"—or mother or whoever—"is in the recovery room, the surgery is over, everything went well." But when I say, "I have just seen her in the recovery room and she is fine," it's another big piece of reassurance. That just tells you how frightened everybody concerned is. Especially elderly patients. An elderly husband and the woman have been married for the last forty, fifty years, and he is petrified that he's never going to see his dear wife again. I go down and tell him, "She's fine, she'll be back as soon as she's awake," and I explain why she's kept in the recovery room for "so long." And I repeat: "She's going to be fine, and when she comes down, we'll start giving her fluid or even a light supper."

And then I'll see the patient every day, for as long as she's in the hospital—five, six, or seven days.

How much time will you spend with a patient?

It depends. With one patient, I finally convinced her to look at the incision with me, and she had such a reaction that I was back and forth seeing her about three or four times that day. I must have spent at least four hours with her, and that was the day before she was supposed to go home. I ended up calling her surgeon at home to say let's keep her another day. We did, and she was okay by the time she left.

Another big thing of mine is if a patient needs that extra support and it is permitted by the surgeon, I make sure a nurse or I help her take a shower before she leaves. Because that first shower is difficult. The area is numb, and to be touching it for the first time . . . it's a funny, eerie feeling. It can be very unpleasant, to say the least. Some patients just fall to pieces. I will never forget this one patient. She had just turned thirty, a single parent with no support system whatsoever, and she was going home to her ten-year-old daughter. Her surgeon usually preferred no shower until the sutures are out. I went to the surgeon and I said, "Please, let me help her take one shower. I just can't imagine letting her go home and face that by herself." And I am going to cry now—every time I talk about it I get upset. Because she shook like a leaf, and she cried all the way through the shower, and then afterward I cried for her.

Do your cancer patients ask, "Why me? What did I do wrong?"

That question is on their mind, I'm sure, to some extent. And some really do get very upset about that issue, especially those patients who feel that they have taken care of themselves well, who have exercised and watched their diets and never "abused" themselves. It's very frustrating: I share the feeling of those people, and I understand what they're saying: What can you do to prevent another incidence? There's no answer now. And the patient knows there's no answer. She really isn't looking for an answer from me, basically, but rather for someone who understands what she's talking about and will allow her to talk. As I said earlier, I think a lot of my function really is to listen, to allow this person to talk it out, get it all out of her system. Because very often, a friend or a family member will immediately pat her and say, "Oh, don't worry. Everything's going to be fine," or, "Well, you know there's no answer, so forget about it," or whatever we tend to say, meaning well, but that stops the patient from talking about it.

So the best thing a friend could do is to resist the urge to soothe, and just listen.

Right. I also tell the husband, "She knows that you love her and nothing's changed, and I know it, too, but I'd like to remind you that this is going to take a lot of your patience." Because sometimes a husband or good friend can become "tired" of listening to the same thing over and over again. He may say, "I've told you ten thousand times already that it doesn't matter, so why are you carrying on?" I think if he just holds her hand and sits by her, she'll stop. She'll realize that there's no answer. She'll get over her need to keep talking—after she's talked enough—and she'll stop. Then she'll be able to go on to the next step in her adjustment.

Do you see a difference in the attitude of women coming in for surgery now and the women you saw in 1971?

Yes. The patients who are going to have a mastectomy now know they can choose to have reconstruction. And the patients who can have their breasts saved are happy they have that option.

Are patients more knowledgeable?

Yes, in general, but you'd be surprised. Some patients will say, "I never watch those programs. I never listen, I never read." It shows that they are afraid.

Do you have patients now who come in for a biopsy and don't know if they'll wake up without a breast?

No, not here. We very rarely do the one-step procedure anymore, unless the person wants it. And once in a while a patient does want that. She chooses a mastectomy because she's learned that she doesn't want radiation; and if she doesn't have the breast removed, the breast is still there and, with it, the possibility of further breast cancer. So she will say, "If a mastectomy is what

I want, why not do it all at once, rather than come back and forth?"

So here comes another big philosophy of mine, and that is, as a nurse, I feel that one of my big functions is to help a patient really understand her options clearly so she can make a fair decision.

You'll discuss the pros and cons of mastectomy versus lumpectomy with her the night before?

Right. Usually the patient has already gone over it all with the surgeon, gynecologist, medical doctor, and oncologist she has been consulting. But if she's not sure about a point—"If I am to have this procedure, this is what it involves: yes or no?"—I'll give her a last-minute clarification.

Do you find that lots of patients arrive after a few weeks or so of rather hectic medical research following the biopsy? That seems painful to us.

Oh, yes, and that's why I would like to meet the patient as soon as she finds the lump—not just the night before she is having the lumpectomy, radiation, or mastectomy. But I haven't been too successful in that because it's difficult to reach them. The biopsy is done either in the doctor's office or as an outpatient.

If you could design the ideal breast cancer care, what would it be?

I would make sure that there is referral right away to somebody like myself—someone who could spend time with the patient. In all fairness, most of our surgeons really do explain things and refer patients to oncologists and/or radiotherapists for information about the different options. But most of the time, the women do need to talk about it. They're terrified. They need to have someone to listen and to help—just to let them talk and maybe just clarify fine points, little things that they are thinking. And there are some women, unfortunately, who are still kind of afraid of asking the doctor too many questions or taking too much time.

Ideally, then, if a woman finds a lump, she would first go to her doctor, have a biopsy, and then talk to somebody like you. Would you suggest to every woman that she discuss her case with a radiologist and a chemotherapist?

That I don't know if I would do. One principle that I have is not to do or say anything that is going to interfere with the patient-doctor relationship, because that relationship is extremely important for the patient. It's very hard on a patient if she has to worry about whether her doctor is competent on top of all her other problems.

So what I will do is, I will talk to the doctor, inform him or her that this patient would like more information about this or that so the doctor can talk to her.

But I do think it's good if the woman feels certain about her choice, whichever way she goes. And before she's certain, she should talk to a surgeon, an oncologist, and a radiotherapist, just so she can hear some different perspectives and have all the information, and most of all, so that she does not regret later on and say, "I should have gone to see So-and-so—maybe I should have done something else." I think the worst thing is to regret.

About reconstruction surgery: you described it as simple.
We've heard some stories that make it sound complicated—
painful and full of hazards.

I suppose there could be complications, but I don't know where those women had their surgery. And there is the issue of how good the plastic surgeon is, and even with the best plastic surgeon, sometimes, yes, maybe there are complications of the prosthesis, the reconstructed breast. In general, though, I can honestly say to *our* patients that the results are usually good and the physical recovery is simple. But of course, I do make sure that the patients do not expect to have a breast replaced. Because it's terrible to be disappointed.

Is anyone doing work like yours at other hospitals?
Unfortunately, I don't think so. At any meetings or conferences I go to, I am looking for someone with whom I can share and learn and relate—and I haven't come across anyone. I think most hospitals have a nurse who takes care of oncology patients, but that covers everything—it's too much.

CANCER RISK ANALYSIS

PATRICIA KELLY, PH.D.

"THERE IS A REAL NEED FOR SOMEONE TO HELP YOU THROUGH THE DECISION-MAKING PROCESS. WHEN A WOMAN HAS BEEN TOLD SHE HAS BREAST CANCER, SHE'S FEARFUL. YOU NEED TO SPEND ENOUGH TIME WITH HER TO HELP HER UNDERSTAND THE SIGNIFICANCE OF THE INFORMATION YOU GIVE HER.

Dr. Patricia T. Kelly's role as part of a team of medical professionals at the Breast Health Center of Children's Hospital and Adult Medical Center of San Francisco has placed the center's work in the early detection of breast cancer at the cutting edge of care and treatment.

What role do you play here at the breast center?
My training was in genetics and genetic counseling—interpreting scientific information and providing counseling for people who had a child with a birth defect and who sought reproductive counseling. I've taken that expertise and applied it to women who are trying to understand their treatment options for breast cancer. I also see women who have a family history of breast or other cancers and who want to know their risks for developing cancer. As part of my work I also talk with people who want to know how to handle cancer in the family: "What are normal reactions?"; "What should I tell the children?"

There is a real need for someone to be there for each woman, to help her through the decision-making process. One of my missions in life is to make people aware that every hospital needs the services of a medical geneticist to help women who have been diagnosed with breast cancer.

I began the breast cancer risk analysis service because women began asking me for it. I realized that the skills I used in helping people to make decisions about reproduction could be used to help women facing breast cancer. You see, it's not enough to pass a law, as we have in California, saying women must be given options. A great deal depends on *how* you tell them about these options. When a woman has been told she has breast cancer, she's fearful. You need to spend enough time with her to help her understand the significance of the information you give her. Women often tell me, "I know I have questions, but I don't know what they are." Women must be given enough background information so they can formulate the questions that are important to them.

What kinds of questions do women with a personal or family history of breast cancer ask you?

"Where did the cancer come from?" "Why did it happen to me or my relatives?" "What are the chances it will happen again?" "What causes cancer?" "Could my job have been the cause?" Was it stress?" "Was it my personality?" "What about diet?" The answers are different for each woman. However, by educating women about the biology of breast cancer and its causes, we can reduce the guilt many seem to feel when they are told they have this disease. People who have a strong family history of breast cancer or other cancer want to learn what their risk is and what kind of health care program they need to protect themselves. They ask what kinds of doctors they should see and how often.

Do you think misinformation about breast cancer is being offered to the public?

It's not so much that incorrect information is given to the public. Instead we are dealing with technical information that can be easily misinterpreted. An example is the American Cancer Society figure that the average woman's risk of breast cancer is one in ten. Many people have heard this statistic and think it means that one in ten women at the PTA meeting or at the gym will develop breast cancer in the next few years. What they don't realize is that it's not meaningful to discuss risk without mentioning time, any more than you can talk about speed without specifying miles per minute, per second, or per hour. That 10 percent risk of breast cancer refers to the average white woman's risk from birth to age one hundred ten! Her risk from birth to age fifty is about 2 percent; from birth to age seventy is 6 percent. From age seventy to one hundred ten, it goes up another 4 percent to make 10 percent. The risk in black women is lower, although quickly approaching that of white women. The risk to Oriental women is also lower, perhaps due to their diet.

Can a woman really influence her chances of developing cancer by eating a certain kind of diet?

Oh, I think that's been shown quite conclusively for breast cancer, ovarian cancer, uterine cancer, and colon cancer. For example, when Japanese women move from Japan to Hawaii and then to the San Francisco Bay Area, the incidence of breast cancer increases. The same has been found in other groups as well. As immigrants give up their traditional diets and begin eating the U.S. diet, which is higher in fat and lower in fiber, their risks for breast cancer increase. For example, in Japan, 20 percent of the calories come from fat; in the United States, 40 percent. It appears that a low-fat, high-fiber diet helps reduce risk. We are just beginning to study the effects of different types of fiber and fat on the body.

If a woman comes in whose mother and grandmother both had breast cancer, how do you determine what her risks are?

First, I ask her about diseases in her relatives. Breast cancer can be passed as easily through the father's side of the family as through the mother's, so I ask about both sides of the family. I then order medical records on a woman's affected relatives. Sometimes the family understanding about the type of cancer or the age of the person when the diagnosis was made is not correct, so the records are important. The records also tell me what kind of cancer a woman's relative had. For example, if it was colon cancer, the records will tell me the type and the part of the colon that was affected. If a woman's relative had breast cancer, I want to know the age at which the disease was diagnosed, whether it was in one breast or both, and whether it was an invasive cancer or in situ (noninvasive) cancer.

Once I determine what a woman's risk is, we talk about methods for early detection—BSE, physician examination, and mammography. With early detection, a woman need not lose her breast or die of breast cancer. Many women with a family history of the disease are amazed to learn that they are not predestined to develop breast cancer. Often a great deal of reeducation is needed to help women realize the advances that have been made in saving lives and in treatments for breast cancer. These women want to do all they can to keep themselves safe from cancer and to improve the quality of their lives by decreasing their anxiety. Because—make no mistake about it—it's extraordinarily traumatic to have one or several close relatives have breast cancer. Women come in saying, "I feel like a walking time bomb."

When a woman who has breast cancer comes to see you with her slides, you send her to your own pathologist for a second opinion. Why do you do that?

A pathology report is somewhat like an architect's drawing. It tells you whether you have a castle or a cottage. For example, several years ago I saw a young woman who had a five-month-old baby and was diagnosed with a huge breast cancer. This woman and her husband had previously consulted with many excellent physicians who all agreed that with a cancer of this sort the future looked grim for her. I followed my normal procedure and asked the pathologist to review the tissue removed during her recent breast biopsy. While we were talking, the pathologist called to say that almost all of the tissue was in situ (noninvasive) cancer. Only a minute amount of invasive cancer was present. Based on the revised pathology, her prognosis changed from grim to great—she'll live to be a grandmother.

The pathologist is often the forgotten specialist in determining breast cancer treatment options. In seeking second opinions, it's essential to include this specialist as well.

Can you tell us more about in situ cancer and how it differs from invasive breast cancer?

I think you will be hearing a great deal about in situ carcinomas in the next few years, as more women have mammography and seek prompt medical care for breast lumps. At this hospital, where we specialize in early detection, more than 20 percent of all breast cancers found are of the in situ type. In situ carcinomas differ from those that are invasive in that they lack the biological capacity to metastasize or spread to other parts of the body. They do, however, increase a woman's risk of developing invasive breast cancer.

There are two types of in situ cancer: ductal and lobular. Interest in ductal carcinoma in situ (DCIS) has grown in the last ten years as an increasing number were found by mammograms. Children's Hospital has the longest-running study on DCIS in the United States. We have followed over seventy women—some for more than ten years—who had small areas of DCIS that were found by the presence of calcifications on a mammogram. (Not all calcifications on a mammogram are associated with ductal carcinoma in situ, but in these women they were.) In this study, women had the DCIS removed, and then they were followed carefully. To date, only four of the women have developed invasive breast cancer. None has died of this disease. From this study and others, it now seems that not all women with DCIS need to have a mastectomy. There are often options.

I understand that Nancy Reagan's breast cancer was DCIS. If she had been seen at our hospital, she would probably have been given the option of having a biopsy and being followed. We would also have tried to help her realize that ductal carcinoma in situ does not metastasize.

Lobular carcinoma in situ (lobular neoplasia, or LCIS) is the other type of noninvasive breast cancer. It does not itself metastasize, but it does increase a woman's risk of developing invasive breast cancer—and the risk is the same to both breasts.

What about getting an opinion from a radiation therapist before surgery?

Unfortunately, many women will see two or three surgeons and medical oncologists, but they'll neglect the radiation oncologist. I think a woman owes it to herself to see at least one of each specialty. If, after that, some questions remain, see another. It's money and time well spent. Women need to realize that for many breast cancers several weeks to a month can safely be used to arrive at a treatment decision. Even in those rare cases where time *is* important, a woman would be wise to consult a radiation oncologist to see what role that therapy could play in her treatment.

As a cancer risk specialist, do you accept the statistic that survival rates for women after a mastectomy and after lumpectomy with radiation are really equal?

Many studies now show quite clearly that the life expectancy is the same whether a woman receives a mastectomy or a lumpectomy followed by radiation therapy. There is no significant difference in the risk of recurrence to the breast itself when either of these treatments is used. Remember, breast cancer is not what kills a woman; it's the cancer's spread to other parts of the body that threatens her life. It's like dandelions on a lawn. If you remove the yellow dandelion flower before the white fluffy seeds develop, you won't have dandelions spread all over the lawn.

Can anyone make an appointment to see you, or do they have to be affiliated with your hospital?

Although this is a hospital-based service, it is open to the community at large—people hear about us and come from all over the country. When people come from out of town, we generally see them for one or two hours a day over a two- or three-day period. The aim is to make sure that a woman has access to and understands the implications of the information she needs to make an informed decision about her own health care.

SCRIPTS
Questions to Ask Your Doctors

"I wish I'd had a script when I went in to the doctor: ask this and this," said a woman frustrated by a lost opportunity to quiz her surgeon. We thought that was a great idea and roughed out scripts for each procedure.

The questions begin when you find a lump in your breast or a routine mammogram turns up something suspicious. From our interviews, we'd suggest going directly to a breast surgeon rather than to an internist, gynecologist, or general surgeon. The surgeon may recommend: a) coming back in a few weeks when you're at a different point in your menstrual cycle; b) performing a needle aspiration to see if the lump is a cyst or a solid tumor; or c) scheduling you for a biopsy. If the surgeon tells you the lump is nothing, and you still feel it, Dr. Kruger advises: Get another opinion.

BEFORE BIOPSY

1. What kind of biopsy are you planning to do? Why? What information will it give us?

2. Where will you do the biopsy? In your office? In the hospital? If in the hospital, how long will I need to stay?

3. What kind of anesthesia will you use?

4. How much does the procedure cost?

AFTER BIOPSY, IF THE PATHOLOGY REPORT IS POSITIVE

1. What kind of cancer is it? Is it invasive or in situ? Is it estrogen-receptor positive or negative? Is it fast- or slow-growing?

2. What are the implications for treatment?

282

INTERVIEWING SURGEONS

1. What do you think my options are?

2. What would you recommend in my case? What are the alternatives?

3. *If mastectomy is recommended:* Under what circumstances are you comfortable doing a lumpectomy? What affects your decision to perform a lumpectomy or a mastectomy—certain pathological aspects, size?

4. Would you describe the surgery to me—what exactly do you remove?

5. Where will you make the incision? What will it look like when it's healed?

6. What complications might arise from the surgery?

7. How extensive a node excision do you think will be necessary?

8. How long do you think I'll be in the hospital?

9. What is your fee?

10. I'd like to get a second opinion: how do I go about getting copies of the pathology report and mammograms?

11. I am considering reconstruction: how do you like to work with a reconstructive surgeon? Do you think there's any reason to wait to have reconstruction?

INTERVIEWING RADIOLOGISTS

1. Do you think lumpectomy and radiation is an option in my case? Why?

2. How many sessions of radiation do you recommend?

3. What will it cost?

4. How long will I have to wait for each treatment?

5. What will the treatment do to my skin? Can you show me a range of pictures of women who've had radiation?

6. What do you think are the possible side effects in my case?

INTERVIEWING THE ANESTHESIOLOGIST

1. Will I be given any medication before going into surgery? What kind?

2. What kind of anesthesia will you be giving me during surgery?

3. Are there alternatives, and what makes this one the best for me?

4. Will you be the one who administers the anesthesia?

5. How will it be administered?

6. Are there any side effects?

7. Are there any risks?

8. After surgery, how long will it take to regain consciousness?

9. What is your fee?

INTERVIEWING CHEMOTHERAPISTS

1. Do you think I should have chemotherapy? Why? For how long? *If answer is longer than six months:* I've read that nothing is gained by more than six months of chemotherapy—why do you think I need more than that?

2. What protocol would you recommend for me?

3. How does it work? How effective is it? How does it affect the rate of recurrence and survival?

4. What are the possible side effects?

5. What's the latest being done to control nausea and vomiting? What can you do to reduce the side effects? What can I do? Do you think marijuana helps? Are there any foods to avoid or to keep on hand?

6. How will the drugs be administered?

7. I've heard that the drugs can be administered through a subclavical catheter rather than IV: what are the advantages and disadvantages of that method?

8. Who will give me the chemo—you or a nurse?

9. Am I a candidate for hormonal therapy instead of chemo-therapy?

10. How much will it cost?

INTERVIEWING RECONSTRUCTION SURGEONS

1. What kind of reconstruction would you recommend for me? Why?

2. When do you think I should have the surgery?

3. Would you want to be present during the mastectomy?

4. What are the possible complications?

5. I'd like to see photographs of your work and meet a few of your patients—would that be possible? *(If the answer is "no," look for another doctor.)*

6. How much will this cost?

The Hospital: Routines, Procedures, and Services

THE ADMITTING PROCESS

INSURANCE PLANS

ONE-STOP CARE

PATIENTS' RIGHTS

A PATIENT'S BILL OF RIGHTS

THE ADMITTING PROCESS

Setting the date for hospital admission and making a reservation for a room—private or semiprivate—as well as arranging a time for preadmittance lab work is usually done through the surgeon's office. The lab work must be done no longer than fourteen days before surgery so the results will be current. Many large metropolitan hospitals make every effort to settle the details concerning admission before check-in day. The procedure varies from hospital to hospital, but, generally, when the hospital takes the reservation, the preadmitting office sends the patient a questionnaire requesting personal data, such as age, sex, marital status, and so forth, and insurance information that is to be returned to the hospital within forty-eight hours. If the surgery is scheduled immediately, this information will be taken over the phone.

The preadmitting office also arranges for private nursing care, a phone, a TV, and any special diet a patient may need—vegetarian, low fat, low salt, kosher, and the like. You can make these arrangements by phone or in person. Make sure to get the name of the person you speak with so if you want to make any changes, you have a contact. Most hospitals hand out a booklet about the hospital's policies regarding fees, visiting hours, use of the telephone, social services, complaints, and so on. If the hospital has a patient representative, that person is your official ombudsman. The phone number for the department is usually prominently displayed in the admissions booklet and in each room. Use it. The patient representative's only job is to make sure your stay in the hospital is as trouble free as possible. (See interview with Ruth Ravitch, patient advocate, page 300.)

A patient has recognized rights when she is treated in a member hospital of the American Hospital Association. These rights are clearly set forth in "A Patient's Bill of Rights" (see page 307). A few women we interviewed complained about people coming in to examine them several times while they were in the hospital. Another woman talked about not understanding the reason blood samples were taken frequently. All of them had the right to refuse examination or treatment, according to "A Patient's Bill of Rights": "Those not directly involved in her care must have the permission of the patient to be present."

PREADMISSION LAB TESTS

These tests are part of the check-in routine for patients undergoing general anesthesia. If a patient is scheduled for local surgery, the tests are generally unnecessary unless the patient is old, has severe hypertension, or has a history of heart problems. In such cases, the patient may be given one or more of the tests to make sure she is able to tolerate the local.

Chest X-ray. Checks that the lungs are healthy and can take the anesthesia. Generally, if a patient has had an X-ray within two or three months, the test need not be repeated.

Electrocardiogram (EKG). Conducted to make sure the patient's heart is healthy enough to withstand surgery. Electrodes are placed directly on the skin of the upper body in a painless procedure to record the heart muscle's activity. An irregular reading may indicate heart problems that need to be reviewed by a cardiologist.

Complete blood count (CBC). A number of different tests are performed on the blood taken from a patient to make sure she can go through the surgery with minimum risk. The most common blood test checks the level of hemoglobin, a protein in the red cells responsible for carrying oxygen to the body's tissues. If a patient is found to be anemic—her hemoglobin level is low— surgery might be delayed until her blood has built up to normal levels, or she might be given a transfusion. A platelet count is also done to check that the blood will clot normally. A hematocrit reading is taken to measure the volumes of blood cells and fluid in the body: a particularly low hematocrit reading may be an indication that a transfusion is necessary.

Urinalysis. Tests for specific gravity (SG)—compares the weight of urine to that of plain water. If the count is low, it indicates urinary obstruction; if high, dehydration. Also checks levels of sugar, acidity, and protein. Abnormal readings may require further evaluation by a doctor before surgery.

These tests *can* be performed on the day a patient is admitted to the hospital, but if any problems require cancellation of surgery, the sudden change can be very stressful for everyone concerned. For this reason hospitals and physicians recommend scheduling necessary tests before admitting day.

WHAT TO TAKE TO THE HOSPITAL

Preadmittance literature at most hospitals includes tips on what to pack and what not to pack. The lists generally recommend taking a lightweight robe, nightgown or pajamas (the hospital provides a gown, but many patients prefer to wear their own), slippers, toilet articles, stationery, and an inexpensive watch or clock. You are asked to bring no more than a few dollars and no jewelry or other valuables.

Many of the women we interviewed admitted they took more than they needed to the hospital. But this is no time to deprive yourself of anything that will make you feel more comfortable about being in the hospital. If you want to take something seemingly unnecessary with you, take it. The women we interviewed had some suggestions, many that might not be on any official hospital list: a Filofax, envelopes of checks for the private nurses, insurance forms already filled out, a Walkman and favorite cassettes, books, their own pillow and fresh pillowcases, vitamins, body cream, makeup, magazines, and tapes designed to calm you before surgery and to help heal you after surgery from the Planetree Health Resource Center in San Francisco. For breast surgery patients: a nightgown that buttons up because it's difficult to lift your arm right after node excision. If you're in a room equipped with a refrigerator, the women suggest stocking up on fruit, juices, and wine to offer guests, plus extra glasses and paper napkins.

CONSENT FORM

The night before surgery you will be asked to sign a consent form similar to the one reprinted on page 224, agreeing to have a specific procedure performed on you. The form may need revisions or additions to bring it into line with the verbal agreement you have made with your doctor—for instance, to remove only the breast lump rather than perform a mastectomy.

INSURANCE PLANS

PAT MC GUIRE

"KNOW WHAT YOUR POLICY COVERS BEFORE YOU HAVE
TO TAKE ADVANTAGE OF IT."

*Pat McGuire is an insurance benefits manager working
with a small brokerage company in Seattle, Washington.
She pointed out that with a good insurance plan, the cost of
a hospital stay can virtually be taken care of, and with
major medical riders, a portion of the doctor's fee can be
reimbursed.*

*How can a consumer get the cheapest but best possible
medical coverage?*
By working for a company or belonging to an organization that
has group insurance covering all hospital costs as well as doctors'
or surgeons' fees.

So group insurance is your recommendation?
Yes. Group insurance may be funded two different ways. The first
is noncontributory, where the company pays 100 percent of the
cost. The advantage of this type of insurance is that the individual does not bear *any* of the cost. Up until two years ago there
was an even greater advantage—a person could get coverage
under this policy without any health statement, so no prior or
current illness could affect your eligibility for coverage. But that
is no longer true because costs have risen so dramatically. To get
this type of insurance today you have to submit evidence of your
insurability. What this means is that at the time of application
there can be no presence of a preexisting condition such as cancer, heart disease, high blood pressure, AIDS, kidney problems,
pregnancy, and so on.

The second type of funding is called contributory. The employer
agrees to pay a percentage of the costs, and the employee picks

293

up the rest. Under contributory insurance, if the employee agrees to take the coverage when it is first offered to her, no health history is required—that is, if the company she works for employs twenty or more employees. This figure depends on the area of the country and the particular policies of the insurer. However, if she works for a company that employs less than twenty people, or for any reason she declines to accept the initial offer and then *later* wants coverage, the application form requires a full health statement. Any prior illness or physical problem listed in that statement could be used as a reason for denying a person coverage if she or he is hospitalized for that illness or problem. So if a woman has a condition such as fibroids or endometriosis that might warrant future surgery, ideally she should be employed by a large company that requires no health statement.

Two common options in group insurance exist. The first offers a basic plan where certain items are paid for at the rate of 100 percent of usual and customary charges—for example, the cost of a semiprivate room—while other things such as the doctor's fee is covered at a percentage of perhaps 80 percent, 85 percent, or even 90 percent. The second common option is comprehensive major medical, where you pay a standard deductible and then everything above that is covered at an agreed-upon percentage.

What happens with individual insurance?

Today, individual insurance rates are more or less even with group insurance—that is, if you are under age forty-five. If you are forty-five or older, the cost of coverage may be greater than group insurance. Anyone applying for individual insurance is required to give the insurer health information. They ask you to tell them the last time you went to a doctor and the names of the doctors you have consulted within the past few years. When you sign your name at the bottom of the statement, you give them the right to go to those doctors to find out the nature of your visit. When the doctor responds, the information received is placed in the computer for future reference. Coverage can be denied if there is proof of illness prior to application. Also, if you have a condition that requires hospitalization or extensive outpatient care, the insurance companies can attach riders to your policy stating they will not pay for treatment for that particular problem again. The obvious conclusion is that if you are over forty-five, with any preexisting medical condition, you could be denied individual insurance and should make every effort to get coverage through a group plan in a company that has more than twenty employees. At any age noncontributory is best because the employee does not pay. Second best is contributory when it is first offered to you.

How are rates for hospital insurance claims determined?
The rates are based on usual and customary charges for a particular area or city. Every three to six months the rates for various procedures are charted. A simple average is calculated. The rates are different across the country. For example, what a doctor or a hospital charges in Los Angeles is much higher than what they might charge in Seattle, whereas in Podunk, Iowa, the rates may be even lower.

Would it be accurate to say that a consumer is dependent on her employer's choice of carrier and plan for adequate medical coverage?
Yes. The portion of our company that works on health benefits helps design plans for individual companies. We advise them of the benefits available and advise them of what's new on the market, what might be better for their employees. The options increase depending on the size of the group. And the company usually makes the decision about what kind of plan or plans they will offer their employees based on the company's financial picture. I'm sure when people are considering the advantages of one job over another, excellent medical coverage is one of the real inducements.

Are there tremendous profits in hospital plans?
Actually the profit margins are small, but the dollars coming in are very large. The insurance companies take that money and invest it. In lots of cases the loss ratio is over 100 percent, which means they have put out far more money than has been paid in, but most insurance companies make their money from investments.

Although Blue Cross/Blue Shield is the most widely publicized of the insurance plans, there are many others.
Is there any advantage to having Blue Cross/Blue Shield?
Not particularly, even though you might think so because Blue Cross/Blue Shield is a nonprofit carrier. All premium rates and benefits for Blue Cross/Blue Shield as well as the for-profit companies like Mutual of Omaha, Traveler's, or Metropolitan Life are based on the usual and customary charges existing in the area on the age/sex ratio of the particular firm they are insuring. And they're based on the benefits within the plan they are selling.

However, for-profit carriers may provide better contracts, and they are worth investigating if you have a choice.

At this time [December 1989], there is a trend with all of the insurance carriers to go to what is called "preferred provider option" for groups. Different companies have different titles for this option, but it means that a particular carrier goes out to the various hospitals, the various doctors in all fields of medicine in a geographic area, and gets those doctors to agree to accept a certain fee for a procedure.

The number of different doctors and hospitals you have to choose from depends on the carrier. Blue Cross/Blue Shield, because of their size and visibility, often represent a great many doctors and hospitals. The preferred provider option plan gives the consumer the greatest number of options. Not only can those doctors who have signed preferred provider contracts work in whatever hospital they have agreed to work in, but they can work in other hospitals that have a similar agreement with the carriers.

So if you have a preferred option plan, you can be assured of a certain rate with an affiliated doctor. But what happens if you go to the same doctor covered by another medical insurance plan?

It's possible that your cost could be higher then. For example, indemnity plans which are offered by for-profit organizations might charge you more. These plans make payments to the consumer on usual and customary charges which are determined by their own figures. If your doctor charges more than their assessment of the costs, you could be responsible for the difference—even if your policy with them states they will pay 100 percent.

What would be your advice to consumers of medical insurance?

To know what your policy covers before you have to take advantage of it. Does it pay for all or a percentage of the hospital costs? Does it pay the doctor's fee? Does it cover private rooms, private nurses? How about lab tests, drugs, and prescriptions? Does your medical plan allow you to choose your own doctors, or is your choice of doctors limited by the plan? What surgical procedures does your plan cover? Are maternity benefits included? Does your plan include physical examinations or any preventive medical procedures? What is the policy regarding preexisting conditions? Also, if you are changing jobs, make sure your current plan continues to give you medical coverage through the transitional period.

ONE-STOP CARE—INSIDE A BREAST HEALTH CENTER

CAROL ROGERS

"A PATIENT CAN COME HERE, SPEND FOUR HOURS, AND WALK OUT WITH A COMPREHENSIVE UNDERSTANDING OF HER OPTIONS FOR SURGERY, CONSERVATION THERAPY, AND INFORMATION ABOUT THE RISKS AND BENEFITS FOR EACH OF THESE CHOICES."

Carol Rogers is manager of the Breast Health Center at Children's Hospital and Adult Medical Center in San Francisco, established in 1981 to teach women breast self-examination. Other services have been added since. In 1988 an expanded, state-of-the-art center opened to centralize all aspects of breast health: breast self-examination education; mammography; and the services of a medical geneticist who specializes in cancer risk analysis. A breast pathologist, radiation oncologists, surgeons, medical oncologists, and nutritional counselors are closely affiliated with the center.

What brings most women to the center?
A great many women come in to learn the Mammacare method of breast self-examination. It is a grid method developed to make it easier for a woman to perform BSE. To teach this method, we place a grid over a lamp and project the light onto her breast. She is then directed to palpate her breast, following the grid. This approach is less haphazard than the conventional circular method because you examine smaller sections of the breast using firmer palpation. The result is a more thorough examination—we find lumps are discovered earlier.

297

Many women come in when they discover a breast lump. Our breast health nurse examines a woman to make sure there actually is a lump and then sends her for a mammogram and to see a surgeon.

Another type of patient is the woman who had a biopsy at another hospital and a diagnosis of cancer was made. She wants a second opinion from us. We set up an appointment for her with our cancer risk analyst, who reads the original pathology report, the mammography reports, and anything else that has to do with her diagnosis and family history. The slides and mammograms will already have been reviewed by our breast pathologist, so the patient has a second opinion on the pathology report. Our cancer risk analyst then has everything she needs to work with the patient to sort out her realistic options.

If the patient is interested in breast conservation therapy, meaning lumpectomy or segmental mastectomy plus radiation, she will be sent to see a radiation oncologist. Also, if she wishes to consult a second surgeon, we can refer her to one. So a patient can come into the breast center, spend four hours, and walk out with a more comprehensive understanding of her options for surgery, conservation therapy, and information about the risks and benefits for each of these choices. We find that helping a woman to obtain and understand the facts is one of the best ways to help her deal constructively with the fear she naturally has when she is told she has breast cancer.

If a woman does not have access to a breast center like yours, what should she do?

Be assertive. Know there are options. Don't let a surgeon tell you, "I'm going in for a biopsy, I'll do a frozen section, and if it's positive, we're going to proceed with the mastectomy." That is not state-of-the-art medicine. Take the time to get other opinions, to read, to get information. It's a stressful process, but it's more stressful if a woman allows a surgeon to remove a breast and then discovers later that there were treatment options open to her. Many breast cancers now do not require mastectomy. However, the fear of the word *cancer* is so great in all of us that when we hear we have breast cancer our immediate reaction is to say, "Take it off. I don't want cancer in my body." Mastectomy is still recommended at times when the cancer is advanced or for other reasons. But many women, with information and time to reflect, find that they need not have a mastectomy. I can't stress strongly enough that there are generally options to be considered. If a woman is uncertain about a diagnosis on her biopsy, she should insist on a review of her slides by a pathologist who specializes in breast disease and breast cancer before making any decision on surgery.

PATIENTS' RIGHTS

RUTH RAVITCH

"WE HUMANIZE THE HOSPITAL EXPERIENCE FOR THE
PATIENT. WE HAVE TO SOLVE THE PROBLEMS THAT
MIGHT BE IMPEDING A PATIENT'S RECOVERY, AND WE
HELP A FAMILY COPE WITH THE HOSPITAL SYSTEM."

*Ruth Ravitch has been the director of the Patient Represen-
tative Department at New York City's Mount Sinai Medical
Center since she developed the program in 1966. Ms. Ravitch was the first president of the National Society of
Patient Representatives of the American Hospital Association and a founder and co-director of the master's
program in health advocacy at Sarah Lawrence College
from 1980-1985. She is currently a special consultant to
that program.*

*We understand that Mount Sinai Hospital was the first in
the country to institute an advocacy program for patients.
How did that come about?*

In 1966 Medicare and Medicaid programs were altering health
care delivery systems, and Mount Sinai was developing a medical school. The director of social services felt that it was important for the hospital to have a department dedicated to
individualizing and humanizing the hospital experience for patients and to create an official channel of communication between the patients and administration. Our function was to be
patient advocates: to handle complaints, solve problems, answer
questions, and act as liaison between patients and staff. We
would also hasten solutions by negotiating the complex hospital
bureaucracy on behalf of the patient or family. Another important aspect of our job would be to assess where the bottlenecks in

the system prevented optimal care and to offer solutions and recommendations for changes from a patient perspective. We would
report our findings to hospital administrators to help them pinpoint problems in their operations and deliver more effective
services.

What kind of authority do you have in the hospital?
The department has the support and cooperation of the hospital's
senior management team. We have access to staff in all departments and at every level as well as access to medical records. We
have an overview of the entire patient care system and the authority to cross departmental lines to advocate for the patient
when necessary. Our role in patient care is to help the hospital
improve its response to patient needs by pointing out the patient's
view to the hospital administration. We try to do this without
assigning blame or complicating issues with emotionalism. It
has been my experience that this way encourages staff to listen
and to help find solutions to the problems.

What aspects of this role do you feel are most important?
First, evaluating the patient's needs and wishes, then presenting
the facts to the appropriate staff member. Another important
facet is learning which staff members are responsive and responsible in implementing plans that have been developed for the
individual patient. A patient's problem frequently involves many
staff members, including doctors, nurses, and aides—often from
several departments. In some cases we arrange a conference in
the patient's room that can include the patient's family, the
nurse, the doctor, the social worker—if there is one on the case—
and a member of our staff. We discuss the patient's perception of
the problem and the needs of the patient. This opens channels of
communication and improves interaction between the patient,
the family, and the staff.

Sometimes the staff labels a patient or family as "troublesome"
or "demanding," and this is reflected in their behavior toward the
patient. When a patient is very sick, or develops an infection or a
reaction to medication after surgery, or falls out of bed, the staff
may feel they have contributed to the problem. Instead of becoming more solicitous of the patient's needs, they can develop negative feelings, making it difficult to talk to the patient. In such
cases—when communication breaks down—the patient representative can get it started again. If an impasse is reached, we

might recommend that the patient be transferred to a different floor where the relationship between patient and staff is more compatible.

Patient representation is such a logical solution to better patient care. How many hospitals across the country have such an organization?

Over one-half of all hospitals in the United States have a patient representative program now. Hospital administrators have multiple problems to deal with—budget, space allocation, research, and meeting the needs of staff as well as patients. A patient representative department focuses on the patient. It is a structured way to deal with patient problems, and more and more hospitals are adopting the concept.

How large a department do you have?

Besides myself we have two coordinators—one for our In-Patient Division, the other for the Ambulatory Care and Emergency Room Division. We also have eight patient representatives, a Spanish interpreter, and an administrative secretary. We are assisted by five volunteers, all of whom have been with us for at least five years; each devotes at least two full days a week to the department. We handle approximately forty thousand cases a year.

How do patients find out your organization exists?

First of all, elective patients receive a packet of information before they are admitted, and the patient representative telephone number is included. Then, when patients are admitted they are given a welcome card that states: "If you have any questions or concerns about hospital services that staff is unable to resolve, please call the Patient Representative, dial 66." Also, the welcome booklet at one's bedside contains information about the services the hospital provides, including the patient "hot line" number that connects directly to our office. That number is also posted on all patient telephones. Patients are also given the Patient's Bill of Rights—in compliance with the New York State Health Code—which again mentions the availability of our services and the number to call. Spanish-speaking patients are given all information in their own language.

Let's say a woman in a hospital lacking a patient representative has what she considers a major problem and can't get anyone to help. What should she do?

Hospitals are complex organizations, and if contact can be made with the appropriate department, the solutions may come faster. If the problem is nursing, the woman or some member of her family can contact the director of nursing. If the problem is with social services, the head of that department should be contacted. Other hospital problems should be taken to the administrator or the director of the hospital. Patients must make their problems and complaints known. That's the only way a hospital can help and serve them better.

But you have to admit that all hospital staff members are not Florence Nightingales.

Absolutely. And very few people are always patient and kind. Nurses and aides and hospital staff sometimes wake up on the wrong side of the bed like everyone else. And at times that's reflected in their attitude. Nursing in particular is a very difficult job. You have to know a tremendous amount these days because the technology is always changing. The nationwide shortage of registered professional nurses is complicating the quality of health care and putting added burdens on those in the field. But I think people who work in a hospital are there to serve patients, not just to get a salary. There are other jobs where people can make the same or even more money without the particularly difficult responsibilities hospital workers assume in treating and caring for people who are ill and upset. Improving the interaction between patients and staff is often only a matter of pointing out the patient's perception.

With fewer nurses, what will happen to patient care?

I think people will become adjusted to accepting alternatives to the traditional modes of care. The number of patient representatives will increase as well as staff members with technical training. These professionals will share some of the nursing responsibilities, relieving the nurse of many of the tasks she now performs. Patients will have to recognize that some parts of today's comprehensive nursing role will be taken over by other players.

How often do nurses get in touch with your department for help with a patient?

About 30 percent of our referrals are from nurses, doctors, ancillary staff, and administration. We are often called on to handle "difficult" patients—people who are excessively anxious and require a great deal of attention and time beyond their medical needs. I had an interesting case last week, which is an example of the kind of work we do as patient representatives. A nurse called to say that a patient had to be moved to another room and that she refused. She had been assigned to a room with one nurse for two patients when she had been very ill. Now she was medically ready to be moved back to the room she had occupied before. When I approached her bed she said, "You want me to move." I explained that because she was much better now we were asking her to give up the room and the private nurse for a much sicker patient. I asked her why she didn't want to move. She said, "Well, the room I had before didn't have a telephone and my television didn't work for a day and I didn't like my bed." Everyone had assumed that she didn't want to move because she wanted the extra care and attention of the private nurse. No one had listened to her reasons for not wanting to move. I assured her that before she was moved, the television and the phone would be working. I offered to move her in the bed she was occupying and gave her credit for the days her phone hadn't worked. Responding to the concern that was shown, she willingly agreed to be moved. The arrangements were made, and the nurse was asked not to make the move until everything that had been promised was in place.

In our interviews we talked with women who want to make sure that surgery is not performed by a resident. Can that be prevented, or is it established procedure in some hospitals?

If you are a private patient, the surgery should be performed by your private physician. However, in a teaching hospital, your surgeon may be working with a resident as part of the training program. When it is determined that the resident has the necessary skills, the resident may be allowed to perform part of an operation such as opening or closing a wound. As the resident becomes proficient, increasingly complicated procedures will be performed. It is important to know that in a reputable hospital if a resident performs any part of a procedure, an experienced surgeon will oversee the operation.

What happens when a patient doesn't like the resident assigned?

At times we are involved in cases where a patient doesn't get along with a particular resident. A patient representative can arrange for another resident to take over the case. Patients should be aware, however, that having residents on call twenty-four hours a day improves the quality of patient care. Attending physicians are not always available, and it is important that a physician who is knowledgeable about a case *is* available at all times.

Is it difficult remaining a true patient advocate when you are being paid by the hospital?

Here at Mount Sinai I know we've been able to maintain our position of patient advocate and assure that patients we see receive the best care and services that the hospital can offer. One way we can maintain our objectivity is to keep a little distance between ourselves and other departments. I think the hospital responds to our recommendations because we manage to maintain our objectivity about the patients, staff, and system. When people work closely together on the same floor or same nursing unit or department, they function as a team that can deliver efficient medical care. The team may make decisions concerning a patient without involving her or her family, and they expect the patient to understand that the best decision regarding her care has been made. When the patient or family expresses concern about that care, the patient representative can mediate and help the team find an alternative way to deal with the situation.

Are there independent patient advocates who don't work for the hospital?

This field is just opening up. There are advocates who see people in nursing homes. Usually they have hospital, nursing, social services, or patient representative experience. Some are paid by families who do not live nearby. In New York State, ombudsmen associated with the Department of Health have access to nursing homes and review the quality of care delivered. A new federal law will mandate this access to all nursing homes in the country. However, I think it's particularly difficult to advocate from outside the institution. Not knowing the staff and not having access to records can be a real stumbling block. Patient representatives working in the institution know the staff and know how the charts are organized. They know where to find laboratory and X-ray reports and whom to contact when a test must be rescheduled or when a patient is dissatisfied with some aspect of her care.

What should you look for in a patient representative?

They should be assertive without being bossy. They must be able to communicate well and have exceptional negotiation skills.

They need analytic and organizational skills and problem-solving abilities as well. They must be tactful and patient, and a good sense of humor is an asset. It's very important that they be non-judgmental and accepting of the values and priorities of both patients and staff members.

Is patient advocacy a real career?

Absolutely. In 1980 I started a graduate program in health advocacy at Sarah Lawrence College in Bronxville, New York. I have two people working in my department now who are graduates of that program. They did their fieldwork here as part of their studies and became members of the staff when the department expanded. In New York City there is a patient representative department in every hospital, and almost all have expanded their programs during the year. The National Society of Patient Representatives of the American Hospital Association has over one thousand members.

What is their training?

Students analyze actual cases and discuss various ways of handling situations that may occur. There are practicums where the students work in a hospital or in an outside advocacy organization. The course in physiology helps students understand the processes and functioning of the body. "The Language of Patient Care" is a course covering surgical and X-ray procedures: what they are and how patients must prepare for them, how it feels to undergo them, and how long they take. Courses in hospital law, health care regulations, medical ethics, psychology, and medical economics are also part of the curriculum.

Sometimes people think patient representation is a hostess job designed to comfort patients or take complaints about food service. We do a lot of that, but as professionals we also have to solve the problems that might be impeding a patient's recovery, and we help a family cope with the hospital system not only while the patient is in the hospital, but in some cases after she is discharged, where continuing care might be necessary. The patient should not be released before she is medically ready to be sent home, but a problem could arise when a patient *is* medically ready for discharge according to her physician, but she doesn't feel well enough to go home. She may find it difficult to stand, to walk, to do housework, or to take care of the children. Social services and home care departments of the hospital are usually responsible for coordinating services at discharge and after the patient is at home. The patient representative is available if there is a systems breakdown or if an appeal to Medicare or other insurance company is necessary.

If a woman is a preparing for an operation at Mount Sinai, can she call you before she comes into the hospital?

Certainly. We would be happy to answer any question about the hospital, but we would encourage her to talk with her doctor about her medical concerns.

And if she isn't sure of the right way to frame a question to her doctor, could you help her with that?

Yes, we can assist by helping her formulate the questions she would want to ask the doctor about treatment and alternatives, prognosis, length of stay, and so forth. The American Hospital Association Patient's Bill of Rights, which follows, can be used as a guide.

A PATIENT'S BILL OF RIGHTS

During the 1970s the board of trustees and house of delegates of the American Hospital Association developed the following statement on patients' rights. It defines the responsibilities of the physicians and medical staff. Implicitly, it expects the patient to share in her own health care by first knowing her rights, then exercising them.

The American Hospital Association presents "A Patient's Bill of Rights" with the expectation that observance of these rights will contribute to more effective patient care and greater satisfaction for the patient, her physician, and the hospital organization. Further, the association presents these rights in the expectation that they will be supported by the hospital on behalf of its patients as an integral part of the healing process. It is recognized that a personal relationship between the physician and the patient is essential for the provision of proper medical care.

The traditional physician-patient relationship takes on a new dimension when care is rendered within an organizational structure. Legal precedent has established that the institution itself also has a responsibility to the patient. It is in recognition of these factors that these rights are affirmed.

1. The patient has the right to considerate and respectful care.

(continued)

---

2. The patient has the right to obtain from her physician complete current information concerning her diagnosis, treatment, and prognosis in terms the patient can be reasonably expected to understand. When it is not medically advisable to give such information to the patient, the information should be made available to an appropriate person in her behalf. She has the right to know, by name, the physician responsible for coordinating her care.

3. The patient has the right to receive from her physician information necessary to give informed consent prior to the start of any procedure and/or treatment. Except in emergencies, such information for informed consent should include, but not necessarily be limited to, the specific procedure and treatment, the medically significant risks involved, and the probable duration of incapacitation. Where medically significant alternatives for care or treatment exist, or when the patient requests information concerning medical alternatives, the patient has the right to such information. The patient also has the right to know the name of the person responsible for the procedures and/or treatment.

4. The patient has the right to refuse treatment to the extent permitted by law and to be informed of the medical consequences of her action.

5. The patient has the right to every consideration of her privacy concerning her own medical care program. Case discussion, consultation, examination, and treatment are confidential and should be conducted discreetly. Those not directly involved in her care must have the permission of the patient to be present.

6. The patient has the right to expect that all communications and records pertaining to her care should be treated as confidential.

7. The patient has the right to expect that within its capacity a hospital must make reasonable response to the request of a patient for services. The hospital must provide evaluation, service, and/or referral as indicated by the urgency of the case. When medically permissible, a patient may be transferred to another facility only after she has received complete information and explanation concerning the needs for and alternatives to such a transfer. The institution to which the patient is to be transferred must first have accepted the patient for transfer.

(continued)

8. The patient has the right to obtain information as to any relationship of her hospital to other health care and educational institutions insofar as her care is concerned. The patient has the right to obtain information as to the existence of any professional relationships among individuals, by name, who are treating her.

9. The patient has the right to be advised if the hospital proposes to engage in or perform human experimentation affecting her care or treatment. The patient has the right to refuse to participate in such research projects.

10. The patient has the right to expect reasonable continuity of care. She has the right to know in advance what appointment times and physicians are available and where. The patient has the right to expect that the hospital will provide a mechanism whereby she is informed by her physician of the patient's continuing health care requirements following discharge.

11. The patient has the right to examine and receive an explanation of her bill, regardless of source of payment.

12. The patient has the right to know what hospital rules and regulations apply to her conduct as a patient.

GLOSSARY
Breaking the Code—Translating
Medicalese into English

ADRIAMYCIN: A chemotherapy drug that works by interfering with DNA synthesis or other essential components of the cell.

AXILLA: The medical term for the underarm and one site of the lymph nodes.

BENADRYL: An antihistamine effective in treating nausea.

BILATERAL MASTECTOMY: The surgical removal of both breasts.

BIOPSY: The removal and microscopic examination of tissue to determine whether it is cancerous or benign.

BONE SCAN: Because breast cancer frequently spreads to the bone, this test—which determines the presence of malignancies in the skeletal system—is often required of patients whose physical symptoms and diagnostic tests indicate the likelihood of metastasis. The patient is injected with a radioactive substance that, under X-ray, highlights abnormal growths.

BOOSTER RADIATION THERAPY: A second phase of radiation therapy, a "booster" dose may be aimed directly at the cancer site with an electron beam or administered internally with an implant of a radioactive material, such as iridium. Implants are put into place while the patient is still in the hospital; external radiation therapy calls for a series of five to ten hospital treatments.

BREAST AUGMENTATION: The enlarging of breasts through the surgical insertion of implants.

CALCIFICATION: Hardening of tissue by a deposit of calcium salts, which can occur in ovarian and breast tumors and other tissues. The distribution, density, and shape of calcium deposits as re-

310

vealed by x-ray may help radiologists to differentiate between malignant and nonmalignant tumors.

CANCER CARE, INC.: A nonprofit social services agency that addresses the psychological and emotional needs of cancer patients. The organization offers free counseling, financial assistance for home patient services, and transportation to and from chemotherapy/radiation treatments; it also supplies information and referrals to health care institutions. Cancer Care has chapters in New York City, Long Island, Connecticut, and New Jersey.

CAT SCAN (COMPUTERIZED AXIAL TOMOGRAPHY): An X-ray procedure that takes thousands of cross-sectional views of the body, which are then merged into a single image by computer. During the test, which takes less than an hour, the patient lies completely still inside a circular X-ray machine. In cases of cancer, staging can be determined by examining the CAT scan for evidence of spread to lymph nodes and other organs.

CHEMOTHERAPIST: A physician, usually a medical oncologist (cancer expert) or hematologist (specialist in blood disorders), who oversees chemotherapy. A chemotherapist should discuss with the patient her options of treatment, how and where the drugs will be administered, possible side effects and complications, and what results can be expected.

CHEMOTHERAPY: Treatment of disease with chemicals (drugs); the term is often used to refer to the use of powerful medications to treat cancer. Because cancer is characterized by cells that undergo uncontrolled division, anticancer drugs are designed to stop this process by interfering with cell growth and reproduction. This is why chemotherapy drugs are often toxic to other rapidly dividing cells, accounting for such side effects as hair loss and sores in the mouth.

CMF: A chemotherapy drug regimen, combining cyclophosphamide (see CYTOXAN), Methotrexate, and 5-Fluorouracil, often more effective than a single drug in treating some breast cancers.

COBALT MACHINE: Commonly used in radiation therapy, it requires a metal (cobalt) to produce and deliver radioactive X-ray beams.

COMMONWEAL: Defines itself as "A center for service and research in health and human ecology." Its Cancer Help Program consists of eight-week residential workshops for people with cancer and their families. "The purpose of the workshops," Commonweal says, "is to reduce the stress of the cancer experience by educating cancer patients about options in therapies, lifestyles, and self-exploration. Participants must be under the care of a physician and be able to care for themselves."

CONSENT FORM: A document stating that a patient agrees to surgery or certain diagnostic procedures. Signing the document indicates that the patient not only agrees to the procedure, but also understands her medical condition, the nature of the test or surgery, its risks and benefits, and its alternatives—a principle known as informed consent.

CYTOXAN: The trade name for cyclophosphamide, a widely used chemotherapy drug that destroys cancer cells by damaging their genetic components (DNA). May be taken intravenously or orally. Possible side effects include nausea and vomiting, bone marrow suppression, hair loss, bladder irritation, and infertility.

DNA (DEOXYRIBONUCLEIC ACID): A chemical that makes up the genes, present in all of the body's cells. By dictating the structure and function of cells, genes determine our characteristics and encode information for traits passed from generation to generation. Many chemotherapy drugs work by interfering with the structure or function of DNA, thus destroying the cell.

DOUBLE-LUMEN IMPLANT: One kind of breast implant used in reconstruction, it consists of a silicone core surrounded by saltwater.

DRAIN: Tubes or suction devices inserted after mastectomy to drain the fluids that accumulate postoperatively. May stay in place several days as needed.

DUCT: In the female breast, milk travels through a system of tubelike ducts from milk glands to milk reservoirs in the nipple area. The duct is the site of most breast cancers (see DUCTAL CARCINOMA).

DUCTAL CARCINOMA: The most common type of breast cancer, it develops as a small, hard tumor in the lining of a breast duct. In its invasive form, it spreads quickly to the lymph nodes and often causes the nipple to appear sunken. The in situ ductal cancers rarely leave the duct site, are too small to be felt, and are most often detected as calcified areas on a mammogram.

ELECTROCARDIOGRAM (EKG): A diagnostic test that charts any irregularities in the heart by tracing the pattern of electrical impulses that move through the heart. Electrodes are placed on the chest, ankles, and wrists. A painless procedure, the electrocardiogram is one of the standard preoperative tests.

ESTROGEN: A hormone produced primarily by ovarian follicle cells; the adrenal glands and body fat also manufacture estrogens, even after menopause. In addition to prompting monthly thickening of the uterine lining and increases in cervical mucus, estrogen causes the development of female characteristics at puberty.

EXPANDER: When there is too little skin covering the breast or insufficient blood supply for a full reconstruction following a mastectomy, an expander may be used to stretch the skin for the eventual breast implant. The saclike device is inserted and gradually inflated with increasing amounts of saline solution over a period of weeks or months, then removed and replaced by the permanent implant. Some new expanders may be left in place permanently, sparing the patient another surgery. The procedure can be performed under general or local anesthesia.

FIBROCYSTIC BREAST DISEASE: A recurring condition characterized by breast tenderness, pain, swelling, and the occasional appearance of cysts or lumps.

5-FLUOROURACIL (5-FU): A commonly administered chemotherapy drug that interferes with the normal metabolism of a cell's DNA. Administered intravenously. May cause diarrhea, mouth sores, bone marrow suppression, nausea.

HALSTED MASTECTOMY: Developed in the late 1800s by Dr. William Stewart Halsted, this "radical" mastectomy removes the breasts, underarm nodes, chest muscles, and sometimes rib sections. It is rarely if ever used now, having been replaced by the equally effective—and less disfiguring—modified radical and simple mastectomies.

HISTOPATHOLOGY: The area of pathology concerned with tissue changes and their relationship to disease. (See also PATHOLOGY.)

HORMONE: A chemical substance produced by the body that can turn organs on and off, thus regulating many body functions, such as digestion, growth, and sexual functioning. Synthetic forms of many hormones are used to treat hormone deficiencies caused by illness or, in the case of menopause, aging.

HORMONE ASSAY: If a tumor is malignant, tests that reveal how much the cancer is influenced by the hormones estrogen and progesterone—called estrogen- and progesterone-receptor assays —should be done right away, as the results are critical for determining treatment methods. Women who test ER-positive, meaning that their cancers are estrogen-dependent, are generally good candidates for hormonal drugs that block estrogen's effects. Those whose results are ER-negative usually respond better to conventional chemotherapy.

HOT FLASHES: A feeling of warmth that begins on the face and radiates to the chest, accompanied by flushing and sweating. According to *Obstetrics and Gynecology* (J. B. Lippincott, 1986), 75 to 85 percent of women experience this symptom following menopause. Many women have only occasional episodes; a minority experience attacks that are frequent and intense enough to interfere with normal functioning. Although the cause of hot flashes is not certain, many believe they are due to a misfiring of the glands involved in temperature regulation in an attempt to reactivate the ovaries.

HYSTERECTOMY: Surgical removal of the uterus and, sometimes, adjacent structures. Total or complete hysterectomy, in which the entire uterus is removed, may be performed to remove symptomatic fibroids or a sagging uterus or to correct severe bleeding. A complete hysterectomy (known technically as a hysterectomy with bilateral salpingo-oophorectomy) involves removal of the uterus, fallopian tubes, and ovaries. When the uterus only is removed, a woman still produces estrogen and ovulates, but the ova are absorbed by the body. When the ovaries are removed, "surgical" menopause occurs.

IN SITU CANCER: A malignancy that does not spread beyond its primary site.

INTRADUCTAL CARCINOMA: (See DUCTAL CARCINOMA.)

IV (INTRAVENOUS): A needle inserted into a vein to administer blood products, nutrients, and medications directly into the blood. The IV is usually placed in the crook of the elbow or top of the hand.

INVASIVE DUCTAL CARCINOMA: (See DUCTAL CARCINOMA.)

IRIDIUM: A radioactive material used in radiation therapy (see BOOSTER RADIATION THERAPY). Bits of iridium are implanted in tiny tubes in and around malignant breast tissues.

KÜBLER-ROSS, ELISABETH: Author of several books on how to cope with death and terminal illness (mentioned as helpful by several cancer patients interviewed here), notably *On Death and Dying,* which explores the common emotional stages experienced by dying patients, and *On Children and Death, Living with Death and Dying,* and *To Live Until We Say Goodbye.*

LINEAR ACCELERATOR: A type of X-ray machine used in radiation therapy that works by converting electricity into high-energy beams.

LIVER SCAN: Because breast cancer often spreads to the liver, this test is recommended for those whose physical symptoms or diagnostic tests indicate the likelihood of metastasis. After a radioisotope is injected into the patient, the normal tissue of the liver will absorb the isotope and appear highlighted; abnormalities will show up as less prominent "cold" spots in areas where the liver is not performing its usual trapping function.

LOBES: Anatomical units of the breast that serve as drainage channels for milk.

LOBULAR CARCINOMA: Cancer that starts in the breast lobules, the small end ducts that branch off the breast lobes. It may be invasive or in situ. The tumors of in situ lobular carcinoma are too small to be felt but generally show up as calcified areas on a mammogram. Some may develop into invasive cancer, but how or when is difficult to predict.

LUMPECTOMY: Removal of the cancer and a clean margin of tissue rather than the entire breast. For tumors that fall into the first two stages of breast cancer and are under four centimeters

(1½ inches), lumpectomy followed by radiation and/or chemo-therapy treatments has proved as effective as mastectomy alone. (See pages 14–15.)

LYMPHEDEMA: Fluid accumulation. When lymph nodes are re-moved from the underarm, the normal fluids transported by the lymph system may build up and cause the affected arm to swell; this condition is called lymphedema. Elevating the arm and using pressure bandages may relieve discomfort. Patients should also avoid wearing tight sleeves, doing heavy manual work, or staying too long in the sun.

LYMPH NODES: Soft, small structures attached to the vessels of the lymphatic system, which help fight disease and act as the body's drainage network. Underarm lymph nodes are the first place cancer is likely to lodge as it spreads from the primary breast site. Because the presence of cancer in the nodes of the axilla means that the malignancy may have traveled to other parts of the body, knowing the number of cancerous nodes is crucial to determine the course of treatment. The only way to test lymph nodes for cancer is to remove them surgically from the affected underarm. This is usually done at the time of the lum-pectomy or mastectomy.

MACROBIOTICS: A severe vegetarian diet that claims to have pow-ers to prevent as well as cure illness. The regimen emphasizes brown rice and other grains, cooked vegetables, beans (including soybeans), and seaweed; it restricts raw fruits and vegetables and suggests avoiding citrus fruit in any form and the "night-shade" vegetables (tomatoes, potatoes, zucchini, eggplant, and peppers).

MAMMOGRAM: A procedure that can detect cancerous tumors be-fore a lump is big enough to feel. The test takes only a few min-utes and is mildly uncomfortable, as it involves "sandwiching" each breast between metal plates while tissue is X-rayed from different directions. Suspicious areas will show up on the film as denser masses of tissue. The American Cancer Society suggests that women have a baseline mammogram between the ages of thirty-five and forty. The National Cancer Institute recommends that women age forty and over have a mammogram every two years and then, after age fifty, annually.

MASTECTOMY: Surgical removal of the breast as a treatment for breast cancer. There are four types: 1) simple—removal of the breast; 2) modified radical—removal of the breast and lymph nodes; 3) radical—modified radical plus removal of the chest muscles and sometimes rib sections; 4) extended radical—radical plus removal of internal mammary lymph nodes under the breast bone.

MENOPAUSE: The end of a woman's reproductive capabilities, in which the elaborate interactions between glands that produced fertility change dramatically. This produces a period of readjustment, during which the body establishes a new hormonal balance. During the transition period, women may experience hot flashes, night sweats, or other symptoms. According to the American Medical Association, menopause usually occurs between ages forty-five and fifty-five and lasts two to three years; however, it can last from ten to fifteen years. During the postmenopausal period, many women experience symptoms due to decreased estrogen production, including osteoporosis (see below) and thinning and drying of the vaginal walls.

METASTASIS: The spreading of cancer to other parts of the body. Breast cancer generally travels via lymphatic channels and the bloodstream, most often metastasizing to the liver and bone. (See also BONE SCAN, LIVER SCAN.)

METHOTREXATE: A chemotherapy drug, given intravenously, that works by interfering with cell metabolism. May cause nausea, vomiting, and mouth sores. Because Methotrexate suppresses bone marrow—which produces white blood cells, red blood cells, and platelets—patients may become more prone to infections, anemia, and bleeding.

MICROCALCIFICATION: Specks of calcium salts that may show up on mammograms and indicate cell activity. Advancements in mammography have made it possible to differentiate one speck from another. Shape, size, and distribution can determine a benign or suspicious condition.

NEEDLE ASPIRATION: Procedure to determine if a lump is a cyst or a solid tumor.

NEEDLE LOCALIZATION: Procedure to pinpoint lump before biopsy.

ONCOLOGIST: A cancer specialist who manages the diagnosis and treatment of cancer patients. May be an internist, general surgeon, or surgery specialist.

ONCOLOGY: The medical specialty dealing with cancer.

OSTEOPOROSIS: The gradual loss of bone mass in women as they age, which can result in fractures and/or curvature of the spine. Osteoporosis is most common in slender white women; other risk factors include a family history of the disease, undergoing early menopause, smoking, and lack of exercise. The disease is partially preventable by a calcium-rich diet, weight-bearing exercise, and, after menopause, going on estrogen replacement therapy.

PATHOLOGY: The branch of medical science concerned with the nature of disease and its effects on body tissue. A pathology report will reveal whether a tissue is benign or malignant, what type of cancer cell is present, the rate at which it is multiplying, its possible penetration into blood vessels or lymph channels, and the extent to which the tumors may be hormone-dependent. (See also HISTOPATHOLOGY.)

PLATELETS: Small particles in the blood that serve a clotting function. Because platelets can be easily damaged during chemotherapy, making the patient more prone to bleeding, it's critical to get a "platelet count" (make sure the level is sufficient)—as well as a measure of white blood cells and red blood cells—before beginning treatment.

PREDNISONE: An adrenal cortical steroid, taken orally, used in cancer treatment that works by mimicking or blocking the effects of naturally occurring hormones. Side effects may include gastrointestinal upset, weight gain, and fluid retention.

PROSTHESIS: An artificial body part. Breast prostheses are generally fitted four to six weeks after mastectomy, when the incision has healed. Most are made of polyester, foam rubber, or pockets filled with liquid or silicone gel. They are available in a variety of sizes and shapes and in dark as well as light flesh tones. They're sold in corset shops, surgical supply stores, and some department stores. Special mastectomy bras have pockets to hold the prostheses.

QUADRANTECTOMY: A lumpectomy that removes one-quarter of the breast surrounding the malignant tumor.

RADIOLOGIST: A physician who specializes in administering and interpreting X-rays.

RADS: The abbreviation for "radiation absorbed dose," the unit of measurement for the amount of radiation absorbed during radiation therapy. Most breast cancer patients receive from 4,400 to 5,000 rads per treatment, each lasting about ten minutes and administered five days a week for roughly five weeks.

REACH TO RECOVERY: In this American Cancer Society program, women who have had breast cancer serve as counselors to those who may be approaching, undergoing, or recuperating from treatment. Volunteers visit patients and offer literature and advice about exercises, prostheses, clothing, and rehabilitation, as well as support to family members. For information, contact your local American Cancer Society chapter.

RECONSTRUCTION: The simulation of a breast through plastic surgery.

ROENTGEN THERAPY: X-rays used in diagnostic procedures and radiation therapy. Named for German physicist Wilhelm Conrad Roentgen (1845–1923).

SALINE IMPLANT: Breast implant filled with saltwater solution. (See interview with David Hidalgo, M.D., page 251.)

SEGMENTAL MASTECTOMY: Another form of lumpectomy. Removal of a cancerous breast lump and a wedge of normal tissue surrounding it. (See also LUMPECTOMY, QUADRANTECTOMY.)

SILICONE: A gel used in some breast implants.

SIMONTONS: Carl Simonton, M.D., is a Texas oncologist who, with his social-worker wife, Stephanie Matthews, developed a highly controversial approach to cancer treatment, which he uses in conjunction with conventional methods. Their work is based on theories that cancer is the result of great stress and enormous life changes. The Simontons theorize that people with a "cancer personality" (emotionally inexpressive and given to helplessness and hopelessness) are particularly prone to the disease. The Simontons train cancer patients to visualize themselves as powerful fighters, asking them, for instance, to imagine their cancer cells as weak and disorganized and their chemotherapy as a white knight riding in to destroy the enemy. The Simontons have not been able to persuade the medical establishment that their work is effective. They are also criticized for seeming to hold cancer patients responsible for their illness.

SONOGRAM: A test in which sound waves are used to detect a breast mass. It is a painless procedure. High-frequency sound waves are emitted and received by a device resembling a microphone (called a transducer), which is moved over the breast.

STAGING: Breast cancer staging is an internationally standardized system by which doctors communicate information about the size, type, and position of a malignancy in the body, whether it has metastasized, and where.

The "TNM" method classifies breast cancer three ways: T, for tumor; N, for nodes; M, for metastasis. Numbers following each letter—T_1, N_0, M_0—provide shorthand information about the size of the tumor, the degree of involvement of the nodes, and the extent of metastasis.

Stage I means a tumor is less than 2 centimeters (T_1), has no lymph node involvement (N_0), and shows no evidence of metastasis (M_0). Stage I is the most curable of cancers, and with the advancements in mammography more and more cancers are discovered at Stage I.

Stage II is a tumor larger than 2 centimeters but less than 5 centimeters (T_2), with negative nodes (N_0) and no metastasis (M_0). Stage II can also mean a tumor less than 5 centimeters with positive nodes (N_1) on the same side of the body but no evidence of metastasis (M_0).

Stage III indicates the tumor is larger than 5 centimeters (T_3), and any number of positive nodes are attached to each other, to skin, or to underlying tissue (N_2), but there's no evidence of metastasis (M_0). Stage III also applies to a tumor of any size that extends into the chest wall or to the skin when the nodes are positive and fixed to each other or to the skin or to underlying tissues (N_2), but where there is no evidence of metastasis (M_0).

Stage IV means any tumor of any size with or without lymph node involvement, but with evidence of metastasis (M_1). Stage IV refers to advanced cancer.

MX indicates that metastasis may exist but can't be detected.

TAMOXIFEN: An anticancer drug used in hormonal therapy that inhibits the effects of circulating estrogens and helps to shrink the estrogen-dependent tumor. Tamoxifen is often prescribed as an alternative to chemotherapy in postmenopausal women. Side effects are generally minimal but may include nausea and vomiting, bone pain, vaginal bleeding or itching, and hot flashes.

TETRAHYDROCANNABINOL (THC): Marijuana derivative used to prevent the nausea and vomiting that may accompany chemotherapy treatments. Some researchers theorize that THC acts on the brain to block the nausea response. A synthetic form is administered orally, in a tablet called Marinol. According to Lester Grinspoon, associate professor of psychiatry at Harvard Medical School and author of *Marijuana Reconsidered* (Harvard University Press, 1977), smoking cannabis is considerably more effective than the synthetic.

BIBLIOGRAPHY

American Cancer Society Cancer Book, The. Doubleday, Garden City, NY, 1986.

Atlas of Breast Reconstruction Following Mastectomy, by Bernard M. McGibbon. University Park Press, Baltimore, MD, 1984.

A Woman's Choice: New Options in the Treatment of Breast Cancer, by Mary Spletter. Beacon Press, Boston, MA, 1982.

Breast Cancer: The Facts, by Michael Baum. Oxford University Press, Oxford/New York, 1981.

Choices: Realistic Alternatives in Cancer Treatments, by Marion Morra and Eve Potts. Avon, New York, 1987 (rev. ed.).

Columbia University College of Physicians and Surgeons Complete Home Medical Guide, The. Crown Publishers, New York, 1985.

Complete Book of Medical Tests, The, by Michael E. Osband, M.D. W. W. Norton & Company, NY, 1984.

Complete Guide to Women's Health, The, by Bruce D. Shephard, M.D., F.A.C.O.G., Carroll A. Shephard, R.N., Ph.D. Plume Books, published in the United States by New American Library, New York, by arrangement with Mariner Publishing Co., Inc., 1985.

Confronting Breast Cancer: New Options in Detection and Treatment, by Sigmund Weitzman, M.D., Irene Kuter, M.D., D.Phil., and H. F. Pizer, P.A.-C. Vintage Books, New York, 1986.

Every Woman's Guide to Breast Cancer: Prevention, Treatment, Recovery, by Vicki L. Seltzer, M.D. Penguin Books, New York, 1987.

Every Woman's Health: The Complete Guide to Body and Mind by 18 Women Doctors, D. S. Thompson, M.D., consulting editor. Doubleday & Company, Inc., Garden City, NY, 1985 (3rd ed.).

Medical Access, by Richard Saul Wurman, ACCESSPRESS Ltd., 1985.

Memory Bank for Chemotherapy, by Fredrica A. Preston and Cecilia Wilfinger. Williams & Wilkins, 428 East Preston Street, Baltimore, MD 21202, 1988.

New Our Bodies, Ourselves, The, by the Boston Women's Health Book Collective, Simon & Schuster, New York, 1984.

Obstetrics and Gynecology, by David Danforth, M.D., and James Scott, M.D. J. B. Lippincott Co., Philadelphia, 1986.

Overcoming Breast Cancer, by Genell J. Subak-Sharpe. Doubleday & Co., New York, 1987.

Oxford Companion to Medicine, The, Volume II. Oxford University Press, Oxford/New York, 1986.

Surviving Breast Cancer, by Carole Spearin McCauley. Dutton, New York, 1979.

Taber's Cyclopedic Medical Dictionary. Davis, Philadelphia, 1985 (5th ed.).

Webster's Medical Desk Dictionary. Merriam Webster, Springfield, MA, 1986.

INDEX

324